# FROM NATIONALISM TO REVOLUTIONARY ISLAM

This study of dominant social movements in the Middle and Near East by a group of social scientists and historians is the first attempt to bring nationalism and the contemporary Islamic movements into a unified thematic perspective. The process of national economic and political integration supplies the unifying context for the analyses of the various social movements to which it gives rise. The examination of nationalism in general, and of the rise of the Arab nationalist movement in Greater Syria in the early decades of the century in particular, is followed by a close analysis of the interplay of ethnic identity and Islam in the local politics of the tribal North-Western Frontier Province of Pakistan. The politicisation of Islam in Algeria, Turkey and Egypt is then explored and explained, together with the characteristics of the emergent Islamic movements. The last three essays cover Shiite Islam in Iran since the opening decade of the century, focusing on various components and aspects of the Islamic movement which culminated in the revolution of 1979. The case-studies thus chart the recent upsurge of revolutionary Islam and the concomitant decline of nationalist movements in the contemporary Middle and Near East. The introduction offers an analytical perspective for the integration of this major theme which is forcefully suggested by the juxtaposition of the essays.

# From Nationalism to Revolutionary Islam

*Edited by*

Said Amir Arjomand

*Foreword by*

Ernest Gellner

State University of New York Press

Albany

First published in U.S.A. by
State University of New York Press, Albany

For information, address State University of New York Press
State University Plaza, Albany, N.Y., 12246

**Library of Congress Cataloging in Publication Data**

Main entry under title:

From nationalism to revolutionary Islam.

  Includes bibliographical references and index.
  Contents: Introduction/Said Amir Arjomand—
Nationalism in the Middle East/Richard Cottam—
Social factors in the rise of the Arab movement in Syria/
Rashid Khalidi—[etc.]
  1. Near East—Politics and government—Addresses,
essays, lectures.  2. Near East—Social conditions—
Addresses, essays, lectures.  I. Arjomand, Said Amir.
DS62.4.F76  1984        956'.04        83-18038
ISBN 0-87395-870-5
ISBN 0-87395-871-3 (pbk.)

# Contents

# Foreword

## ERNEST GELLNER

The central theme of the history of the twentieth century is now totally plain and obvious. In the course of it, industrial/scientific societies, hitherto largely confined to what may loosely be called the North Atlantic world, spread to the rest of the globe. It does not look as if the transformation of the rest of the world will have been completed by the end of the century; but there can be no shadow of doubt that the disruption of the traditional agrarian societies will by then be largely accomplished.

The process which we are witnessing is the replacement of agrarian societies by industrial or industrialising ones. What is the difference between them?

Agrarian societies contain a majority of direct agricultural producers; they had a fairly stable technological base, cognitive and technical innovation being a rarity rather than a normality; they were generally hierarchical, authoritarian, dogmatic and stability-oriented. They possessed belief-systems claiming absolute and transcendental grounding which were linked to the authority and hierarchy structures of their societies and provided them with their legitimation.

Industrial societies are defined by the possession of ever-growing and ever more powerful technical equipment, depending in turn on a form of cognition ('science') committed or doomed to perpetual growth. They employ a diminishing proportion of the population in agriculture. Although their political and cultural superstructure is not homogeneous, it is marked by at least the potentiality of a certain liberalisation (political and doctrinal pluralism and choice, the replacement of the stick of fear by the carrot of material bribery, and the anticipation of radical enrichment), by a diminution of the chasm between a 'Great' Tradition and a 'Folk' Tradition, a larger population, a much increased social mobility and a tendency towards widespread secularisation.

So much is obvious and general. But there are great and profoundly important differences within both agrarian (which includes pastoral) and industrial/industrialising societies. Marxism is perhaps the greatest observer-participant in the overall process – a belief-system which is both a theory *of* the process and an important actor *within* it. Its significance as an actor within the drama can hardly be in dispute. Its accuracy as an account of the whole process is more questionable.

Two central ideas within it in particular seem open to doubt. One is the employment of the notions of 'feudalism', 'capitalism' and 'socialism' as designations of types of society, putatively defined in terms of their mode of production. The facts of history have by now forced virtually everyone (including nominal Marxists) to treat *agrarian* and *industrial* as the real designations of forms of production: capitalism and socialism are only names of the optional socio-political superstructures accompanying the latter one. (The idea that 'feudalism' is some kind of general matrix of the emergence of industrial societies is similarly questionable, and can only be sustained by extending the meaning of the term so widely that it is deprived of much of its utility.) The second questionable idea is that modes of production, or societies defined in terms of their productive base, uniquely determine the 'superstructure'.

In other words, we now need to operate in terms of a simple social typology, agrarian/industrial, which only revived and conquered our speech after the Second World War, and we are quite clear that, whilst each of these types may determine the *problems* faced by a society, they do not uniquely determine its *solutions*.

Despite the great diversity displayed by ex-agrarian, industrialising societies, one can nevertheless offer a certain simple formula for their doctrinal, ideological predicament. The reason why they are obliged to undergo change is of course to be sought in the technical, economic and military superiority of industrial society. They are changing, because they, or their members, wish to be as rich and powerful as industrial, 'developed' lands. The ideological consequence of this situation is obvious. These societies are torn between 'westernisation' and (in a broad sense) populism, that is, the idealisation of the local folk tradition. (The old local 'Great' Tradition is generally damned by its failure to resist the West and by its doctrinal and organisational rigidity, once a source of strength, now a great weakness.) The emulation of the developed world flows from the desire to steal its sacred and power-conferring fire; the romanticisation of the local tradition, real or imagined, is a consequence of the desire to maintain self-respect to possess an identity *not* borrowed from abroad, to avoid being a mere imitation, second-rate, a reproduction of an alien model.

These two ideological trends or temptations are mutually incompatible; nevertheless, most ideologies prevalent in the Third World contain some blend or mixture of the two. The tension between them is manifest and painful. In the far-off days, over a century and a half ago, when the Third World began on the Rhine, the dilemma took the form of the conflict between classicism and romanticism, between the aping of French models and the reverence for the local folk spirit. By the time the dilemma came to be felt in Russia, it was articulated in the terms which we still recognise today.

But there is one section of the ancient world which seems at least in part to have escaped this predicament: namely, Islamic societies, notably those of the arid zone. This interesting exception has not yet been widely noticed. But there is an aspect of it which is conspicuous and which really cries out for more thorough investigation. It is the curious, yet supremely important fact that, of all the great traditional belief systems, Islam alone, far from weakening, has become an increasingly powerful social and political mobilising force. The other traditional faiths have had to retreat before diverse mixtures of modernism and populism; Islam, on the other hand, has retained and enhanced its social vitality, and moreover is vigorously invoked both by conservative and radical regimes.

Is this an accident? I think not. Islam, like other faiths, was divided between a folk variant and a central, literacy-sustained tradition. But the central, scholarly version was rather special: it was not rigidly tied to any one political *ancien régime*, it was carried by an open class of scholars/jurists/theologians which would in principle come to embrace the entire society, and it contained an egalitarian doctrine of equal access to God by all believers willing to heed the publicly available and definitely and finally delimited Word. Its scripturalist, orderly, restrained theology made it compatible with the requirements both of centralising regimes and of developmental programmes.

Its sober and restrained unitarianism, its moralism and abstention from spiritual opportunism, manipulativeness and propitiation, in brief its 'protestant' traits, give it an affinity with the modern world. It did not engender the modern world, but it may yet, of all the faiths, turn out to be the one best adapted to it. It can dissociate itself from both folk 'superstitions' and its archaic hierarchies, and it is not dragged down by them.

What had once, in the days when literacy was a specialist accomplishment, been the faith and stance of a restricted clerical élite, could now, in the age of widespread urbanisation and literacy, become the folk culture of the *entire* society. It could simultaneously define it against foreign enemies, against over-westernised local rulers, and against the rejected moral corruption of the real local past; and yet it could also be used to invoke an uncorrupt ideal past, whose image had always haunted the society, and thus affirm both past roots and future aspirations, both continuity and transformation, identity and purification, under one single banner.

This, in rough outline, is in my view the explanation of the unique and enormously important standing of Islam in the modern world, its potential of both mobilisation and conservation. (The accident of oil explains the power of Moslems; it does *not* explain the powerful hold of Islam over its adherents.) All this fact has not, of course, saved the Moslem lands from the impact of either nationalism or socialist radicalism. The call for culturally homogeneous communities, endowed with a state-sustained and endorsed culture, in other words nationalism, has been felt in the Middle East and North Africa as powerfully as elsewhere. The requirement that the fruits and benefits of the yearned-for industrial cornucopia should be distributed according to moral and political requirements, and not be left to the vagaries of the market – in other words the imperative of socialism – has been affirmed all the more strongly in societies long habituated to the view that the duty of the state is to proscribe evil and enforce good, and which may consequently be receptive to the idea that the good of industrial society should be decreed by norm, rather than be the fruit of accidental, unplanned interactions. Here the state had ever been moralistic in tone, even if in fact it was based on kin and patronage networks and their usurpation of the benefits of power.

The Moslem world is not alone in possessing conservative vested interests, nationalist turbulence and chiliastic social strivings. It is unique in that the fusion of these trends with a genuinely traditional religion, or rather, with its erstwhile top layer, now available to the entire society, is more intimate, more pervasive, more profound, more convincing, than it is anywhere else. How their interaction will concretely mould the future can only be grasped by looking at each case in detail.

The generalities which I have proposed may or may not be valid. Their soundness will not be determined by their logical neatness but by whether or not they fit the facts. Many of the relevant facts have been assembled in this volume.

The struggle of diverse political and ideological trends for the soul of the Middle East is intricate and multiform. These trends can only be properly understood in their diverse complexity. The present outstanding collection of essays explores the microstructure of the various conflicts which are being played out in the Middle East, and provides us with data and insights not available to the superficial view. It indisputably makes a very major and significant contribution to our understanding of a fascinating and as yet far from decided struggle, whose outcome may in the end be decisive for the fate of our world.

ERNEST GELLNER

# Publishers' Acknowledgements

The conference on which this volume is based, and the preparation of the volume itself, were supported by the Joint Committee on the Near and Middle East of the American Council of Learned Societies and the Social Science Research Council (USA).

# Editor's Acknowledgements

The pages in this volume, with one exception, were first presented at a Conference on Social Movements and Political Culture in the Contemporary Near and Middle East held in Mt Kisco, New York, on 14–17 May 1981. I am most grateful to the Joint Committee on the Near and Middle East of the American Council of Learned Societies and the Social Science Research Council for organising the conference and for its material assistance in preparing the manuscript for publication, to Ernest Gellner for kindly agreeing to write the Foreword, and to Ali Banuazizi, Eric Davis, and Peter von Sivers for their editorial advice. I am also much indebted to the members of the Centre for Middle Eastern Studies, St Antony's College, Oxford, especially the late Hamid Enayat, and to the Warden and Fellows of St Antony's College, where, as a Visiting Fellow in 1981–2, I could complete the editorial work and write the Introduction in a congenial and stimulating atmosphere.

SAID AMIR ARJOMAND

# Notes on the Contributors

**Akbar Ahmed,** a Visiting Scholar at the Department of Anthropology, Harvard University, is also a member of the Civil Service of Pakistan. His last post was Political Agent, South Waziristan. He has written extensively on Pakistan and his most recent book is *Religion and Politics in Muslim Society: Order and Conflict in Pakistan* (1983).

**Said Amir Arjomand** is Assistant Professor of Sociology at the State University of New York at Stony Brook. He was a Visiting Fellow of St Antony's College, Oxford, in 1981–2, and is the author of *Shadow of God and the Hidden Imam* (1984).

**Shaul Bakhash** has been a Visiting Associate Professor at the Department of Near Eastern Studies at Princeton University, and is the author of *Iran: Monarchy, Bureaucracy and Reform Under the Qajars, 1858–1896, The Politics of Oil and Revolution in Iran* and numerous articles on Iranian history and politics.

**Richard Cottam** is University Professor of Political Science at the University of Pittsburgh. His fields include the politics of Iran, foreign policy in the Middle East and international relations theory.

**Eric Davis** is Associate Professor of Political Science at Rutgers University, New Brunswick, New Jersey. A specialist in problems of political and economic development, he is author of *Challenging Colonialism: Bank Misr and Egyptian Industrialization, 1920–1941* (1982).

**Farhad Kazemi** is Associate Professor of Politics and director of the Hagop Kevorkian Center for Near Eastern Studies at New York University. He is the author of *Poverty and Revolution in Iran: The Migrant Poor, Urban Marginality and Politics* and the editor of *Iranian Revolution in Perspective.* He is also an editor of *Iranian Studies.*

**Rashid Khalidi** teaches politics at the American University of Beirut, where his research interests include modern Arab politics and history, and Soviet Middle East policy. He is the author of *British Policy Towards Syria and Palestine 1906–1914* (1980) and a number of papers and monographs.

**Binnaz Toprak** is Assistant Professor of Political Science at Boğaziçi University in Istanbul. She received her Ph.D. in political science from the City University of New York. She is the author of *Islam and Political Development in Turkey* (1981) and has written on religion, women, and politics in contemporary Turkish society.

**Peter von Sivers** is Associate Professor, Middle East History, University of Utah. He has done research and published in the field of social history (Egypt, Iraq, Syria, 750–1500; Algeria, 1830–1914), and has written articles on the Abbasid Thughur in *Journal of the Economic and Social History of the Orient*, 25 (1982) and on the Bou Amama revolt 1881 in *Peuples méditerranéens* (1982).

# Note on Transliteration

Turkish words have been written in the modern Turkish alphabet. Two separate simplified transliteration systems have been adopted for Persian and Arabic. Maximum effort has been made to be consistent within each of these systems. However, exceptions have had to be made for such common words as imam, Islam, *jihad* and ayatollah, and for proper names such as Muhammad, Husayn, Mosaddeq, Nasser and Khomeini which have been spelt uniformly throughout. Diacritical marks have been omitted, and "'" is used both for the *hamza* and the *'ain*.

# Glossary

| | |
|---|---|
| *'Adalat Khaneh* | House of Justice |
| *adda* | Market |
| *Akıncılar* | The Raiders (youth organisation) |
| *al-amir* | The commander |
| *al-Ahd* | The Covenant |
| *al-'id* | The festival (either of the breaking of the fast or the sacrificial festival) |
| *'alim* | 'Learned' or religious scholar |
| *al-infinitah* | The Open Door |
| *al-jihaz al-sirri* | The Secret Organisation |
| *al-umma al-mu'mina* | The Community of the Faithful |
| *al-umma al-jahiliyya* | The Community of Unbelievers |
| *al-usra* | The family |
| *al-wasita* | Mediator |
| *Amir al-mu'minin* | Commander of the Faithful |
| *anjoman* | (Political) society |
| anomie | Absence of social standards; normlessness |
| *Ansar Khumayni* | Helpers of Khomeini |
| *aqayid* | Ideas; ideology |
| *'ashura* | The day of commemoration of the martyrdom of Imam Husayn |
| *'atabat* | Shi'ite holy centres in Iraq |
| *'avamm* | Common masses |
| *ayatollah* | 'Sign of God', title of Shi'ite religious dignitaries |
| *badshah* | King |
| *bast* | Taking of sanctuary |
| *Ba'th* | Rebirth; the ruling party in Iraq and Syria |
| *beghairat* | Shameless |
| *dar al-harb* | Realm of war |
| *da'wa* | Mission |
| *ezan* | Call to prayer |

xvii

| | |
|---|---|
| *Fada'iyan-e Islam* | Devotees of Islam |
| *Fara'iziyya* | A movement for observation of religious duties (*fara'iz*) in Bengal in early nineteenth century |
| *farangi* | 'Frankish'; European |
| *fatwa(h)* | (Legal) injunction |
| *friperie* | Used cloth |
| *gourbi* | Dwelling built by Algerian peasants |
| *Hak İş* | (Turkish) Labour Union |
| *hadith* | Tradition (saying or deeds) of the Prophet |
| *hay'at mazhabi* | Religious association |
| *hefz-e bayza-ye Eslam* | Protection of the citadel of Islam |
| *hijra/hijrat* | Migration after the model of Muhammad's migration from Mecca to Medina |
| *Hizb al-tahir al-Islami* | Islamic Liberation Party |
| *hudud* | Punishments of the Sacred Law |
| *ijtihad* | 'Endeavour'; exercise of independent legal judgement |
| *İktisatçilar Kültür Vakfi* | (Turkish) Cultural Foundation of Economists |
| *İlim Yayma Cemiyeti* | (Turkish) Society for the Propagation of Knowledge |
| *imam* | (Prayer) leader |
| *imam hatip* | Prayer leader/preacher |
| *imamat* | Leadership of the community of believers |
| *'irfan* | Philosophical Sufism |
| *jahili* | Pertaining to pre-Islamic ignorance |
| *jahiliyya* | Pre-Islamic ignorance |
| *Jama'at al-jihad* | The Holy War Association |
| *Jama'at al-muslimin li'l-takfir* | The Society of Moslems which Charges Society with Unbelief |
| *Jama'at al-takfir wa'l-hijra* | Society of excommunication and withdrawal |
| *javan mardi* | Manly valour |
| *jazirat al'-arab* | The Arabian peninsula |
| *jihad* | Holy war |
| *Jund Allah* | God's Soldiers |
| *kafir* | Infidel |
| *khal'-e yadd* | Takeover from; dispossession |

| | |
|---|---|
| *khassadar* | Tribal levy (of troops) |
| *khavass* | The élite |
| *khilafat* | Caliphate |
| *lashkar* | Army |
| *madrassah/medrese* | Religious school; colleges of religious education |
| *mahdi* | The messianic 'leader' at the End of Time |
| *mai-baap* | Mother–father |
| *Majlis* | Lower House (of Parliament) |
| *majles-e ma'delat* | Assembly of Justice |
| *maktab al-rishad* | The Guidance Council |
| *malik* | King |
| *marja' (-e taqlid)* | Shi'ite authoritative jurist |
| *mashayikh* | The elder; authorities |
| *mashuru'a* | In accordance with Sacred Law |
| *mashurta* | Constitutional |
| *maulvi* | Man of religion |
| *Mekfureci Öğret- menler Derneği* | Organisation of Idealist Teachers (Turkish) |
| *mian* | Man of spiritual gifts and holy descent |
| *Milli Gürüş Almanya Teşkilatları* | Organisation of National Outlook in Germany |
| *Milli Nizam Partisi* | National Order Party |
| *Milli Selamet Partisi (MSP)* | National Salvation Party (NSP) |
| *MSP Gençlik Lokal- leri* | NSP Youth Clubs |
| *MSP Işçi Komisyo- ulair* | NSP Workers' Commission |
| *Milli Turk Talebe Birliği* | National Turkish Union of Students |
| *mosleh-e kabir* | The Great Reformer |
| *mujaddid/mojadded* | Renewer |
| *mujtahed* | Jurist; he who is competent to exercise *ijtihad* |
| *mulaqat* | Meeting |
| *mullah* | Moslem cleric |
| *musawat* | Equality |
| *mustaz'afin* | The disinherited |
| *nadi* | Assembly hall |
| *Naksibendi* | A Sufi order |
| *namaz* | Daily prayers |

| | |
|---|---|
| *nang* | A tribal branch of the Pukhtuns |
| *nazr* | Cash donations for a vow |
| *niswar* | Snuff |
| *Nizam-e Mustafa* | Prophetic Order |
| *Nurcu* | 'Seeker of light', a follower of Bediüzzeman Saidi Nursi in Turkey |
| *pir* | Saint, spiritual guide |
| *qazi* | Judge |
| *rawza-khani* | Shi'ite religious ceremonies usually devoted to recitation of the tragedy of Karbala and martyrdom of Imam Husayn and his family |
| *ruhaniyyat* | Clergy |
| *ruz-nameh* | Journal, newspaper |
| *salafiyya* | An Islamic movement enjoining the imitations of the ways and the pristine Islam of the 'Pious Ancestors' |
| *sartor* | Black head (symbol of grief) |
| *sayyed* | Descendant of the Prophet |
| *şeyh* | Shaykh; Sufi guide |
| *shaheed* | Martyr |
| *Shari'a* | Holy law |
| *Sufi* | Islamic mystic |
| *tabliq* | Missionary activity |
| *tafsir* | Interpretation of Koran |
| *takfir* | Excommunication |
| *talib* | Seminarian |
| *Tanzimat* | The Reforms |
| *tarikat* | (Sufi) Brotherhood |
| *tawhid* | Unity (of God) |
| *tasu'a* | The day of mourning preceding 'ashura |
| *ta'ziyeh* | Passion play on the martyrdom of Husayn and his family |
| *teeman* | Tribe-at-large |
| *Teknik Elemanlar Birliği* | Union of Technical Personnel (Turkish) |
| *thana* | Eulogy |
| *tollab* | Seminarians |
| *Tudeh* | Iranian Communist Party |
| *Türk Yazarlar Sendikase* | Syndicate of Turkish Writers |
| *Türkiye Yazarlar Birliği* | Writers' Union of Turkey |

| | |
|---|---|
| *'ulama* | 'The learned', plural of *'alim*; religious authorities |
| *'umad* | Plural of *'umda*; village magnate |
| *umma(h)* | Community of believers |
| *Usuli* | Pertaining to rationalism in jurisprudence |
| *Usuli* movement | A movement of jurisprudential rationalism in late eighteenth- and nineteenth-century Shi'ism |
| *vali* | Guardian, custodian |
| *velayat* | Guardianship, authority, mandate |
| *velayat-e faqih* | Authority, sovereignty of the jurist |
| *wilaya* | Province |
| *zakat* | A religious tax |
| *zawiya* | Sufi convent |
| *zendeh bad* | Long Live . . .! |

# 1 Introduction: Social Movements in the Contemporary Near and Middle East

## SAID AMIR ARJOMAND

The essays presented in this volume focus on the endogenous factors in the emergence and growth of social movements in the contemporary Near and Middle East. The broader context of the incorporation of the Middle East into the world economic system and, more recently, the increasing importance of the region in world politics are taken for granted and not subjected to analysis. Of the variety of contemporary social movements considered by the participants, those whose driving force was nationalism or Islam emerged as the most important and effective. Furthermore, a pattern of the declining significance of nationalism and the concomitant shift to Islam as the focus of the popular movements during the last two decades emerged with clarity. This shift from nationalism to revolutionary Islam thus appeared as the most appropriate thematic principle for the selection of the case-studies. However, no attempt was made to impose a single explanatory framework throughout the volume. The contributors, representing a variety of disciplines and theoretical and methodological orientations, have in fact followed differing approaches to the problem.

## CULTURE, COLLECTIVE IDENTITY, IDEOLOGY AND ORGANISATION

National integration constitutes the socio-historical context of the movements studied in this volume. 'The integrative revolution', to use

1

Geertz's felicitous phrase (Geertz, 1963), has deeply affected the Near
and Middle East in the twentieth century as it has the rest of the world.
Its period of inception, pace and continuity or disruptiveness have
differed considerably from country to country but its varying impact is
by now felt throughout the region. In the process of national integration, politics inevitably become public: urbanisation and the
increasing integration of the rural periphery into a national economy,
the spread of literacy and higher education results in the considerable
enlargement, if not the creation, of a public sphere. There is a great
increase in popular political awareness and the masses – especially the
urban masses – are, in one form or another, integrated into political
society. National integration intensifies the need for 'a cognitive and
moral map of the universe' (Shils, 1972), and gives birth to modern
political ideologies. More fundamentally, it necessitates drastic changes
in the cultural context of all socio-political activity. Politico-cultural
movements seeking to disseminate a sense of collective identity and a
corresponding form of consciousness and/or espousing political ideologies are thus set in motion.[1]

The social movements studied in this volume, with one exception, fall
into the category of 'general social movements' – movements, that is,
which aim at arousing and disseminating a new consciousness (Blumer,
1939; Wilson, 1973, p. 12).[2] They are akin to the classical type of broad
politico-cultural movements such as nationalism, liberalism, socialism,
communism and fascism which are characteristic of the comparable
stage of national integration in the West and which constitute the subject
matter of Heberle's important early study, *Social Movements: An
Introduction to Political Sociology* (1951). Although the more limited or
'specific' social movements of the variety currently under study by most
American sociologists (Marx and Wood, 1975) are not entirely absent in
the Middle East, they are relatively insignificant.[3]

It is not difficult to explain this fact. The differentiation of the social
structure and the degree of institutional political pluralism is not such as
to allow the mobilisation of a substantial segment of the population for
a considerable length of time on the basis of a specific issue brought into
relief against the background of a consensual normative order. The
structural and organisational obstacles to the generation of concerted
socio-political action are such that, as a rule, they can be overcome
either by an appeal to the most general and broadest principles, or not at
all.

An important feature of the social movements in the contemporary
Middle East derives from the less differentiated social organisation of

the contemporary Middle East: rudimentary or heteronomous organi-sation.[4] The movements under consideration in this volume, unless they succeed in the take-over of the state and appropriation and extension of its apparatus, are sustained by weak and rudimentary organisational structures. Adopting Hobsbawm's (1959) useful analogy, we may say that these loosely-structured and tenuously independent organisational frameworks often suffice to keep their respective movements 'endemic' until propitious conditions facilitate either the take-over of the state by its proponents or the 'epidemic' spread of the movement and its temporary control over a wider organisational network of sympathetic institutions. Curiously enough, the communist movement which has had the strongest autonomous organisational structure in the form of a reasonably well-disciplined political party, with clandestine cells, is also the one whose record has so far been marked by lack of success except in South Yemen and Afghanistan.

In addition to the somewhat minimal importance of the organi-sational factor, one is also struck – at least in retrospect – by the relative ineffectiveness of Western-inspired political ideologies such as lib-eralism, socialism and communism to generate popular movements in the Middle East.

Liberalism and the ideas of representative democracy did produce constitutionalist movements amongst the literate segments of Middle Eastern societies in the latter part of the nineteenth and early decades of the twentieth centuries. Their force, however, was by and large spent before the process of national integration came into full swing after the Second World War. Where and to the extent that liberalism and the advocacy of parliamentary democracy survived, as in Mosaddeq's Iran, it did so under the protective wing of nationalism.

The Middle Eastern communist parties, it is true, can boast of considerable success in Iran in the 1940s and early 1950s. The same is true of communism in Iraq in the late 1940s to the early 1960s. Batatu, who devotes an entire third of his monumental book on Iraq to the communist party and its activities until 1955, justifies doing so not only by pointing out that 'the communists alone had the true characteristics of an organised political party', (Batatu, 1978, p. 478) but also because they 'provided the Iraqis with not a few of their categories of thought' (Batatu, 1978, p. 466). The initiative of the communist parties in propagation of political ideas and creation of viable organised parties cannot be denied. Nor should the influence of such initiative on other social movements and political parties be minimised. Nevertheless, in both Iran and Iraq, the initial success of the communists, due to their possession of a coherent political ideology as well as their organisational advantage and party discipline, can be explained by the absence of significant rivals in either respect. In Turkey, the contending rivalry of Kemalism inhibited the growth of the communist movement (Tunçay, 1981). The rivalry of the *Ba'th* in Syria, the Syrian National Party and the *Phalange* in Lebanon, and the *Wafd* and the Muslim Brotherhood in Egypt had the same effect (Batatu, 1978, p. 478).

In contrast to communism, socialism has, in a number of important instances, been successful in the Middle East. But socialism has been successful only when combined with a strong, indeed a predominant, dose of nationalism. It cannot be disputed that the confrontation with imperialism and pan-Arab nationalism constituted the basis of the popular appeal of Nasserite socialism. As for the *Ba'th* movement,[5] its chief ideologue Michel Aflaq is explicit 'The *Ba'th* is scientific socialism plus spirit'. Furthermore, this socialism is not 'the first philosophy, the view that guides all life, [but merely a] tributary deferring to a source, which is the national idea' (cited in Batatu, 1978, p. 736).

When turning from the organisational and ideological factors to those pertaining to culture and collective identity, we seem to tumble upon the key factors underlying the strength of the contemporary social movements in the Middle East and North Africa. In this connection, we cannot do better than begin with Ernest Gellner's theory of nationalism, first stated in *Thought and Change* (1964). This is especially so because the theory enables us to go beyond nationalism, and towards a more general understanding of the importance of collective cultural identity – be it predominantly tribal, national or religious – in contemporary social movements. According to Gellner, urbanisation and industrialisation, national economic and political integration, accompanied as they are by the spread of literacy and expansion of higher education, brings about a radical change in the mode of interpersonal relations. The burden shifts from the structural context of the relationship to the system of communication. Culture thus becomes the crucial element in the new mode as the determinant of the *identity* of the interacting individuals.[6] This sets the precondition for the politicisation of ethnic, national or religious culture and therefore identity. Although Gellner's attention is centred only on the politicisation of ethnic and national identity and culture, the last possibility – that is, the possibility of politicisation of religious identity – is also especially strong in the Middle East as Islam has always been and remains a primary basis of communal identity and loyalty.

The successful politicisation of any one of these forms of collective identity, or more usually the politicisation of collective identity composed of overlapping elements of all these forms, can effectively generate and propel social movements.

## NATIONALISM AND THE ISLAMIC MOVEMENTS

The twentieth century opens with the prominence of nationalist movement in the Middle East, with the Constitutional Revolution in Iran in 1905–6, the Young Turks' Revolution in 1908 and the onset of the Arab national movement in the Greater Syria. It is therefore appropriate for us to begin with an examination of nationalism.

Students of nationalism are often struck by the vagueness and malleability of nationalist ideologies. Not only is it possible to combine loyalty to ethnic and religious communities with loyalty to the nation-state, but the resultant varieties of nationalism can be associated, in yet another dimension, with a variety of political ideas. The national bond can be harnessed to political action in varying ideological mixtures, that is, in association with radical as well as with conservative political ideas. As Cottam puts it in Chapter 2, 'behavioural manifestations flowing from nationalism vary greatly depending on other components of the ideology'. (As we shall see, however, the characteristic of malleability is not exclusively confined to nationalism but is also encountered in the ideologies of other types of movements.)

It is generally accepted that the intelligentsia is unfailingly over-represented in nationalist movements, and that 'the ideology of nationalism is born of their situation and problems' (Smith, 1971, p. 136). However, the *success* of nationalism is determined by factors extraneous to the aspirations of the intelligentsia. In the period after the First World War, the immediate success of the nationalist movements was essentially due to the collapse of empires (Smith, 1976, pp. 50–3). In Chapter 3, Khalidi traces the emergence of the Arab nationalist movement in Syria on the eve of the disintegration of the Ottoman Empire. His analysis brings out the importance of the intelligentsia by concentrating on an important stage of the process of national integration in the Middle East: the creation of a public sphere and the incorporation of the intelligentsia into political society. After the Young Turks' Revolution in 1908, political participation increased markedly with the institution of parliamentary and local elections and with the freeing of the press from political censorship. This provided the context for 'an integrative process [which] consisted of the movement into the political stage of members of the military, journalists, teachers and professionals, all of whom had played little or no part in the traditional politics of the Ottoman Empire'. In this context, the intelligentsia – and, incidentally, the army officers as 'intellectuals in uniform' – acted, to use Cottam's phrase, as 'the opinion-formulating élite' of an Arab nationalist movement in opposition to Ottoman domination. A new dimension was superimposed on the traditional politics of the area. The 'politics of the notables' (Hourani, 1968) was thus transformed into a more fully public politics. Furthermore, Khalidi notes the lack of political significance of religious identity in that period (many of the ideologues of Arab nationalism were Christians), and the social heterogeneity of the advocates of nationalism – a feature which contrasts sharply with the homogeneity of the Islamic leadership in Iran.

If the nationalist ideology reflects the normative needs and political outlook of the intelligentsia, the national sentiment or ethos, which determines the responsiveness of the other segments of the population to nationalism, derives from independent socio-historical factors. Cottam's behavioural approach to nationalism focuses on the strength of the national bond and the consequences of the nationalist ethos, defined in terms of primary loyalty to an actual or potential political community. As Cottam emphasises, the individual's simultaneous membership of overlapping ethnic, national and religious communities – that is, his multiple and therefore indeterminate collective identity – makes possible the profession of primary loyalty to more than one political community at any given time.[7] This makes for the continued efficiency of national ethos and loyalty even when the national identity is not politicised. However, without the politicisation of nationality as the primary component of collective identity, no explicitly nationalist movement can be engendered.

Cottam's behavioural analysis clearly implies that the intelligentsia are much more important as a factor in the *emergence* of nationalist ideologies than for the *diffusion and strength* of nationalism. The diffusion of nationalism, its strength as an *idée-force* and its success in consolidating a nation-state depend crucially on the existence of a popular audience receptive to nationalist ideologies, which in turn is determined by the structural features of contemporary societies identified by Gellner. Other elements in the complex set of factors which determine the strength of nationalism in each state are analysed by Cottam. While he sees considerable variation among the present Middle Eastern states regarding viability (territorial, economic, demographic), uniqueness (historical, cultural, linguistic) and the complementarity of identity (religious, racial, ethnic), Cottam's assessment points to uniformity among the Middle Eastern countries as regards increasing political participation, and to near-uniformity as regards the existence of an attentive public.

Chapter 4 by Ahmed examines the interplay of ethnic, tribal and religious identity in a local movement in the North Western Frontier Province of Pakistan which culminated in the open defiance of central government in the name of Islam in 1975–6. This local movement arose in the context of traditional agnate rivalry between the Wazirs and the Mahsuds in the tribal Waziristan, and was led by the Mullah of Wana who, at one point, came to consider himself 'the uncrowned king of Wana'.

Ahmed argues that, in contrast to the nineteenth century Islamic movements, the Islamic movements of the present time cannot be analysed solely or even primarily as anti-Western and anti-colonial, but would have to be looked at in terms of the internal dynamics of moslem societies. Ahmed believes that close anthropological analysis of small Moslem groups engaged in specific Islamic movements illuminates aspects of the phenomenon not observed by the conventional, macro-sociological approach. However, he is equally mindful of the significance of the integration of local groups into the nation-state, and accordingly focuses his analysis at the intermediate level of the administrative district. The impact of national integration is therefore taken into account, with a rudimentary form of public politics added to the traditional intertribal conflict. Ahmed's microsociological analysis also demonstrates that the use of the Islamic idiom for the political mobilisation of a tribal ethnic group is by no means without ambiguities and contradictions.

The case of the movement led by the Mullah of Wana illustrates the possibility of a traditional religious leader challenging the representative of the state on parochial issues on behalf of Wazir tribesmen and in the name of local society. In speaking for local society, and in claiming that he alone can speak for society, the Mullah of Wana resorted to the adaptation of an Islamic idiom to match the generalised legitimatory claims of the state and its representative, who was accused of championing the particularistic interests of the Mahsuds. As a case of overlapping identity, of ethnic, tribal and religious (Islamic) identity, and as a case in which collective social action based on primordial ethnic ties is justified and given greater ideological generality in terms not of an ideology of ethnic nationalism but of Islam, Ahmed's contribution bridges the transition from the chapters on nationalism to those on Islamic movements.

The chapters on Islamic movements are arranged along a continuum of increasing significance. In Chapter 5, von Sivers sets the relative tardiness of the social movements of the traditionalist, Islamic type in the context of a meticulously detailed picture of the conditions of national economic and political integration in Algeria. The same picture is then used to assess the prospects for the rise of an Islamic traditionalist movement in the 1980s. Von Sivers makes the remark that 'for the historian it is a commonplace that tradition is constantly modernised and modernity is constantly traditionalised'. One could only wish all social scientists were equally aware of this commonplace. In Chapter 10, I put forward 'revolutionary traditionalism' as an ideal typical characterisation of the movement led by Khomeini, and suggest that, more generally, 'traditionalism' be used to designate the type of reactive revitalisation movement which arises when Islam as a religious tradition becomes fully self-conscious as a result both of serious threats of erosion from within and of rival Western cultural penetration. Adopting this conceptualisation, von Sivers broadens it beyond the exclusive focus on the religious tradition. He identifies three (unself-conscious) traditions – or aspects of tradition – in rural Algeria: traditions of self-sufficiency, political non-involvement and religious parochialism. In other words, in addition to the tradition of religious parochialism, von Sivers considers the economic tradition of rural self-sufficiency and the political tradition of non-involvement as possible bases for the development of an 'articulated ideology of traditionalism'. This prospect implies the tempting possibility of the use of 'tradition as an instrument of self-protection against the shortcomings of government planning'.

Von Sivers pays close attention to the unequal relation between the rural and urban areas of Algeria and to the economic conditions in the traditional agricultural sector with a view to assessing the likelihood of their thus giving rise to an Islamic traditionalist movement in opposition to the state-controlled official Islam whose contrasting feature is the emphasis on ecumenical, national and secular elements. In this perspective, traditionalism is seen as a centrifugal tendency in reaction to the attempts by the Algerian government to break through self-sufficiency in the agricultural sector, and to bring about its integration into the national market economy. This tendency is sustained, on the one hand, by the 'reluctance towards integration and preference for backsliding into self-sufficiency in the [agricultural] "public sector"', and, on the other, by the struggle of the middle peasantry against the urban bureaucrats. Von Sivers sees potential recruits for an Islamic traditionalist movement among the rural migrants, mostly self-employed in irregular jobs in construction or in commerce and handicraft – 'the bazaar sector' – who constitute about one third of the total urban labour force. Furthermore, those sons of the parochial middle peasantry who go to cities, often to study in universities, but do not succumb to the ideology of the urban techno-bureaucrats, tend to play a leading role in the formulation of an alternative Islamic ideology. He thus sees the protesting students as the tip of an 'Arab Islamic traditionalist volcano' which may well erupt in the 1980s.

Since von Sivers' article was written, the agitation of the Islamic student militants has assumed a sufficiently alarming proportion to elicit a sharply worded threat from President Ben-Jadid of Algeria in early December, 1982. It is very interesting to note that in the proclamations accompanying their violent agitation in November 1982, the Islamic militants not only attacked the 'Marxist ideology of the government' and demanded that the *Qur'an* be the constitution of Algeria, but they also vehemently attacked the government land reform and demanded the restoration of all the government-acquired land to their expropriated original owners (*Le Monde*, 7 December, 1982). The position of the Islamic militants of Algeria on land reform and redistribution, which has puzzled many observers because it is at odds with the position of the Islamic revolutionaries elsewhere in the Middle East, becomes fully intelligible in the light of von Sivers' analysis.

Moving from Algeria to Turkey, where the meteoric rise of the National Salvation Party in the political arena in the 1970s attracted considerable attention, one can observe the political role of Islam in the only aggressively secular state of the Middle East. In Chapter 6, after a brief mention of the *Tanzimat* – the Reforms – instituted by the nineteenth-century Ottoman westernisers and the disestablishment of Islam as the state religion by their twentieth-century heir, Ataturk, Toprak sees the ideology of the National Salvation Party in a direct line of continuity with the late nineteenth-century Islamists who opposed the westernisers. As heirs to the nineteenth-century Islamists – whom we may call, in Gellnerian fashion, the Islamic '*Narodniks*' – the endeavour of the ideologues of the National Salvation Party is seen as 'a revival of the pre-Republican search for an Islamic model of modernity'. She emphasises the importance attached by this Turkish Islamic party to industrialisation as a means of attaining autarky and national glory, and points out that 'the problem of industrialisation occupies the most important dimension of the Party's ideology'. This is presented as consonant with the social background of the leaders of the National Salvation Party who are predominantly drawn from professional groups. In explaining the appeal of the Party and the bases of its social support in the 1970s, however, Toprak notes the salience of traditional rural areas, *especially those undergoing rapid change and economic growth.* (Chapter 6; see further, Toprak, 1981, pp. 110–21). We shall return to the significance of this last point.

In Chapter 7, Davis attempts to put the rise of Islamic militancy in Egypt in a global, world-market perspective. He proposes accumulation, legitimation and authenticity as the central concepts of a neo-Marxian model to explain Islamic radicalism (a term he uses in preference to fundamentalism). World economic forces and the consequent economic inequalities within the Egyptian social structure have conspired to delegitimise both capitalist (liberal) and socialist (state-capitalist) models of development, and have produced a 'crisis of authenticity'. Disaffected social strata have come to consider liberalism and socialism as 'imported' value systems to be replaced by their own authentic ideology, the Islamic ideology. Such an endogenous ideology performs the following functions: it reflects the class interests of the Islamic radicals, it compensates for the 'status deprivation' from which its adherents suffer, it offers a familiar cognitive map for interpreting reality, and it offers a mechanism for re-establishing a sense of community and corporate identity to overcome the fragmentation of traditional institutions such as the extended family.

Davis notes a consistent pattern of recruitment into the Moslem Brotherhood and the affiliated radical Islamic groups from the 1930s through to the 1960s. This pattern is marked by the prominence of urban professional middle class: schoolteachers, clerks, low-level bureaucrats and more recently – with the development of technical education – engineers. He further notes an important qualification. Most of the Islamic militants are recent migrants into urban areas who have had a traditional upbringing in the rural areas. They are thus from conservative and traditionally-oriented social backgrounds. There is a high representation of teachers among the rural members of the Moslem Brotherhood, and the urban militants fully maintain their links with their families who reside in rural areas and are frequently in teaching professions. In Davis's analysis, the Islamic radicals, though predominantly urban, middle-class professionals, are considered the bearers of the ideological outlook of the rural *petite-bourgeoisie* which has conditioned the traditional socialisation of many of them.

Liberalism, Arab socialism and Marxism came under heavy attack in the writings of the Islamic radicals but the most striking feature of their ideology is its 'unitary, holistic character'. Davis thus sees the veering of the Islamic reformism of Shaykh Muhammad 'Abduh (d. 1905) in the direction of the fundamentalism of the present day offshoots of the Moslem Brotherhood as an attempt to regenerate a corporate unity that repairs the breakdown of traditional institutions such as the extended family rather than a pathological and xenophobic response to alien views (which are nevertheless firmly rejected). All this, he insists, is to be understood not as 'revival or resurgence but rather as the *politicisation* of Islam'.

Consonantly with Ahmed's reminder, Davis is attentive to the role of internal factors. British imperialism or Western capitalism can no longer be blamed for all the social and political ills as in the 1930s. The major problem of our time is seen as one of the corruption of domestic society in reaction to which a typical response has been the disavowal and anathematisation (*takfir*) of society and the withdrawal (*hijra*) from it in the form of avoidance of corrupting contacts and the refusal to serve the state and the army, as these are considered under the control of 'infidels'.

The Islamic revolution in Iran is by far the most spectacular manifestation of revolutionary Islam as the fountainhead of popular movements in the contemporary Middle East. As the Islamic revolution represents the culmination of the ousting of nationalism by re-volutionary Islam, the last three chapters of the book are devoted to a more detailed analysis of various components of the movement which led to it. In Chapter 8, Kazemi gives us the first comprehensive account of a terrorist group, the *Fada'iyan-e Islam* (Devotees of Islam), to be published. The *Fada'iyan* were the first Islamic group in Iran to preach, in the 1940s, the necessity of violence as a means of extirpating corrupt statesmen and, more generally, of establishing a truly Islamic govern-ment. They can and should be regarded as the forerunners of the Islamic revolutionaries who followed Ayatollah Khomeini two decades later. Khomeini himself had admired the group and temporarily broke with the leading Shi'ite dignitary Ayatollah Borujerdi when the latter refused to intercede with the Shah to save the life of their leader, Navvah Safavi (executed in January 1956). Mortimer (1982, p. 349) has noted the prominent display of Navvab Safavi's portrait in Khomeini's house in Qum in the spring and summer of 1979, and Kazemi mentions the revival of the *Fada'iyan-e Islam* under an older member, Sadeq Khalkhali, the Judge Blood of the Islamic Revolution. Furthermore, as I point out in Chapter 10, the Devotees' blueprint for an Islamic government was to be implemented, by and large, by the Islamic Republican Party after the Islamic revolution of 1979.

At least two important points emerge from Kazemi's analysis. The first is the endemic continuation of Islamic militancy in the 1960s as manifested in the assassination of the Prime Minister Mansur in 1965 by an Islamic zealot belonging to an offshoot of the *Fada'iyan-e Islam*. The second is the instability and unease in the alliance between the *Fada'iyan* and the leading clerical statesman of the period, Ayatollah Kashani. Although, as Kazemi points out, Kashani on a number of occasions applauded the acts of violence committed by the Devotees and secured the release of the culprits, and although Kashani's sympathisers might occasionally turn up in the demonstrations organised by the Devotees, the truly makeshift nature of the alliance stands in sharp contrast to the organic incorporation of the young militants into Khomeini's Islamic movement in the 1970s.

In Chapter 9, Bakhash focuses on the decisive year of the revolution, 1978, by the end of which the fate of monarchy was sealed.[8] Bakhash's richly detailed account of the role of sermons and pamphleteering in the revolutionary mass mobilisation of that year underscores the role of the Shi'ite clerics in keeping riots endemic from early January to September 1978 when the entire country was engulfed in the revolutionary movement. The rhythm of these endemic outbursts is shown to have been set by the forty-day cycles of mourning ceremonies for the 'martyrs' and by religiously significant dates when commemorative ceremonies would expand into the streets as violent agitation. Bakhash also shows that the more cautious stand of the senior clerics would give way under the pressure of radicalisation from the lesser clerics and militant seminarians who took the leading part in transcribing sermons of the mosque preachers, and in extensive pamphleteering activity. These activities succeeded in propagating the idea of Islamic government, and in discrediting all thought of compromise and moderation.

Finally, in Chapter 10, I view the Islamic revolution of 1979 as the culmination of a traditionalist movement which has its inception in the clerical reaction to parliamentarianism during the first decade of the present century. The progressive, albeit undulating, ideological and organisational coherence of the movement, its leadership by an increasingly dispossessed clerical estate, the special appeal of the movement to the solidly traditional religious sentiment to the stolidly religious social strata, and, finally, the critical events making for the revolutionary politicisation of the traditionalist movement are analysed. The chapter concludes with suggestions for putting Islamic revolutionary traditionalism in broad comparative perspective.

## THE ISLAMIC MOVEMENTS IN ANALYTICAL PERSPECTIVE

I have so far tried to tie together summaries of the individual contributions in the perspective of national integration implicit in most if not all of them. I now propose to go beyond this modest attempt at integration of the material on my own, and to explore its broader analytical implications.

A quarter of a century ago, in his celebrated study of the 'archaic forms of social movements', Hobsbawm (1959) characterised the religious and religiously-oriented popular movement of nineteenth-century Europe as 'pre-political', the contrasting point of reference being socialism and Marxism as the modern and therefore 'political' form of popular social movements.[9] In the 1960s, the relation between religious movements and nationalism was widely prejudged, as seems clear in retrospect, in a similar manner. Abun-Nasr (1963), for example, was predisposed to see orthodox reformism, the *Salafiyya* movement, as the religious preamble to the Moroccan nationalist movement. Ali Merad (1967, p. 147) would maintain that it was 'relatively easy to establish a connection between the expansion of [Islamic] reformism in Algeria and the progress of nationalist ideas among the Moslem masses' (cited in Gellner, 1975, p. 287). Keddie (1969) would similarly consider pan-Islam as proto-nationalism. In his important article on Algeria, Gellner considered the pre-World War Two orthodox reformism 'a form of proto-nationalism' (Gellner, 1975, p. 293). More recently, he has reiterated his view that orthodox reformism overlapped with nationalism and that 'Reformism indeed appeared to be the early form of nationalism' (Gellner, 1981, p. 58).

The above views no longer seem plausible with regard to the self-consciously politicised revolutionary Islam of the present time. In fact, if anything, reversing the order of the prejudgement seems to make more sense. At any rate, such a reversal is often explicitly made by the ideologues of the Islamic movements who present nationalism as a less evolved and misguided precursor. Rather than accepting either of these opposing views, it seems to me that one would be much closer to truth if one considered the Islamic movements as fully religious movements which are inevitably politically conditioned. To persuade the reader that this is the case, I cannot do better than let Hasan al-Banna (d. 1949), the founder of the Moslem Brotherhood speak:

If someone should say to you: This is politics!, say: This is Islam, and we do not recognize such divisions. If someone should say to you: You are agents of revolution!, say: We are agents of the truth and of peace in which we believe and which we exact . . .

'Say: "This is my way: I summon unto God according to a clear evidence – I and whosoever follows me. Glory unto God, I am not of the polytheists." ' (Qur'an 12: 108) . . .

I say once more that the world today is surfeited with propaganda of all kinds – political, nationalist, patriotic, economic, military, and pacifist. And what is the mission of the Moslem Brotherhood alongside this confused welter? . . .

Listen, Brother! Our mission is one described by the term 'Islamic' . . . We believe that Islam is an all-embracing concept which regulates every aspect of life . . . Whatever is in accord with it is welcome; but whatever clashes with it, we are absolved therefrom . . .

O our people, we are calling out to you with the *Qur'an* in our right hand and the *Sunna* in our left, and with the deeds of the pious ancestors of the sons of this *umma* [community of believers] as our example. We summon you to Islam, the teaching of Islam, the laws of Islam and the guidance of Islam, and if this smacks of 'politics' in your eyes, then it is our 'policy'! (al-Banna, 1978, pp. 36, 40, 46–7, 75)

The above passages demonstrate that religion as a meaningful pattern of beliefs is more inclusive than political ideology. It may or may not endow political action with religious – ethical and soteriological – significance. At the same time, the fact that Islam as interpreted by Hasan al-Banna clearly does give politics derivative but nevertheless critical significance attests to the far-reaching political conditioning of his mission (*da'wa*).

Once we accept the primacy of the religious motive as well as the inevitable political conditioning of the contemporary Islamic movements, it appears more appropriate to follow a suggestion strongly implied in the classical formulations of sociology of religion: that political ideologies such as nationalism and communism are functional equivalents of religion, at least with regard to the political sphere. Along this line and in a Weberian vein, A. D. Smith (1971) presents the nationalist ideology as a solution to the problem of meaning of political life. The same can be said of the liberal democratic, the Marxist, socialist, and now Islamic *ideologies* as they all define the meaning and norms of political life. Whatever the respective genetic priority of these ideological systems or the chronological order of their introduction to the Middle East, none can be justifiably endowed with any essential sociological primacy over the others. Democratic nationalism, national Marxism, national socialism, Islamic nationalism, Islamic socialism, Islamic Marxism, Islamic democracy and democratic socialism or Marxism are all possible and actual ideological permutations, but there does not seem to be any empirical warrant for attributing ultimacy to any one of the above components over the others. In the last analysis, democratic, nationalist, socialist, Marxist and Islamic ideologies perform the *same* function of provision of a moral and cognitive map of the socio-political universe, and have, to state the matter generously, a comparable redemptive appeal. As such, they are *rival* systems.

Owing to the simultaneous activities of their respective proponents in the contemporary Middle East, the nationalist, socialist and Islamic movements have become fully conscious of this rivalry and tend to move towards more sharply and mutually exclusive self-definitions. A cyclical rather than a unilinear view of the preponderance of one of the three types of ideology may well be more in order. In principle, any of the three elements can take the upper hand and subordinate the other two. The picture is not static and the relative prospects for these elements undoubtedly change from period to period. What cannot be contested, however, is a far greater receptivity of the masses throughout the Middle East towards Islamic ideologies in the present decade. The chapters by Ahmed, von Sivers, Toprak, Davis and myself discuss some of the socio-political factors underlying this increased receptivity to Islamic ideologies and the consequent politicisation of Islam.

If the assumption of eventual supersession of Islamic movements by those more familiar in the course of Western history may have seemed warranted a decade ago, it was because of the absence of conspicuous self-conscious and exclusionary Islamic movements. Such is no longer the case. Most leaders of the Islamic movements are now wise to and apprehensive of the familiar stratagem of presenting nationalist, socialist and communist ideas in an Islamic garb with the hope of initiating an 'archaic' social movement which could in due course undergo the kind of supersession Hobsbawm and Gellner were taking for granted.

Perhaps because a variety of official and individual reconciliations of Islam with democracy, nationalism and socialism have been frequently encountered in the present century, most observers have so far remained inattentive to the self-conscious and fiercely exclusionary character of the contemporary Islamic movements, beginning with the Moslem Brotherhood. The passages quoted from al-Banna imply resistance to

16 *Introduction*

any change in what is perceived to be the configuration of the core elements of Islam. Al-Banna proceeds to point out that if nationalism and other political ideologies are prefigured in Islam, then, and only to that extent, they have a place in it. But why attach a weight different from what they have in the Islamic configuration, and why present them in a new configuration?

The pursuit of science, on the one hand, and patriotism and nationalism on the other, are both prefigured in the *Qur'an* and the *Hadith*. But whereas al-Banna sanctions the learning of natural sciences at their most advanced stage, he refuses to grant the same status to nationalism because the nationalist political ideology is a rival political system. 'People are at times seduced by the appeal to patriotism, at other times by that of nationalism.' But the virtues of patriotism are 'to be found in Islam in a state more complete, more pure, more lofty, and more exalted than anything that can be found in the utterances of the Westerners and the books of Europeans' (al-Banna, 1978, pp. 47–8). It is no surprise that 'the notion of nationalism ... melts away and disappears just as snow disappears after strong, sparkling sunlight falls upon it, by contrast with Islamic brotherhood, which the *Qur'an* instils in the souls of all those who follow it' (cited in Mortimer, 1982, p. 230). Similarly, 'internationalism, nationalism, socialism, capitalism, Bolshevism, war, the distribution of wealth, the link between producer and consumer ... we believe that all of these have been dealt with thoroughly by Islam' (al-Banna, 1978, p. 87). In the same period, and very much in the same vein, Mawlana Abu'l-A'la' Mawdudi, the founder of the *Jama' at-i Islamic* of Pakistan would write: 'in their spirit and their aims Islam and nationalism are diametrically opposed to each other' (Donohue and Espisito, 1982, p. 94).

As I show in Chapter 10, the leaders of the Islamic movement in Iran in the 1970s similarly sought to define the Islamic character of their movement in sharp contradistinction to nationalism and thus preclude the possibility envisaged by Gellner. In fact, as I point out, the Constitution of the Islamic Republic of Iran reverses Gellner's view, considers the nationalist movement of the earlier decades as proto-Islamic and celebrates its supersession by the Islamic revolutionary movement under the leadership of Khomeini.

The Islamic movements have adopted a similar posture *vis-a-vis* socialism somewhat more recently. As I try to show in Chapter 10, the Islamic ideologues have cast the basic teachings of Islam into an ideological framework on the nineteenth century European model. As a consequence of this rearrangement of topics, resulting from their employment of 'modern, systematic method', they have produced blueprints for the Islamic economic, social and political 'system'. Fiercely exclusionary definitions of the Islamic socio-economic system have determined the position of the Islamic movement towards socialism. One of the best examples of such elaborations is Sayyid Qutb's *Social Justice in Islam* (1973 [1944]) in which terms like social and economic justice and social co-operation are chosen, systematically fleshed out with the appropriate teachings of the *Qur'an* and *Hadith* and illustrated by suitable examples from early Islamic history. (Qutb was executed in 1966.) There is little substantive adaptation of Western ideas; and where there is such adaptation – as with the vague maxim 'from each according to his ability, to each according to his need', it takes the form of outright appropriation without any dialogue or acknowledgement. This is what fundamentalist Islamic ideology has amounted to. Its adherents have never wavered from their fundamental premise that Islam constitutes the last revelation and the eternally most perfect religion. Therefore, like nationalism, socialism could only be an imperfect conception of the principles of social justice perfectly stated in Islam. This is well brought out by Enayat's summary of Sayyid Qutb's social thought:

> Islam and socialism are two separate, comprehensive and indivisible systems of thought and living . . . Genuine belief in Islam starts with absolute submission to the will and sovereignty of God above . . . In the realm of ideas, the real choice is between Islam and *jahiliyya* (i.e., pre-Islamic ignorance). The latter now pervades the whole human community, including the societies which call themselves Moslem but in practice violate the *Shari'a*. Socialism, like Communism and Capitalism, is an excrescence of *jahili* thought, and therefore carries all the vestiges of its corrupt origin. It stresses such notions as social welfare and material prosperity at the expense of moral salvation. (Enayat, 1982, p. 151)

In Pakistan, the years of Bhutto's rule witness a sharp confrontation between Islamic and socialist ideologies, ending with the abrupt victory of the former in 1977. In the course of this confrontation, A. K. Brohi would write:

> Why is the word 'Islam', which is substantive, being degraded into becoming an adjective of 'socialism' is a question that no one that I know of in this country can . . . honestly answer . . . I suspect that the

'Islam' is in Pakistan constantly being utilized as a cloak for importing alien stuff – be these ideologies or institutions. (Donohue and Esposito, 1982, pp. 137–8)

Similarly, the chief ideologue of the Islamic movement in Pakistan, Mawlana Mawdudi, would assert in 1970:

They found out that their socialism cannot dance naked ... After realising this they started calling socialism 'Islamic' ... If it is really based on the *Qur'an* and the *Sunna* [of the Prophet] then what is the need for calling it socialism? ... Now when they can see that this too does not work they have started calling it Islamic equality (*musawat*) and *Muhammadi musawat*. The object is the same – pure socialism. (cited in Esposito, 1980, p. 150)

This passage demonstrates that Mawdudi, like Sayyid Qutb before him, was determined to prevent precisely what Hobsbawm would consider a natural step in the evolution of political movements. Nearly a decade later, Ayatollah Khomeini showed exactly the same determination as Mawdudi and Brohi had manifested with regard to Socialism in foiling the stratagem of presenting democratic ideas in an Islamic garb. He did so by insisting, at the time of the deliberations over a new constitution, that the term 'Islamic *Democratic* Republic' be rejected. If democracy were already contained in the principles of Islam, he argued, there was no need and no justification for any such qualification.

If the contemporary Islamic movements are neither proto-socialist nor proto-nationalist, how are we to characterise them? Very shortly before the onset of the Islamic revolution in Iran, Charles Tilly (1978) mockingly quoted a passage from Durkheim to deride and discard its implications. The derided implication was that 'restorative collective action' could take place in response to anomic conditions engendered by rapid social change and differentiation of the social structure and in order to reduce anomie:

When a society is going through circumstances which sadden, perplex or irritate it, it exercises a pressure over its members, to make them bear witness, by significant acts, to their sorrow, perplexity or anger. It imposes on them the duty of weeping, groaning or inflicting wounds upon themselves or others; for these collective manifestations, and the moral communion which they show and strengthen, restore to the group the energy which circumstances threaten to take away from it, and thus they enable it to become settled. (cited in Tilly, 1978, p. 17)

Yet one could not wish for a better statement to illustrate the central issue in the present resurgence of Islam in response to the rapid and perplexing social change which is sweeping through Iran and the rest of the Middle and Near East. The search for authenticity, the attempt at the recovery and reaffirmation of the authentic collective conscience, whose source is seen as Islam, is at the heart of all the contemporary Islamic movements. Despite their differences, therefore, all the contemporary Islamic movements can be considered revitalisation movements (Wallace, 1956), propelled by rapid social change and in response to Western cultural influences which are perceived as gravely menacing and are virulently rejected.

Like so many other social phenomena, the Islamic revival is Janus-faced: its self-consciousness in the present century was induced by Western contacts, yet it also set itself the goal of denunciation and purification of peripheral, superstitious religion of the masses in the earlier decades of the century. In the later decades, its second face has been turned to what was viewed as internal political corruption. The efforts in the present century to revive and reinvigorate Islam are therefore simultaneously a reaction against Western influences and against internal corruption in the form first of popular superstitions and then of socio-political pollution and corruption (Gellner, 1975, p. 294; Chapter 10 below). Furthermore, beyond this double negative orientation, the ideology of the Islamic movements, like nationalism, is in many secondary respects malleable.[10] This malleability enables Islamic ideologies to adjust to the outlook of their proponents in various countries. In fact, the outlook of their respective bearers is the one variable which enables us to arrive at a sociologically meaningful typology (see Chapter 10) of the Islamic activist groups all of which consider themselves engaged in *the* Islamic movement of our time.[11] The differences between Islamic traditionalism treated in my own chapter and Islamic fundamentalism or radicalism analysed by Davis is largely accountable by the different outlooks and interests of their respective bearers: the *'ulama* as the guardians of the Shi'ite tradition in the one case and, in the other, the mildly anti-clerical young laymen with rudimentary knowledge of religious jurisprudence. Noting the absence of recognised traditional leadership except for a few old families of *'ulama* in Constantine and Tlemcen, von Sivers speculates that in their struggle against the state and the political élite, the Algerian rural middle class may emerge as bearers of Islamic traditionalism in North Africa. Should this happen, as recent signs increasingly indicate, the emergent type of Islamic traditionalism could also accommodate the imprint of its rural bearers – most notably on the reversal of the land reform and the

reaffirmation of the inviolability of agricultural private property.
Against a similar background of insignificance of the '*ulama*, due to their
disestablishment in the Turkish Republic, but otherwise in contrast to
the parochial traditionalism of the Algerian rural middle class, the
Islamic fundamentalism of the relatively prosperous bourgeois professionals who led the National Salvation Party in the 1970s is combined
with a strong anti-parochial emphasis on national power (made possible
by the historical heritage of the Ottoman Empire) on the basis of
industrialisation and economic autarky.

Owing to the afore-mentioned variations in the ideologies of various
Islamic movements, Western observers, wont to consider political and
especially economic issues as the only 'real' things that matter, have
tended to overemphasise the differences and seriously underestimate the
large measure of consensus among the Islamic movement. They have
not been appreciative of the fact that from the viewpoint of the
participants, these differences are secondary and do not relate to the
'constitutive ideas' (Heberle, 1950, p. 13) of the Islamic movement which
underly the consensus among the traditionalists and the fundamentalists
on the implementation of the Sacred Law, the strict public enforcement
of morals, and the resumption of the universal mission of Islam: 'This is
what He, The Almighty, says: "Fight them until there is no longer
discord, and the religion is God's" (*Qur'an* 2: 193)' (al-Banna', 1978, p.
50).

Our account of the types of Islamic movements and the corresponding
outlooks of their respective bearers has omitted Islamic modernism
which is only touched upon by me in Chapter 10, and, by Toprak in
Chapter 6. The reason is that the attention Islamic modernism has
received as an intellectual trend in the conventional wisdom of Middle
Eastern scholarship seems inordinate in relation to its sociological
insignificance in the present decades. Islamic fundamentalism has
received some attention but deserves still more analysis of the kind
supplied in Chapter 7. If the volume can claim to bring a neglected
aspect of the resurgence of Islam to public attention, it is by throwing
light on the traditional basis of support for the Islamic movements and
the pronounced traditionalistic features found in most of them. Toprak
points to the traditionalist support from rural areas disturbed by greater
than average social change for the National Salvation Party the outlook
of whose leaders shows a mixture of Islamic modernism and fundamentalism. I myself supply indices relating to the strength of traditional
religious sentiments and an increased propensity to traditional religious
activity among the Iranian population in the 1970s. This indicates that

Islamic movement, whatever their more precise orientation, have considerable traditional constituencies. As regards the leadership of some of these movements, I focus on the obvious case of the traditional leadership of the shi'ite clergy at the national level in Iran. Another kind of traditional leadership, this time of a local mullah, is to be found in Ahmed's chapter. It is important to note that the chicaneries of the mullahs of Waziristan mentioned by Ahmed, or the Navvab Safavi's talisman as described by Kazemi, are far cries from either orthodox reformism of the pre-World War Two *Salafiyya*, or the Islamic modernism of Erbakan, Bazargan and Bani Sadr. Whereas the latter types of Islamic orientation are congenial to Gellner's hypothesis which considers them proto-nationalistic, the traditionalist orientation of the masses newly incorporated into political society can, under suitable circumstances such as occurred in Iran, express itself on the political arena in new forms which are completely at variance with nationalism. (See Chapters 5 and 10.)

Let us return to the characteristics shared by the traditionalist and fundamentalist movements as movements of revitalisation. As attempts to extirpate alien norms and to overcome the normative disturbance caused by their intrusion and by urbanisation, these movements advocate the restoration and rigorous enforcement of Islamic norms. They are, to use Hofstadter's phrase, the latest and most striking, albeit non-Western, manifestation of 'the fundamentalist revolt against modernity' (Bell, 1964, p. 103). As such, there are some striking sociological similarities between the contemporary Islamic movements and the European fascism and the American radical right.

Talcott Parsons (1942), when he was still thinking about substantive sociological problems instead of engaging in abstract system-building, made a number of acute observations on the sociological aspects of the fascist movements. He noted that fascism, like movements of religious proselytism tend to develop out of social disorganisation and anomie – and, he could have added, the intrusion of alien norms. He saw in fundamentalism, as one type of reaction to trends 'subversive' of traditional value, an alternative to fascism. Last but not least, he pointed out that all these types of reactive movements were at least as deeply rooted in the social structure and dynamics of modern society as was socialism at an earlier stage (Parsons, 1964 [1942], pp. 134, 137–8). Far more widely known than Parsons' essay is William Kornhauser's *Politics of Mass Society* (1959) in which the idea of anomie was coupled with the notion of the atomisation of mass society. He put forward the hypothesis that urbanisation and industrialisation atomise society into individuals whose social isolation and alienation make them available for recruitment into mass movements. This hypothesis has come under attack as regards the assumption of atomisation of the recruits to mass political movements, and has been refuted by the findings of recent studies of contemporary American movements, many of which show that 'membership in secondary and even primary groups can *facilitate* recruitment to political movements' (Marx and Wood, 1975, p. 392). These empirical studies have given support to Shils' (1974) contrary view on the continued strength of primordial ties in the integrated societies of modern times, as do the studies by Davis and Kazemi with regard to the Middle East. Davis's chapter on the offshoots of the Moslem Brotherhood in Egypt and Kazemi's chapter on the *Fada'iyan-e Islam* in Iran, bring out the importance of primordial ties of family and kinship in the recruitment of members and in the diffusion of the ideologies of the respective movements. We may point out that Batatu's study of the communist movement in Iraq also highlights the importance of primordial ties while underscoring the significance of local ties, be they regional or those of a specific city-quarter (Batatu, 1978, especially pp. 403, 412, 424, 995–8).

However, there is no necessary logical connection between anomie and atomisation. We gain the strong impression from the material presented in this volume that the Islamic militants are among the least atomised members of Middle Eastern society, with strong family and local ties. But their lack of atomisation does not by any means indicate the absence of normative disturbance. On the contrary, they are vehemently reacting to what they consider an alien social world dominated by alien norms and in which the authentic norms are subverted or abandoned. The movement for the revitalisation of Islam is their response to this predicament.

We can now ask who are the bearers of the movement for the revitalisation of Islam, and which traits of the movement derive from the outlook and interests of the social strata which adhere to it. I have deliberately started with the cultural source to be revitalised, namely Islam, because the social scientists looking at kindred movements of the 'dispossessed' (Bell, 1964, p. 22) in the West have not paid enough attention to the cultural factor. Richard Hofstadter, who coined the phrase 'status politics' in 1955, decided seven years later, in 1962, that the proposed phrase required supplementation to stress the role of the cultural factor, and proposed the term 'cultural politics', (Bell, 1964, pp. 84, 99) which, however, has not attracted much attention. Lipset, the chief sociological theoretician of the radical right, has retained his focus on status politics, putting forward the notion of 'status preservatism' which we shall henceforth modify to 'preservationism' (Bell, 1964, pp. 307–446; Lipset and Raab, 1970, p. 487) while giving cursory attention to the 'cultural baggage' accompanying the attempt by a declining social group to preserve their status. Some recent critics of Lipset have censured this neglect of the cultural factor and proposed closer attention to the 'politics of life-style' which are seen not merely as angry responses of declining status groups but also attempts to 'build and sustain moral orders' (Lo, 1982, p. 111). Coupled with earlier criticism for the neglect of the important use of political institution by radical right movements such as McCarthyism, (Lo, 1982, p. 110) these critical studies indicate that the movements of the dispossessed are not merely impulsive responses by anomic individuals, but *counteranomic* movements led by a declining social group which nevertheless remains cohesive and has at its disposal institutional and local networks – and we may add, especially as regards the Middle East, primordial and family ties – as an organisational resource to mobilise support. As the chapters by Toprak, Davis, Kazemi and myself pay enough attention to the counternomic elaboration of Islamic ideologies, we may here turn to the question of the social status of their bearers.

The leading elements of the Islamic movements in Iran, Egypt and Algeria fit nicely to the category of 'dispossessed'. In Chapter 10 I emphasise the progressive exclusion of the Shi'ite clergy from the Pahlavi regime and argue that their increasing dispossession was the chief cause of their turning to revolutionary populism. Von Sivers's account clearly indicates that the Algerian middle peasantry acutely resents the urban bureaucrats whom it considers responsible for its dispossession. It is therefore not surprising that these social strata turn to the Islamic equivalent of nativism – characterised by Lipset and Raab as the choice of distinctive cultural symbols to show the uniqueness of their society and the revival of cultural elements which can serve as symbols for the period of greatness of that society. Lipset attributes this propensity to nativism to the '*Qundam Complex*' typical of 'those who have a greater symbolic investment in the past than in the present' (Lipset and Raab, 1970, p. 504). This complex indicates that, for the group concerned, the primary symbolic status investment is in the past and is related to a reference group whose status has declined. It produces 'status preservationism' manifested in the impulse to reverse the direction of social change which is seen as the cause of the decline in the status of the group. Lipset's conceptualisation fits the cases of Islamic traditionalism remarkably well. Especially in view of the remarkable group cohesiveness and social homogeneity they have shown to this day, the enterprise of the leading core of the contemporary Islamic traditionalist movements can be described as 'corporate status preservationism' – a term Lipset and Raab (1970, p. 48a) use with reference to the American movements of the 1930s and in contradistinction to 'anomic status preservationism' reserved for the radical right of the 1950s.

Moving from the consideration of their bearers to that of their ideological outlook, it is above all the strength of the monistic impulse and the pronounced political moralism of the Islamic traditionalist and fundamentalist movements which makes them akin to fascism and the radical right alike. In a typical statement revealing of the monistic impulse which led Halpern (1963, pp. 134–155) to characterise his movement aptly as 'neo-Islamic totalitarianism', the founder of the Moslem Brothers described theirs as 'a mission which does not tolerate divided loyalty since its very nature is that of total unity, and whosoever is prepared to accept it will live through it as it lives through him' (al-Banna', 1978, p. 44). Decades later, Davis is as struck by the Moslem Brothers' 'tenacious emphasis on the integrated nature of Islam', as I am by the intolerant monism of Khomeini's regime. The monistic impulse of fascism is too evident to require elaboration. Lipset and Raab (1970, p. 14) note a parallel monistic impulse at the heart of the political moralism of the American radical right for whom differences, cleavages, pluralism and 'ambiguity based on evil intent' are illegitimate and cannot be tolerated.

Incidentally, the advocacy of simplistic solutions to political problems is another shared characteristic. The honest grocer who, as Kazemi tells us, would, according to the *Fada'iyan-e Islam*, solve all the economic problems of Iran if appointed the Minister of Finance, finds its counterpart in 'the hick pharmacist in Podunk Corner' who, according to Ms Elizabeth Linington has more sense and competence than 'just about any one congressman picked at random' (Lipset and Raab, 1970, pp. 7–8).

Contemporaneity against the background of comparable extents of national economic and political integration does not exhaustively delimit the range of phenomena to which the outlook of our movements can be profitably compared. If their socio-economic dispossession makes the Islamic militants similar to the European fascist activists in sociological profile and their political moralism and advocacy of revolutionary populism makes them similar in ideological orientation, the more fundamental premises of contemporary Islamic thought and out-look demonstrate certain affinity with Western conservatism during the first half of the nineteenth century. The contemporary Islamic movements are characterised by profound social and cultural conservatism. Their revolutionary populism and political militancy should not divert our attention from the central fact that these are fundamentally reactive movements which aim at the recovery and subsequent conservation of the Islamic tradition. In this connection, it is worth mentioning that in his classic essay on *Conservative Thought*, Karl Mannheim (1953, pp. 90–2) maintains that Marxian revolutionary thought has 'a significant affinity with conservative and reactionary thought', that is, with the early nineteenth-century 'counter-revolution'. This is so because the socialists were in fact not the first to criticise the capitalist rationalisation of socio-economic life: such criticisms were initiated by conservative romanticism and only later taken over by the left.

Like romanticism and modern conservatism in the West, which were born in reaction to the enlightenment in early nineteenth century, the contemporary Islamic revival is strongly conditioned by its reaction to other modern political ideologies and therefore assumes the character of a counter-movement in conscious opposition to them, and in self-conscious defence of traditional norms.[12] The integral tone of the ideology of the Islamic movements, their horror of fragmentation and decay, their quest for totality, all point to the similarity between the contemporary Islamic ideologies and the Western integralist and organistic philosophies which are associated not only with dispossessed fascists and rightist radicals but also with possessing conservatives. So does the fact, emphasised by Davis, that the offshoots of the Moslem Brotherhood in Egypt have chosen to refer to their primary organi-sational unit as 'the family' (*al-usra*) – a term also adopted by the Islamic militant in faraway Malaysia. However, when comparing the themes of these Islamic integralist ideologies with those presented in Mannheim's essay, one is struck by the fundamental *secularity* of modern Western conservatism[13] in contrast to the *Islamic* character of reactive con-servative thought in the Middle East. This is not the place to undertake a systematic discussion of the causes and implications of this latter crucial difference. Suffice it to say that this absence of secularity – not to mention the vehement rejection of secularism by the Islamic militants – makes for the continued politicisation of Islam and poses a constant threat to all present institutional arrangements designed to assure some measure of separation of religion and politics in the contemporary Middle East.

26 *Introduction*

## NOTES

1. At the same time, national integration could set in motion centrifugal forces which may find embodiment in ethnic movements propounding ideologies of ethnic nationalism and separatism and demanding national autonomy or independence. This topic is touched upon in Chapter 4 by Ahmed but is not otherwise treated in the present volume.
2. The distinction between 'general' and 'specific' social movements was first made by Herbert Blumer (1951 [1939]). However, Blumer conceives of the former category more restrictively and of the latter more generally than seems warranted. His treatment of revival and nationalistic movements under 'the merging of specific movements' (Blumer, 1951 [1939] p. 219) is unsatisfactory or at any rate not useful from our historical, comparative perspective. What is important methodologically with regard to general social movements is that the search needs to be directed away from the developments giving rise to specific movements and affecting their vicissitudes and towards broader changes in culture and social structure; to 'focal problems of an era' (Turner and Killian, 1972, p. 282).
3. Concentrating on this latter type of social movement in contemporary America, McCarthy and Zald (1973) have put forward an interesting organisational and entrepreneurial theory of social movements. They study a variety of movements in contemporary America and argue that these 'professional social movements' are generated by career specialists in creation of grievances, whose definition of grievances 'will expand to meet the funds [from foundations, churches, the government, etc.] and support personnel available' (McCarthy and Zald, 1973, p. 23). Not so in the Middle East, which is the land neither of free enterprise nor of complex organisation and where career mobilisers, when and if they come into existence, are unlikely to curtail their ambitions short of the attainment of political power and total control over state and society.
4. This is in sharp contrast to the type of movements analysed by McCarthy and Zald and mentioned in the preceding note.
5. The *Ba'th* movement has enjoyed unusual success, and has attained supreme political power in both Iraq and Syria. However, in view of the recent publication of Batatu's (1978) study of the movement, it has not been covered in this volume in spite of its importance.
6. 'In other words, a very large proportion of one's relationships and encounters – in fact, they *are* more frequently encounters than relationships – are ephemeral, non-repetitive, and optional. This has an important consequence: communication, the symbols, language (in the literal or in the extended sense) that is employed, become crucial. The burden of comprehension is shifted from the context, to the communication itself: when interlocutors and contexts are all unfamiliar, the message itself must become intelligible – it is no longer understood, as was the case in traditional societies, before it was even articulated – and those who communicate must speak the same language, in some sense or other' (Gellner, 1964, p. 155). Furthermore, 'If a man is not firmly set in a social niche, whose relationship as it were endows him with his identity, he is obliged to carry his identity with him, in his whole style of conduct and expression: in other words, his "culture" becomes his identity' (Gellner, 1964, p. 157).

7. The actualisation of this possibility is well illustrated in the Kurdish national movement, in which the double identity of the Kurds manifests itself in conflicting demands by Kurdish groups for complete independence or for autonomy within the nation-states of Iran, Iraq or Turkey (Kutschera, 1979).

8. The Shah, however, did not depart until 16 January 1979, and his government of his last Prime Minister, Bakhtiar, collapsed on 11 February 1979.

9. It is interesting to note that a few years before the publication of *Primitive Rebels*, members of the Iraqi Communist Party were concerned with the very same issues but from the viewpoint of practical politics. Batatu (1978, pp. 694–8) reports a debate on religion amongst the Iraqi communists in jail in 1954. What we may anachronistically call the Hobsbawmian position was advocated by one of the debaters who accordingly favoured an attempt to use religion especially in the form of the flagellant processions commemorating the martyrdom of Imam Husayn for the purpose of mass mobilisation. However, the proponent of the use of religion and of religious symbolism for revolutionary purposes was overruled, and the Iraqi communists simply decided to remain silent on the question of religions so as not to arouse unnecessary hostility. Since 1979, the Iranian Communist Party, the *Tudeh*, has adopted the Hobsbawmian position and unreservedly applauded the Islamic revolutionaries. The present plight of the *Tudeh* is strongly suggestive of their folly in comparison to the wisdom of their Iraqi counterparts in the 1950s.

10. Lest the reader should think Marxism exempt from a similar malleability, let him read the proclamations of the *Tudeh* designed to explain their unrequited love for Khomeini's revolution.

11. The international character of the Islamic movements is unmistakable. As has been pointed out, ideological influences have been freely crossing frontiers. Davis notes the salience of non-Egyptians among the Moslem Brothers arrested in 1965 (Chapter 7). Mortimer (1982, p. 182) similarly notes the presence of many non-Saudis among the Islamic student activists who occupied the Holy Mosque in Mecca in November 1979.

12. As the reference to Mannheim is crucially important, the following remarks are necessary to forestall a possible terminological confusion. Unfortunately for us, Mannheim (1953, p. 95, note) decided to ignore the sense in which the term 'traditionalism' was used by de Maistre and Bonald – the sense corresponding exactly to our usage – and, instead, follows Weber in using 'traditionalism' as unself-conscious traditional, habitual behaviour in contrast to conservatism as self-conscious meaningful action (Mannheim, 1953, pp. 98–103). It is therefore Mannheim's 'conservatism' which corresponds to 'traditionalism' as defined by me and endorsed by von Sivers.

13. Defence of religion *does* loom large in Western conservative thought, but it is a defence of religion as a foundation of social order on *rational* grounds, subsequently to be absorbed into a secular political culture.

# 2 Nationalism in the Middle East: A Behavioural Approach

## RICHARD COTTAM

### PROBLEMS IN DEFINING NATIONALISM

Harold Guetzkow, a pioneer in the art of man-machine international political simulation, lamented years ago that he had not been able to develop a scheme by which he could incorporate the nationalism variable in his simulation exercises (Guetzkow, 1963). Like so many other social scientists, he believed that few phenomena are more important than nationalism if one is to understand inter-state behaviour, but constructing an operationally useful definition of nationalism is apparently a most elusive task.

In my view, a primary obstacle to understanding the concept of nationalism is the almost irresistible tendency to reify it. 'Nationalism' and 'value' are alike in this regard. Everyone, analyst and layman alike, senses that nationalism is a central 'fact' of contemporary socio-political life but very little progress is being made in describing that 'fact'. The truth is, of course, that nationalism is an analytic concept, not a fact. Acute observers of human behaviour have long noted certain behavioural patterns that seem to be associated with an intense identification with politically relevant communities by large sections of a population. When these communities are called nations and especially when these national communities have achieved independent statehood, the associated behavioural patterns are termed nationalistic. We need the concept of nationalism in order to aggregate and to analyse this nationalistic behaviour. Yet oddly in the literature on nationalism there is an almost total neglect of the behavioural patterns we think of as nationalistic. Instead we spend much effort in attempting to 'discover' the definition of nationalism,[1] to decide who is and who is not a nationalist (Smith, 1971), to describe the rhythm of nationalistic growth (Smith, 1979), to describe just how it is spread (Deutsch, 1953), and to categorize nationalism for example as integral, liberal or traditional (Hayes, 1948).

With regard to the non-European world, this tendency to reify is most manifest in the assertion that nationalism is essentially an import from Europe. This assertion relates to a basic truth: that conflict with an explicitly nationalistic people tends to generate an awareness of one's own nationalism. But to treat nationalism in the Third World as an import from Europe is to trivialise it. Those doing so regard nationalistic behaviour as essentially imitative rather than as behavioural patterns that appear naturally and universally when certain specifiable pre-conditions have been realised. As I see it, 'nationalistic' behaviour consists of a set of behavioural patterns associated with an intense identification with a community that has achieved or seeks independent statehood. These patterns are likely to appear regardless of whether the individual members of the community think of that community as a nation. For example, pro-regime Iranians in the Khomeini era behaved nationalistically especially in response to the Iraqi attack even though they had consciously rejected 'nationalism' in obedience to Khomeini's command.

Consistent with this reasoning, I consider any definition of nationalism arbitrary. It will incorporate an area of politically relevant behaviour but will necessarily exclude areas of behaviour that are almost indistinguishably close to the area included. I define nationalism, like ideology, in terms of perception and of value. Nationalism occurs when a large number of people perceive they belong to a community that is entitled to and capable of maintaining independent statehood and who grant that community *a* primary and *the* primary terminal loyalty. The phrase '*the* primary terminal loyalty' is meant to convey the meaning that a nationalist as defined can hold a primary attachment to only one community for which he desires independent statehood. This definition therefore excludes those who have a first intensity attachment for a community, for example the Assyrian, for which its members see no real possibility of independent statehood. It also excludes those whose attachment to a community is at a secondary or tertiary level. For example, the intensity of attachment which many, perhaps most, Egyptians have for the broad Arab community is at a secondary or tertiary level. By this definition these Egyptians cannot be classified as

Arab nationalists. Also excluded are individuals who have an equally intense, primary attachment to two nation-states. For example, a Turkish Jew identifying intensely with both Israel and Turkey is not classified as either an Israeli or Turkish nationalist. The assumption in each case is that the behaviour of the individuals excluded will differ substantially from the core behaviour to be described as nationalistic. The Turkish Jew must somehow reconcile two often competing loyalties and in so doing will follow patterns sharply different from those of either Israeli or Turkish nationalists.

The definition does not exclude simultaneous attachments at a first intensity level to two or more politically relevant communities so long as independent statehood is desired only for one. A Kurd in Iran, for example, may be a first intensity Kurdish patriot but simultaneously an Iranian nationalist if he does not aspire to independence for Kurdistan. Similarly, he may also have a primary attachment to the Islamic community but so long as he does not favour that community's becoming an independent state, he can still be classified as an Iranian nationalist.

Is nationalism an ideology? Few questions are more unnecessarily perplexing. The answer of course depends on the operating definitions, and most of the confusion on the point reflects a previous failure to define. I see ideology as incorporating a politically relevant world view and an associated set of politically relevant values, together suggesting a general course of action in the political realm. As such, nationalism, as defined here, when present is an aspect of ideology and a major determinant of action; but it is clearly not itself an ideology. Thus defined both nationalism and ideology are associated perceptual systems, that is, world views or partial world views, and value systems. The difficulty of dealing with nationalism analytically lies in the difficulty of disaggregating perceptual and value sub-systems from the overall politically relevant perceptual and value systems. The general course of action induced by ideology reflects, by definition, the interaction of all salient system components. A nationalist will place a first intensity value on the dignity, welfare and security of the nation but programmatic meaning is given to such terms as 'welfare of the nation' by other components of the system of values of the ideology. An ideology which does not incorporate nationalism will differ sharply from one that does. But behavioural manifestations flowing from nationalism vary greatly depending on other component parts of the ideology. For example, when overall ideology incorporates nationalism/humanism/liberalism/democracy, the general course of action induced will be very different from that induced by nationalism/authoritarianism/corporatism/militarism. Our tendency in the past has been to deal with these differences by referring to the first combination as liberal nationalism and the second, perhaps, as integral nationalism. But that is no more than a minor classificatory triumph. Our understanding of what is meant by nationalistic behaviour is hardly advanced. What we do know is that nationalism is associated histori-cally with a very broad assortment of ideologies.

Admitting then the extraordinary distortion involved in disaggregat-ing nationalism from ideology, clarity and understanding none the less require that the effort be made. We need to answer the question 'what are the behavioural tendencies associated with identifying with a nation at a first intensity level?' In other words, what is core nationalistic behaviour?

## 1. Elements of World View

When individuals are deeply concerned with the security, dignity, prestige and welfare of the nation (defined as a politically relevant community to which they are loyal at a first intensity level and which they believe is entitled to and capable of defending independent statehood) how does this affect their world view? Or how would the world view of a nationalist and a non-nationalist differ? My proposed answer here is that the nationalist will be more sensitive to threat, often perceiving it when it is absent, more inclined to see slights and indignities, more likely to conjure up glories and more sensitive to indications of relative deprivation of the national populace than the non-nationalist. The nationalist thus is more likely to see threats to, and opportunities for the nation state than is the non-nationalist for the state of which he is a citizen.

Arab, Iranian and Turkish nationalists have a shared tendency to see their nations as victims of imperial conspiracies of such strength and elaborateness as to deny them control of their own destinies. The particular conspiracies perceived will of course vary with nationality, but the patterns will be parallel. Outside observers often find difficulty believing in the sincerity of these views. But in fact the conspiracy view of the Soviet Union held by many American nationalists in the cold war era falls into patterns that are in essential features parallel, such as seeing their tormentors in stereotypical terms. Non-nationalists living in Arab countries, Iran and Turkey are unlikely to share the conspiracy views of their nationalistic countrymen.

## 2. Foreign Policy Motivation

It follows from the above that the pre-dispositional base of a government of a nationalistic people is more likely to lead to a concern for
national security and national grandeur than is that of a government of a
non-nationalist people. Since the grandeur factor is frequently present in
highly activist foreign policies, this is a matter of some importance.
Bluntly, it suggests that a nationalistic government is more likely to be
aggressive since it is more able to attract popular excitement from a
populace interested in national glory. Similarly the nationalistic government is more likely to respond strongly to matters of 'face'. When threat
is involved, the proposition suggests a nationalistic populace is more
likely to see the threatener in 'diabolical enemy' stereotypical terms and
hence to think strategically of achieving 'total victory' and of conducting
'all-out warfare'. The non-nationalistic government, presumably, would
be able to consider more options since it would 'see' a more complex
antagonist.

## 3. Internal Political Control

Etzioni suggests that internal control can be thought of usefully in terms
of four inclusive factors (Etzioni, 1961). These are coercion, utilitarian,
normative habitual (a universal acceptance of customs and norms to the
degree that control is manifested in the form of following the prevailing
norms and customs non-consciously) and normative active. The latter
factor refers to the ability of authorities to control a population through
the manipulation of broadly accepted symbols. Thus if a society is in
disarray (norms have broken down), the economy is in shambles (low
utilitarian) and the coercive forces inadequate, survival of the authority
structure is likely to rest on the ability of authorities to appeal to a
population symbolically. This indeed is one way of looking at legitimacy. Historically those symbols that on such occasions have been
most useful are ones that refer to communities, ways of life or religious
beliefs – the very elements of a value system that most satisfy an
individual's personal security needs. In our era national symbols have at
least rivalled if not bested religious symbols for this purpose. If such
symbols are unavailable because a populace is not nationalistic or not
responsive to an individual leader because of policies he has followed –
as was the case with the Shah of Iran – control of the crisis is likely to be
more difficult. Examples of Middle Eastern leaders who were able to

make heavy use of nationalist symbols for internal control purposes are Ataturk, Nasser, Mossadeq and Ben Gurion. Examples of leaders who had difficulty manipulating such symbols for control purposes or, in other words, had problems with nationalist legitimacy are Nuri Said, Hossein and, with respect to Arab rather than Egyptian symbols, Sadat. Khomeini's symbol manipulation is almost exclusively Islamic rather than Iranian. Were he successful in his revolutionary purpose a new nation would emerge in the area, in which the Islamic community, not the ethnic Iranian, would be the core community.

## 4. Willingness to Sacrifice

The same tendency is to be seen in the ability of a nationalistic government to call on its people to endure great sacrifices in the interest of the community's welfare. Austerity programmes, therefore, are more likely to be acceptable and effective if the populace is nationalistic. Note for example the greater willingness to accept sacrifices by a population in the Middle East *after* as compared with *before* independence.

## 5. Decisional Latitude

Given the strong determining force of nationalism, decisional latitude must of necessity be affected. In the area of foreign policy, nationalism when present should grant decision-makers an ability to take risks and demand sacrifices to a degree denied decision-makers of non-nationalistic publics. Conversely, decision-makers of nationalistic publics cannot easily advocate policies that would result in humiliation or an acceptance of defeat. A dramatic illustration of these points was given in American and Soviet responses to the Cuban missile crisis. John Kennedy indicated that had he followed a compromising policy such as that suggested by Adlai Stevenson, he could have been impeached (Kennedy, 1969). But the Soviets were able to turn their ships around in the middle of the Atlantic with the world's television cameras recording their actions. Since I see the Soviet Union as non-nationalistic and the United States as nationalistic, this behaviour conforms to my expectations. In domestic policy, nationalistic publics will, as suggested above, allow their leaders to pursue policies of austerity to a degree denied the leaders of non-nationalistic states. Conversely, the inability of Arab leaders in Jordan or Saudi Arabia to follow Sadat into accepting the Camp David formula in spite of the parochial advantages for Jordan and Saudi Arabia in their doing so, suggests strongly that Arab nationalism is much more pervasive in Jordan and Saudi Arabia than in Egypt and hence more restrictive of decisional latitude.

## 6. Power Determinant

Nationalism affects state power in two ways. Nationalistic young men are far more likely to volunteer or accept conscription than are their counterparts who do not identify with a primary intensity with the community on which their government is based. Furthermore, nationalistic armies are less likely to suffer problems of morale. Second, the nationalistic government has a bargaining advantage over the non-nationalistic. This is expressed in the form of greater credibility for threats that are based on expectations of prolonged popular support for a government's self-sacrificing and risk-taking stance.

This outline of suggested nationalistic behaviour is of course propositional since evidence for it is historically selective and not the result of testing. But supporting historical evidence appears sufficiently extensive to enable us to conclude that the pattern of behaviour of governments of nation-states and governments of non-nation-states will differ in important respects. It follows then that it is important for purposes of prediction to construct a device for looking at the nationalistic predispositional base of states. This will be done in a later section of the essay. First, however, I want to return to the consideration of value system and perceptual system in order to reduce some of the distortion that appears in the previous discussion.

## IDENTITY PROFILE

Especially given the arbitrary definition of nationalism used here, the distinction between nation-state and non-nation-state is nowhere nearly as clear as the above comparisons suggest. Human identity, even when confined to identification with politically relevant communities, is always complex. Nationalists may be inclined to denounce dual loyalty but in fact loyalties will always be far greater than dual. In order to suggest the wide range of behaviour induced by different identity patterns, I am going to propose a variety of such patterns which I believe are empirically identifiable among Egyptians, Palestinians, Lebanese and Iranians. The procedure to be followed is one of looking at the identity profiles of several hypothetical individuals for each of the four cases. The identity profiles will include value intensity ratings for politically-relevant communities and for four non-community, politically-relevant values. The individuals are treated as prototypes of existing identity-pattern tendencies in the four societies. If one were to imagine that each individual in turn were the modal individual for his society the range of behavioural implications resulting from different value systems would become apparent.

Intensity is attributed at four levels. The first or primary intensity can roughly be considered as the level at which an individual might be willing to risk life and/or career should there be a terrible threat to the community. Secondary intensity is present when the individual would not risk life or career but would be willing to make material sacrifices (as through taxes) at a level that would adversely affect life-style. Tertiary intensity indicates a willingness to give time, effort and to make some material sacrifice but not at the life-style level. Fourth-level intensity exists when the individual makes little time, energy or material sacrifice but does suffer a loss of peace of mind. The communities considered are adapted to the four societies. But for each, the non-community values considered are change, order, tolerance and freedom. These four values were chosen because at this stage in the history of nationalism in the Middle East they appear to correlate significantly with different manifestations of nationalist behaviour. Since I view this in system terms, an individual ranked high in terms of change for example, would be a progressive generally, but will favour some areas of change and oppose others. For example, if individual 'A' is ranked change (1), order (4), tolerance (2), and freedom (1), the change favoured will be very different from that favoured by individual 'B' who is ranked change (1), order (1), tolerance (3), freedom (4).

## Egypt

The three alternately modal individuals I consider here are:

TABLE 2.1

|   | Islam | Egypt | Arab | Change | Order | Tolerance | Freedom |
|---|-------|-------|------|--------|-------|-----------|---------|
| A | 1 | 2 | 2 | 1 | 1 | 3 | 3 |
| B | 3 | 1 | 1.5 | 1 | 4 | 1 | 1 |
| C | 3 | 1 | 3 | 2 | 1 | 3 | 3 |

Individual 'A' in all probability favours a political system grounded in Islamic principles and based on the Islamic community. His image is radical (change 1), not conservative, and he probably thinks in terms of a state embracing Moslems beyond the present boundaries of Egypt. Almost certainly he opposes the Camp David formula and rapprochement with Israel, and sees a far greater community of interest with other, especially Arab, Moslems than with Egyptian Copts. However were he modal in Egypt any proposal for a broader political union would produce internal tensions (note the 'Egypt 2' rating).

Individual 'B' is an Egyptian nationalist of the variety often referred to as Nasserite. His attachment to the Arab ethnic group is sufficiently intense to make likely his strong opposition to the Camp David formula. He doubtless seeks a liberal system in which no distinction is made between Christians and Moslems.

Individual 'C' is unequivocally Egyptian nationalist and would probably be comfortable with the Camp David formula. The treatment of the Coptic community is likely to correlate with that community's willingness to accept the prevailing political regime. Egypt under Sadat behaved as if individual 'C' were the modal individual.

The strange flow of Egyptian identity-patterns may well relate to the rhythm of growth in the size of the politically participant population and suggests the following descriptive proposition. In the 1920s with Zaghlul a charismatic figure and the *Wafd* Party in its prime, the modal identity-profile seems to have been Egypt (1), Arab (3 or 4). But as the growth in awareness and participation extended deeply in the population, newly aware or participant elements seemed to view 'Egypt', 'Arab', and 'Islam' as virtually co-terminous descriptors of the community with which they identified.[2] Their profile then could be depicted as Egypt (1), Islam (1), Arab (1). Responding to this development Egyptian politics became more Arab. But the secular trend in Egypt as elsewhere continued. As it did so one section (the largest) of the highly attentive, secular public seems to have remained as in Zaghlul's day, Egypt (1), Arab (3) – the group most likely to support the Camp David approach. However, another smaller group became Egypt (1), Arab (1.5) as with Egyptian individual 'B' described above. Then with the continued growth in political participation and a further crystallisation of the sense of identity of the deeply religious section of the population, that group became less Egyptian, less Arab and more Islamic. Individual 'A' with Islam (1), Egypt (2), Arab (2) is assumed to represent this trend. Were this individual to become modal, a new nation based on an Islamic community might well emerge. However, 'A's' attachment to the

Egyptian community and the Arab community would still complicate this development.

## Palestine

Each of these individuals is recognisable. 'A' may well demonstrate the ambivalence in his Palestinian and Arab identities by calling for risks by Palestinians in the interests of the Arab nation that 'B' would find unforgivable. 'B' is likely to be unequivocal in his Palestinian nationalism since there is no real possibility of forming a separate Christian state in the area. Furthermore, as a liberal he is likely to accept and respect the sectarian diversity among Arabic-speaking Palestinians. 'C' is quite likely a notable and the variety of Palestinian many Israelis wish were modal. He is unlikely to favour an Islamic state, given his conservatism (and in contrast to Egyptian individual 'A') and might well be comfortable with the kind of autonomy the Begin government offered Palestinians.

## Lebanon

There are here two Lebanese nationalists ('C' and 'D'), two Arab nationalists ('E' and 'F'), one parochial (Maronite) nationalist ('B'), and individual 'A' is torn in several directions. Obviously there is enormous variation among individuals within each sectarian community and the listing of these six individuals is designed in part to suggest the terrible strain identity variation must produce within Lebanon. No modal individual is likely to be discoverable there now or for the foreseeable future. In this sense, therefore, Lebanon is an excellent example of a non-nation-state.

## Iran

Individual 'A' is the Iranian Ayatollah Khomeini prefers (and may be himself). He is not an Iranian nationalist, preferring instead an Islamic state. But he is in favour of both radical change and a tight new order. 'B' is probably a Kurdish nationalist, but one whose behaviour will be affected by an Iranian attachment. Both 'C' and 'D' are Iranian nationalists, although 'D' (who could be ex-President Bani Sadr) will be somewhat ambivalent on the question of an Islamic state. 'C' could be a follower of Dr Mosaddeq's National Front.

There is of course no inevitability in the common assumption above

The three Palestinians looked at are:

TABLE 2.2

| | Islam | Christianity | Palestine | Arab | Greater Syria | Change | Order | Tolerance | Freedom |
|---|---|---|---|---|---|---|---|---|---|
| A | 3 | — | 1 | 1 | 2 | 1 | 1 | 3 | 3 |
| B | — | 1 | 1 | 3 | 4 | 1 | 4 | 1 | 1 |
| C | 1 | — | 2 | 3 | 3 | 3 | 1 | 3 | 4 |

The six Lebanese considered are:

TABLE 2.3

| | Sect | Locale | Lebanon | Arab | Greater Syria | Change | Order | Tolerance | Freedom |
|---|---|---|---|---|---|---|---|---|---|
| A | Druze (1) | 1 | 2 | 1 | 1 | 1 | 3 | 2 | 2 |
| B | Maronite (1) | 1 | 2 | — | — | 1 | 1 | 4 | 4 |
| C | Orthodox (3) | 3 | 1 | 2 | 2 | 3 | 1 | 3 | 2 |
| D | Shia (1) | 4 | 1 | 2 | 4 | 2 | 1 | 2 | 3 |
| E | Sunni (1) | 2 | 2 | 1 | 2 | 3 | 1 | 3 | 3 |
| F | Sunni (3) | 4 | 2 | 1 | 2 | 1 | 3 | 1 | 1 |

The four Iranians to be looked at are:

TABLE 2.4

| | Islam | Kurdistan | Iran | Change | Order | Tolerance | Freedom |
|---|---|---|---|---|---|---|---|
| A | Shia (1) | — | 3 | 1 | 1 | 3 | 4 |
| B | Sunni (1) | 1 | 3 | 1 | 2 | 3 | 3 |
| C | Shia (3) | — | 1 | 1 | 3 | 1 | 1 |
| D | Shia (1) | — | 1 | 1 | 3 | 2 | 3 |

that if one holds a primary attachment to Egypt, Palestine, Lebanon, or Iran that individual will favour independent statehood for his community. Rather his favoured perceived-role for his community will be a consequence of a psychological balancing process. But in any event such a first intensity attachment will incline the individual toward what I have described as nationalistic behaviour.

## CHECK-LIST DEVELOPMENT

What the foregoing section indicates is that the most one can claim is that some polities are more inclined towards nationalistic behaviour than others. But in every polity there will be a diversity of behavioural tendencies relevant to nationalism and a pure case of nationalistic behaviour cannot exist. In effect, therefore, the nationalistic behaviour outlined should be viewed as an ideal type and polities should be described in terms of the strength of the tendency to act in the direction of nationalistic behaviour. In this section, I develop a check-list which should allow one to predict the strength of this tendency.

### 1. Strength of Nationalism among Attentive Publics

The first element of the check-list, attentive public attitudes, is based on an assumption regarding the rhythm of nationalistic development. That assumption is that nationalism as it appears in a society is likely first to be embraced by elements of the society that are deeply interested in and well-informed about politics, that are change-oriented and that tend to value tolerance and freedom more than order. There is no implicit theory underlying this assumption. The point is instead empirical. It is based on the observation that socio-economic change in the past era has resulted in an increasingly natural identification with larger politically relevant communities. Almost by definition those elements of the public that are most interested, change-oriented and least attached to authoritarian values would be likely to lead the way towards viewing parochial communities as irrelevant. But their personal identity needs would impel them towards attachments to new communities but communities that are larger and more relevant to changes in the economy. These new communities to which they become attached should nevertheless be communities with which identification is natural and easy. Ethnic communities seem to serve this purpose most readily *if* they are of sufficient size and possess territorial resources sufficient for economic and defence purposes. Less attentive, less change-oriented and more authority-oriented elements of the population then gradually embrace the nation. As they do so the former vanguard of nationalism – still change-oriented – tends to move beyond the nation and towards communities defined more universally. Thus nationalism at first is a progressive and later a profoundly conservative phenomenon. Since national values once established relate most obviously to individual security needs, providing as they do one of the easiest answers to the question 'who am I?' they are most unlikely to be easily discarded.

Failure to follow this rhythmic pattern is common enough. For example, if there is a serious threat, external or internal, to the survival of the nation the change-oriented element is likely to remain highly nationalistic, as in Israel. But if the rhythm is followed, it will be associated in middle age with a departure from the national ranks of vital elements of the opinion-formulating élite. In fact, though it may be somewhat of a tautology, the most obvious indicator of the importance of the opinion-formulating élite in nationalist movements is the nationalist versus universalist content of articles in the media servicing the liberal intelligentsia of any country.

The case is easily made that the relative influence of the change-oriented, anti-authoritarian and highly-attentive elements of society is in fairly rapid decline in nationalist movements throughout the Middle East. Mustafa Kamal in Turkey, Sa'ad Zaghlul in Egypt, Mosaddeq in Iran, Rashid Ali al-Gaylani in Iraq and Nabulsi in Jordan – examples of the often upper-class leaders who were most admired by these elements of the population – are part of an increasingly distant past. Nevertheless this opinion-formulating element of the population includes even in this era a disproportionate number of individuals who can be described as opinion-formulating. They are, for example, likely to be over-represented in the press of all Middle Eastern states.

## 2. Political Participation

The corollary element to this is the extensiveness of political partici-pation. The assumption here is that change in our era is also characterised by a steadily broadening base of political participation. What is meant here is a move away from ascriptive behaviour by the mass of any society and towards an acceptance of a view that all individuals can have some influence over their own destinies. This naturally is associated with moving away from a parochial communal identity, such as the extended family or feudal estate, towards a larger community more in tune with the needs of a changing economic system. Since their more attentive brethren will have preceded them in this process, there will be for the non-attentive mass a ready-made community to which they can transfer their loyalties. There is no reason to assume, however, that the earlier parochial loyalties will be discarded. Rather there is really an addition of the nation to the communities of political relevance with which the individual identifies.

The primary difference between the successful Iranian revolution of 1951 and that of 1978 is in the extensiveness of mass participation. Whereas in 1951 only a veneer of the population, probably no more than 15 per cent, was participant, by 1979 the percentage was close to, if not as high as, that of Western European states. When participation is at this level the potential strength of nationalist movements will be very great if the participant mass responds to nationalist symbols.

## 3. Viability

The definition of nationalism used in this essay includes the perception of an ability to maintain independent statehood based on the national community. No element of the definition is more important. If the members of the community do not believe that a state based on that community can defend itself or can develop the socio-economic base on which independence can rest, the set of behaviour termed as nationalistic is unlikely to prevail. Instead the individual members of the community will of necessity be compelled to accommodate to a government with a broader community base. Quite possibly their attachment to such a community, likely to be a conglomerate identity community, will not be at a primary intensity level and the state will then be a non-nation state. In the Middle East some examples of ethnic communities too small to be nations are the Turkmen, Qashqa'i, Assyrian, Druze and Alawi communities. Other communities are at the marginal level. These include Kurdish, Baluchi, Israeli and Palestinian and their struggles to achieve and/or maintain independent statehood incorporate much of the basis of turmoil in the area.

The elements of the viability base are three: population, territory and economy. The requisite population base for viability is situationally relative. Iceland, a distant island with a population of around a quarter of a million, has a sufficient population. But Kurdistan with anything from five to twelve million may be insufficient. On the other hand Turks, Arabs, and Iranians have sufficiently large population bases that should they desire independent nation statehood, it could be denied them only by extra regional forces. Israelis, Palestinians and Baluchis can probably maintain independence only with extra regional assistance.

The territory should be sufficiently large, defensible and possess sufficient agricultural and other resources to allow for defence and economic viability within the regional context. Here again Kurdistan with its contiguous territory, highly defensible topography and oil resources would rate as viable in this factor in many situational settings. But in the Middle East the Kurdish territory is the meeting point of Turkic, Iranian, Arab and even Slavic peoples and must be considered territorially insufficient. Here too Israeli territory would seem clearly insufficient and necessitating extra regional support should its neighbours prove enduringly hostile.

The economy should provide the basis for granting its population an acceptable living standard without external assistance. Left alone, Kurdistan might well constitute such an economic base. Baluchistan in an era of rising expectations probably cannot.

## 4. Uniqueness

For the set of behaviour described as nationalistic to prevail, a people must think of itself as a unique and distinctive people. If the people of a state are heterogeneous and find great difficulty seeing any common personality, nationalistic behaviour is unlikely. Similarly if the people of a state see very little that distinguishes them from the peoples of other states, they are unlikely to be predisposed to behave in nationalistic patterns. There are three basic elements in this category: history, culture, language.

### History

The uniqueness aspect is perceptual. Thus history relevant as a predictor of nationalistic behaviour is as perceived. A nationalistic people is likely to have a memory of a common past of at least several generations duration. If that memory incorporates episodes of great shared tragedies and, probably less important, great triumphs the predispositional base is strengthened. In any event to qualify as a nation a people must expect to share a common life in the future. The expectation common among Arabs in several states, that within a generation or so the state might be absorbed into a larger state, is destructive to nationalism associated with the contemporary state. Expectations among citizens of Iran that some of the ethnic components of that state may break away to form their own states is similarly damaging to an Iranian nationalism associated with the current multi-ethnic state of Iran. On the other hand Turks, Egyptians and Israelis evince little doubt that they are members of viable nation-states that are likely to persist for the foreseeable future.

*Culture*

Here there are two dimensions of importance in terms of uniqueness as an aspect of a predispositional base for behaving in a nationalistic manner. One is the perception of great cultural achievements as in the realms of art, architecture, literature and science. The second is a perception that the people of the community have a distinctive national culture. Defining a national culture is, of course, unnecessary for the task of evaluating this factor. What is necessary is ascertaining the perception of national cultural uniqueness. Quite typically a people which accept the fact of a strongly unique culture will have great difficulty in spelling out its features. But asked to characterise those of other peoples they believe to be less unique, they will have no difficulty. This is a consequence of viewing others stereotypically while at the same time understanding that the elements that comprise a national culture are too vaguely spelled out and difficult to evaluate when one views one's own people. However, if there is a perception of either a conglomerate culture or a culture shared with peoples of other states, the nationalistic predispositional base is weakened.

*Language*

Multi-lingual nations do exist but linguistic diversity is a major impediment for a nationalistic predispositional base. Conversely a people who have a single language which is unique to them have a major predispositional base advantage. The revival of Hebrew by Israelis is without question one of the major cohesive factors for the Israeli nation, and the pride and affection which Arabic speakers have for their language has much to do with the persistence of Arab nationalism in spite of an extraordinary range of impediments.

## 5. Complementarity of Identity Groups

The final element of the check-list concerns the range of politically relevant communities with which the people of a state identify. The major communities of concern here are religious, racial and ethnic. If the people of a state are diverse in religion, race and ethnicity, the problem of generating a nationalistic predispositional base may be a serious one. As the example of the United States demonstrates, however, nationalism may nevertheless be strong. However, when the people of a state have a common religion, race and ethnicity, as the Japanese are close to having, the advantage for a nationalistic predispositional base is enormous. The critical variable is that of community identity complementarity.

## Religious Communities

Since many religions aspire to universality, the members of associated religious communities are likely to manifest some tension with regard to their national and religious community identities. If both communities aspire to independent statehood, the individual loyal to both may well be forced into the position of making an exceedingly painful choice. In terms of the rhythm of development or change, the probability is highest of national–religious community tension in later stages of nationalistic development. As the mass of the population becomes increasingly participant, the proportion of the participant population that identifies intensely with religion is likely to increase. At the same time a common pattern is for a secular trend to develop among the most attentive section of the population. But the secular trend appears to develop at a rate that resembles an arithmetic progression whereas the participatory trend developes at a rate resembling a geometric progression. Thus a polity may appear to be intensifying in its religiosity when in fact there is a strong secular trend at work and religious intensity is in actual decline. This can be depicted as shown in Figure 2.1.

The dualism of political and spiritual authority in Christianity, reflected in the concept of the Two Swords, is surely a factor in making for complementarity of religion and nation in politics in which the religious community is predominantly Christian. But the point can easily be overdrawn. Church–state conflict is likely whenever both religious and national communities attract primary intensity identification. The Khomeini phenomenon in Iran is of unique quality because of the extraordinary coincidence of charisma and the perception of the charismatic figure that the religious community is the popular base on which a state should rest. But in my view Iranian development is prototypical of the proposition depicted graphically above. And also in my view very few Iranians are in the category of individual 'A' in the previous section (Islam (1), Iran (3)). The majority are close to

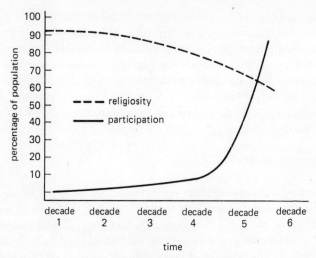

FIGURE 2.1

individual 'D' (Islam (1), Iran (1)) with individual 'C' (Islam (3), Iran (1)) heavily represented within the highly attentive population. If this is valid, the Iranian national and religious communities are likely to complement and hence reinforce the nationalistic predispositional base. As stated earlier, it may well be true that people of the Islam (1), Iran (1) category under Khomeini explicitly denied their nationalism. But their behaviour none the less identifies them as nationalistic. Iranian responses to the Iraqi attack were in close harmony with this point. However, should there be a growth in the percentage of the population that is Islam (1), Iran (3), identity competitiveness rather than complementarity will develop and Iranian national survival would be in jeopardy.

When there is religious diversity in a state a factor to note is that of religious distance as mutually perceived. If the majority or the core group[3] of the state population are members of a single religious community and view other religious communities within the state as exotic or at least very different, complementarity will be unlikely. Members of religious minorities are in such an event likely to perceive non-acceptance. In addition, if the achievement levels of majority or core group and minority are significantly different, complementarity is reduced. The problem is more serious if the minority is modally more achieving, as with Maronites and Copts, than when it is less achieving than the majority or core group, as with Druze or Alawi.

## Racial Communities

Racial communitics are natural foci of identity when perceived. Patterns of complementarity and competitiveness of national/racial communities are similar to those of national/religious communities when there is a strong racial perception. However, that phenomenon is rather rare. The biological basis for racial distinctiveness is so weak that the perceptual basis is hard to come by. There were indications that the Aryan race might supersede the German nation as the base of future statehood had Hitler been successful. But the difficulty of drawing boundaries was such that the definition of 'Aryan' became increasingly problematic. Racial distance as perceived is if anything even more of a problem for identity complementarity than religious distance as perceived. Racial minorities viewed as exotic will have great difficulty in being accepted by, and accepting, majority nationalism. In the Middle East this factor is of little concern.

## Ethnic Communities

The problem of ethnicity/nation is somewhat different. When there is ethnic homogeneity in a state, as with Japan and Norway for example, the ethnic community is the national community. But when a state is multi-ethnic, complementarity of national and ethnic communities depends on several factors. First, if the ethnic community is sufficiently large, territorially-based and capable of satisfying economic aspirations, community members can think in terms of independent statehood and the national and ethnic communities may well become competitors – as in Canada and in Lebanon. For complementarity of ethnic and national communities in a multi-ethnic state, the problem is much simplified if ethnic communities are not able to entertain realistic thoughts of seeking independence. When ethnic groups can reasonably aspire to independence, survival of the multi-ethnic state will be in question. A survival strategy may well call for downgrading nationalistic appeals to the majority or core ethnic community and to seek instead to cultivate a less intense attachment to the multi-ethnic state. Such an attachment would not meet the requirements of the definition of nationalism advanced here but could be described by the broader term 'patriotist'. This appears to be the case today in the Soviet Union and may be the case in Nigeria and even India. Multi-ethnicity in Iran may in the future present Iranian nationalism with this alternative.

When multi-ethnicity exists and there is sub-marginal perception of viability, complementarity is likely to be related to the distance factor in parallel fashion to that described for religion. Evidence suggests that here too the problem of maintaining complementarity deepens in later stages of nationalistic development. Two patterns deserve to be described.

First is the case in which a minority tends to be more achieving or more rapidly developing than other elements of the population. Examples are Armenians in Turkey, Jews in Iraq, Maronites (considered here more as an ethnic group than a religious community) in Lebanon. If the minority is able to think reasonably that independent statehood is possible for that community, nationalism centred on the ethnic community is likely to appear. This was apparently the case for Armenians in Turkey and is quite clearly the case for much of the Maronite community in Lebanon. In this event, the situation is highly competitive and the minority may well be risking a genocidal reaction. However, if the member of the community cannot reasonably think in terms of statehood, there is likely to be an accommodation with the new nationalism that is embracing the majority or core community. Nevertheless, the members of such overachieving minority communities are likely to view the majority with a combination of fear and contempt. Identification with majority or core-based nationalism is extremely difficult because of this contempt. Furthermore fear of violence, even genocide, is not unreasonable and that fear may well deepen as the mass base of majoritarian nationalism grows. Safety for the minority is likely to be found in the persistence of the norms of tolerance within the majority community, and tolerance norms are likely to be endangered as the populist base of nationalism broadens. The problem is seriously exacerbated if the over-achieving minority is perceived to identify with an outside state especially if that outside state is threatening. Jews in Iraq, with many individual exceptions of course, tended not to identify with emerging Arab nationalism even though in its early stages that nationalism was most strongly advocated by members of the Moslem liberal intelligentsia and many leading members of the Jewish community were closely associated with them socially. Then when Israel appeared on the scene the situation rapidly became intolerable and most Jews felt there was no alternative to emigration.

Happily more common and less threatening is the pattern in which the ethnic minority is less-achieving or is modernising at a slower rate than the majority or core elements of the population. A typical development pattern is that of the Azerbaijanis relative to the Farsi-speaking Iranian community. In this case the developmental lag is a narrow one. Other ethnic minorities in Iran, such as Arabs, Turkmen, Kurds and Baluchis are more slowly developing relative to the core element. In these cases as Iranian nationalism develops, typically led by members of the modernising, highly attentive population, modernising and highly attentive members of the minority communities may well be co-opted into the emerging Iranian nation. But if the minority perceives itself as relatively deprived, economically, socially and/or politically, as political participation becomes more pervasive, a counter élite is likely to appear that will argue a case for separation. In this event the outcome is likely to depend on the minority's perception of the possibility of separating, defending the new political entity and providing the society of that entity with a viable economy. If separation is clearly impractical on any of these grounds, the effort will still be likely to be made to achieve some form of autonomy within an umbrella state organisation. There is no inevitability of outcome in such an event. If the majority or core-based government follows a utilitarian strategy and offers a better and more influential future to the minority, those élites arguing for association with a larger, multi-ethnic national community may well prevail. Iran, in its current agony, is faced with this very challenge. The Kurds in Turkey, Iraq and Syria are following in the pattern.

## APPLICATION OF THE CHECK-LIST

In the following application the symbol ' + + ' is used to indicate that an element of the check list is strongly favourable for a nationalist predispositional base and the symbol ' — — ' is used to indicate strongly unfavourable. The check-list then can serve as a guide to expected nationalistic behaviour and as a means for identifying areas of difficulty for the nation.

With Japan and the USA as comparative referrents, this amounts to a very preliminary proposition. Indicator usage is intuitive and arbitrary and the most obvious early development for this scheme is to reduce the judgemental quality by standardising coding procedures. Still it may be suggestive. It certainly argues a greater potential for Arab nationalism than is commonly assumed. It suggests a healthy base for Turkish nationalism (which would be further enhanced by a more utilitarian strategy toward the Kurds) and fairly good prospects for a multi-ethnic Iranian nationalism. For individual Arab states (except Egypt) the judgement is less sanguine. The case of Arab nationalism is particularly intriguing. The existing behavioural parameters induced by Arab

TABLE 2.5

| | Japan | USA | Israel (Only Jews) | Israel (All) | Arab | Egypt | Lebanon | Iran | Turkey | Palestine | Jordan |
|---|---|---|---|---|---|---|---|---|---|---|---|
| Attentive Publics | + | + | + | + | + | + | − | + | + | + | O |
| Political Participation | + | + | + | + | + | + | + | + | + | + | + |
| Viability | | | | | | | | | | | |
| Population | + | + | − | − | + | + | O | + | + | − | − |
| Territory | + | + | − | − | + | + | O | + | + | − | − |
| Economy | + | + | − | − | + | O | O | + | + | − | − |
| Uniqueness | | | | | | | | | | | |
| History | + | + | + | + | + | + | − | + | + | + | O |
| Culture | + | + | + | + | + | + | − | + | + | + | O |
| Language | + | + | + | + | + | + | + | + | + | + | + |
| Identity | | | | | | | | | | | |
| Complementary | | | | | | | | | | | |
| Religion | + | O | + | O | + | O | − | + | + | O | O |
| Race | + | − | + | O | O | O | O | O | + | O | O |
| Ethnicity | + | − | + | − | O | O | − | O | + | O | − |

nationalism have been fairly well sketched by Arab policies. Arab nationalism is too strong to allow Arab leaders, other than the late Sadat, to follow a course of action that would doom any hopes for Palestinian independence. But it is not strong enough to overcome personal, sectarian and ethnic vested interests that would be damaged by the creation of a large Arab nation-state.

Special note should be taken of the strong showing of Arab nationalism in the viability section of the check-list. Whereas the proposed rating is a high one, mid-twentieth century Arab history with its direct or indirect dominance by external powers has left Arabs with little sense of a strong viability base for an Arab nation-state. Indeed modern Arab history has given Arabs a particularly low sense of efficacy. Western imperial interests are perceived as opposing Arab unity and sufficiently strong to have this wish prevail. Were Arab nationalists to gain a heightened sense of efficacy, it follows, they would see less reason to accommodate to present state divisions and become more energetic in pursuing a goal of an Arab nation-state. If so, a shift of identities in the direction of first intensity for Arab would be a natural consequence. The point here is the one already made. For nationalism to remain strong, a people must believe it has the capability of establishing and defending a nation-state able to provide a satisfactory standard of living. In part because of their experience with imperial powers, Arabs have not been able to sustain a sense of an ability to establish and defend an Arab nation state. Yet the viability base, it is proposed here, is potentially a very good one and if Arabs were able to see this and hence to believe that an Arab nation-state is a practical possibility, Arab nationalism could become a significantly more pervasive phenomenon.

## CONCLUSION

My purpose in this essay was to propose an identity framework within which nationalism in the Middle East could be viewed. My assumption is that identification with politically relevant communities inclines individuals in certain political behavioural directions. But overall behaviour is better viewed as flowing from a system of values and an associated world view (system of perceptions); and efforts to look at behaviour related specifically to nationalism out of the system-context produces serious distortion. My attempt therefore has been to try to look at nationalistic behaviour in the system-context and with particular attention to variations induced by other community attachments, notably religious ones.

## NOTES

1. For a catalogue of definitions see Shafer (1972, ch. 1).
2. For supporting survey research data from Egypt in the inter-war period see Ismail (1962).
3. For a development of the concept of ethnic core see Gordon (1964).

# 3 Social Factors in the Rise of the Arab Movement in Syria

## RASHID KHALIDI

During the Ottoman Constitutional era, the politics of the Arab lands of the Ottoman Empire – of Syria, Palestine and Lebanon in particular – were dominated by a deep cleavage. This political cleavage, mirrored in the local press which flourished in the wake of the lifting of the Hamidian censorship, and recorded in the diplomatic despatches of foreign observers, grew deeper and more intractable in the years following the 1908 revolution, until it culminated in the Arab Revolt and the hanging by the Ottoman authorities, in 1915 and 1916, of dozens of its leaders.

On the surface, this conflict seemed to oppose the Ottoman central government and the ruling party – the Committee of Union and Progress (CUP) – to local elements in the Syrian and other Arab provinces who allied themselves to the opposition party: the *Entente Liberale*, for most of the period 1903–1914. But a closer look at the main sources, be they foreign diplomatic despatches, contemporary histories or the local press, reveals that in fact there was a cleavage of at least equal importance between two rival local groupings. Dawn (1973) designated these rival groupings the 'Arabists' and the 'Ottomanists' – the proponents of Arab nationalism, and those who favoured the status quo. It is possible to infer the positions of each group by examining the issues over which politics became polarised during this period. These were briefly the questions of language, nationality, provincial autonomy as against greater centralisation, religion and foreign penetration; issues which, in one form or another, dominated the politics of all the outlying minority regions of the Empire in this period, whether in the Balkans,

53

Armenia or the Arab provinces. The differences between the Arabists and the Ottomanists on these issues have been discussed extensively by Dawn in his article in 'The Rise of Arabism in Syria', who argues that the clash between the Arabist and Ottomanist factions in Syrian society was essentially 'a traditional inter-élite conflict' (Dawn, 1973, p. 173).

It is the argument of this paper that the Arab movement in Syria during the pre-war period was not only the instrument of one faction in a traditional inter-élite rivalry, but also a vehicle for the entry into Arab politics of new forces and of groups representing a different social base. This process became possible only because of the post-1908 transformation of the Ottoman political system, which provided for parliamentary and local elections, freed the press from the restrictions of political censorship, and was itself the result of the eruption of the military into politics.

Thus, there was a conflict between two rival groups within the Syrian élite, groups whose contours may well have been determined, as Dawn suggests, by the holding or non-holding of public office. On the one side stood those members of the élite who had a vested interest in perpetuation of the status quo, and on the other, those without such vested interest. However, alongside this conflict, there was another process taking place, not fully appreciated by Dawn. This latter integrative process consisted of the movement on to the political stage of journalists, teachers, professionals and members of the military, all of whom had played little or no part in the traditional politics of the Ottoman Empire.[1]

Furthermore, it seems that a larger proportion of these men, members of what we can loosely term the new intelligentsia, were attracted to the Arabist cause, although this would be hard to prove conclusively without further research. The evidence which we will present, however, does seem to indicate that for a variety of reasons, these mostly young and radical members of the intelligentsia found more in common with the Arabists than with their opponents, the Ottomanists, who were partisans of the status quo. Our evidence tends to confirm that, as a result of the adhesion of the intelligentsia to the movement, the Arabists had striking success in the press, among army officers, and in other fields where such individuals played a vital role.

We will now proceed to examine how the changes in the political process in the Empire as a whole led to changes in Syria, and how these changes in turn superimposed a new dimension on the traditional politics of the area. All this will help us to understand how and why the Arabist movement represented and was led by men from new and heretofore unrepresented strata of Syrian society. It will also help us to explain how this era marks the beginning of the transition from traditional to modern politics in an important part of the Arab world.

An examination of the extensive political press of the 1908–14 period, and of the British and French consular correspondence from the cities of Syria, indicates clearly that the reimposition of the Ottoman Constitution changed, at the very least the form, and perhaps some of the content, of the political process.[2] As a result, we witness the first signs of a transformation of what Hourani (1968) called 'the politics of the notables', in the form of two or more coalitions of the urban élite roughly balancing one another and acting as intermediaries between the supreme political power in the capital and the local population.

Among the signs of this transformation was the fact that alongside traditional channels of communications between factions of the élite and their respective constituencies, the press became an important, perhaps the most important, medium for influencing public opinion. At the same time, the forum of public discussion began to shift from the home, the mosque and the coffee-shop, to the election meeting (there were three general elections in the Empire between 1908 and 1914 – in 1908, 1912 and 1914), the political club, the party meeting and the schools and institutes of higher education which were growing rapidly in number in Syria in the late nineteenth and early twentieth centuries (Tibawi, 1969, pp. 181–2, 194–6). As an example of the spread of education, by 1914 there were in the province of Beirut alone 359 state primary and secondary schools for an estimated population of about 800 000, all of them established within the preceding three decades (Tamimi and Bahjat, 1917, pp. 151–3).

Moreover, even in the older centres of political debate, in the home, the mosque and the coffee-shop, the newly-freed and fast-growing press provided new subjects for discussion, new ideas and new ideologies, and new forms for discourse, even where the subject was not a new one. Thus, we find polemical newspaper editorials in a leading Beirut Arabist paper, *al-Mufid*, being read aloud in the home, and in many cases memorised, by excited young people (Khalidi, 1981b, p. 44). The impact of the press can perhaps be better gauged if we realise the extent to which it grew during this period.

Using as our source the standard history of the Arabic press (Tarazi, 1933, pp. 8–71), it is possible to enumerate at least 100 newspapers of a serious nature and published for a considerable period which were established in the cities of Syria between 1908 and 1914. Beirut leads with thirty, followed by Damascus with twenty, Aleppo with twelve,

Tripoli and Jerusalem with seven each, and Jaffa, Homs, Haifa, Hama and Latakia with from four to six each.

As all the afore-mentioned developments (particularly the broadened potential role of public opinion and of the urban masses) drastically widened the scope of politics and expanded what Deutsch (1980, pp. 48 ff.) calls the 'politically relevant strata' of the population, a new dimension was being super-imposed on the traditional 'politics of the notables'. Indeed, politics for the first time seems to have been moving out of the latter's control, to the benefit of heretofore powerless groups, or of groups which had newly risen in the society.

In the Empire as a whole, the 1908 revolution ushered in features of 'modern' politics to which we have since become accustomed in the Middle East. These include (i) the repeated intrusion of the military into public life; (ii) the prevalence of ideologies of a nationalist and populist nature; and (iii) the process we have just mentioned – the broadened participation in politics by new sectors and strata. Clearly, this process was most evident regarding the Turkish regions of the Empire in the years 1908–18, as has been demonstrated by Ahmad (1969). Nevertheless, during this same period we can perceive the same changes, albeit perhaps somewhat later and to a lesser degree, taking place in Syria, Iraq and some other Arab areas. This can best be shown by a brief account of how all three processes emerged in Syria during the constitutional period.

As an obvious example of the involvement of the military in politics, we have the activities of the Arab nationalist secret societies among Arab officers in the Ottoman Army, most notably *al-'Ahd* (the Covenant).[3] Not surprisingly, these bodies bear a striking resemblance to the underground groups of Turkish officers which were instrumental in carrying out the 1908 revolution. Another similarity with the Arab nationalist secret societies can be found in the close links between Turkish civilian and military groupings in opposition to the Sultan before 1908 (Ahmad, 1969; Ramsaur, 1957).

Some sources tend to underestimate the importance of the Arab military officers' groupings. Dawn (1973, pp. 174–5), for example, includes only twelve members of *al-'Ahd* in his list of the Syrian membership of the pre-1914 Arab nationalist movement. But we know from French diplomatic despatches written in the spring of 1913 (*Ministère des Affaires Étrangères*, hereafter MAE, 1913a; MAE, 1913c; MAE, 1913e) that at least forty Arab officers in the Ottoman Army which defended Constantinople during the Balkan wars were actively involved in planning for the nationalist goal of the creation of an Arab state extending from Egypt to Baghdad in the event of the collapse of the

Empire. Another source (Sa'id, 1934, p. 47) affirms that of 490 Arab officers stationed in the Istanbul area in 1914, 315 belonged to *al-'Ahd*.[4]

One of the most striking examples of how far the politicisation of the military and their involvement in Arab nationalist politics had gone by the end of this period was the celebrated Col. 'Aziz 'Ali al-Masri affair of 1913, discussed in Khadduri (1965). This combined intense public agitation and the active involvement of the press with a serious exacerbation of the Arab-Turkish issue in the Empire as a whole.

There is no need to stress the nationalist nature of the ideology espoused by the Arabists. It also seems clear that their cause was popular in Syria, and had a certain mass appeal. This is logical, since the main issue over which the public divide emerged between the Arabists and Ottomanists in 1909–12 was the question of language. Specifically, the dispute arose over new regulations imposing Turkish as the only language allowed in local schools and government offices (Musa, 1970, pp. 58–9; Daghir, 1916, pp. 53–4). The demand of the Arabists for the retention of Arabic found a powerful response among several different constituencies, thus causing an uproar in Syria. For pious Moslems, the use of Arabic, the language of the Prophet and the *Qur'an*, had strong religious overtones, and the issue was easily projected in such a light. We find indeed that the newspaper *al-Mufid*, the organ of the main Arab nationalist secret society, *al-Jam'iya al-'Arabiya al-Fatat*, extensively employed such religious appeals (e.g. *al-Mufid*, 1911a; *al-Mufid*, 1911d), as did other nationalist or nationalist-leaning newspapers in Syria (e.g. *al-Ittihad al-'Uthmani*, 1910; *al-Ittihad al-'Uthmani*, 1911).

For another constituency, that of the large number of young men newly-educated in the expanded local school system in Syria (whose families were unable to send them on to higher education where they would have learned Turkish, as did many of the sons of the élite), the call for the continued governmental use of Arabic was also attractive. For whether as aspiring bureaucrats, or simply as private citizens in their dealings with the state, such individuals would have been seriously disadvantaged by the language reforms implemented by the government in 1909 and 1910. Even part of the élite was affected by these measures, for not all had received an education in the governmental secondary and professional schools where Turkish was taught. At the very least, those who received a traditional or Western missionary education, and thus had learned no Turkish, were clearly likely to be negatively affected. Not surprisingly, Dawn's data indicates (1973, p. 161) that 'Western and traditional education both tended to produce Arab nationalists; state education pro-Ottomans.'

There is another indication of the relative popularity of the Arabists and Ottomanists in Syria, although it is one which is perhaps not methodologically ideal – the election results, particularly those before 1912. (The governing CUP rigged the two following elections.) Of the twenty-one Arab deputies elected in Syria in 1908 and in the three by-elections before 1912, only seven can be identified as supporters of the government party, and thus as Ottomanists, while at least thirteen were members of the opposition and can be described as Arabists.[5] Of the latter, five were sentenced to death and one to permanent exile for Arab nationalist activities during the First World War.

It can of course be argued that the fact that the majority of the representatives of the Syrian provinces before the 1912 election were Arabists is no indication of the political orientation of their constituents at the time of their election, for in 1908, when eighteen of the twenty-one were elected, the lines between the Ottomanist and Arabist factions had not yet been clearly drawn. While this is true, strictly speaking, it is certainly a fact of significance that a clear majority of the elected representatives of the people of Syria should have aligned themselves with the Arabist current over a four-year period. Like all politicians, they had an eye on re-election, and the public stands they took must in some measure have been a reflection of the attitudes of their constituents in the Syrian provinces.

The fact that most of these deputies were members of upper-class families, and that the two-stage indirect election system provided for by the Ottoman election law weighted the political system in favour of these same families and the social class they represented, does not diminish the significance of our observation. Even if large property-owners and other notcables were over-represented in the final analysis – for although all male tax-payers over the age of 25 chose their secondary electors in the first stage, in the second stage only individuals of substantial local means were likely to be elected by the latter group – the very fact that initially an appeal had to be made to the general populace meant that whichever candidate could combine popular themes with an outstanding local reputation had a distinct advantage.

It is not surprising, therefore, that we find the Arab deputies in the Ottoman Chamber forming a parliamentary bloc, opposing the government over a number of issues of concern to the Arab provinces such as river concessions to the British in Iraq or Zionist settlement in Palestine (*al-Muqtabas*, 1911a; *al-Muqtabas*, 1911b; Ahmad, 1969, pp. 66–7, 93; Khalidi, 1980, pp. 212–28; Mandel, 1976, pp. 112–16), and in 1911 and 1912 moving more and more into opposition to the CUP and the Ottomanist trend associated with it. We have to assume that by these acts they were not only responding to their own developing nationalist outlook, but also to perceived shifts in public opinion at home. We know from the daily press that the speeches of the Syrian deputies, and even their more mundane political activities in the capital, were extensively reported, as they must have been aware themselves (e.g., *al-Mufid*, 1911b; *al-Mufid*, 1911c; *al-Muqtabas*, 1911c). Thus, although the later political orientation of these thirteen deputies is perhaps not representative of the outlook of their constituents when most were first elected in 1908, and though they are not strictly representative of the people who elected them in terms of social origin, it seems reasonable to assume that the shift in their thinking and their adoption of an overt Arabist stand by 1912 is indicative of the trend of public opinion in the Syrian provinces.

This view was certainly shared by foreign observers at the time. Both British and French consuls in virtually all the cities of Syria reported a growing Arabist trend from 1909 until 1912 (Khalidi, 1980, pp. 217–41). Their despatches during these years are filled with comments such as: 'the antagonistic sentiment as between Arab and Turk is beginning to permeate downwards to the lower classes' (British Consul, Damascus, in Foreign Office – hereafter FO, 1910b); 'Among the population in general a good deal of bitterness and discontent is caused by the policy of the present Government . . . popular feeling . . . is just now rising sharply against the local authority' (British Consul, Beirut in FO, 1910a); 'the separatist idea which, in the minds of many, lurks in the mind of every Syrian Arab' (British Consul, Beirut, in FO, 1911a); 'the recent stir of pro-Arab or anti-Turkish sentiment' (British Consul, Damascus, in FO, 1911b); 'the CUP are in disfavour . . . owing to their anti-Arab policy' (British Consul, Beirut, in FO, 1912c); and *'D'une façon générale les esprits sont inquiets, la désaffection des populations arabes vis-à-vis de la Turquie me parait s'accroître . . .'* (French Consul, Beirut, in MAE, 1912a).

The consular despatches also give us an excellent and detailed picture of how their declining popularity pushed the CUP to rig the 1912 elections; a French Consular despatch from Aleppo relates for example that the *vali* of Aleppo, Mazhar Pasha, told him he had resigned rather than lend himself to *'certaines manœuvres destinées à fausser ces elections'* (MAE, 1912b). Although the CUP swept the elections throughout the Empire as a result of these 'manœuvres (Ahmad, 1969, pp. 102–4), the campaign which preceded this 'victory' was revealing of popular feeling in Syria. Again according to the foreign consuls, the CUP candidates uniformly failed to arouse public enthusiasm, while prominent Arabists were repeatedly enthusiastically received. In Beirut, two anti-CUP orators, Lutfi Fikri Bey and Shukri al'Asali, were carried on the shoulders of a cheering crowd after rousing speeches which were enthusiastically received; in Aleppo, on the other hand, the Ottomanists initially had difficulty finding anyone who could speak properly in public; while the three leading Arab CUP members of Parliament, Shaykh As'ad Shuqayr of Acre, Sherif Ja'far Pasha of Mecca and 'Ali Effendi Jenani of Aleppo, who spoke to an electoral rally in Beirut, were apparently incapable of arousing any positive response from the crowds (FO, 1912a, 1912b, 1912c; MAE, 1912c, 1912d; see also *al-Muqtabas*, 1912a, 1912b, 1912c; and *al-Mufid*, 1912a, 1912b, 1912c, 1912d).[6]

As evidence substantiating the impact of Arab nationalist ideology and the involvement of the masses in Syrian politics, it would be appropriate at this point to quote the comment by the French Consul-General in Beirut in the spring of 1913. This was written after the Ottoman Government's closure of the Beirut Reform Club had led to the entire Beirut press (with the exception of two pro-CUP papers) appearing with black borders, and with the official closure order as their only front-page news item. The closure of one paper (the Arabist *al-Mufid*) which followed, and the arrest of five of the leaders of the movement then led to six days of feverish demonstrations which nearly degenerated into riots. Speaking of the disturbance, the Consul declared (MAE, 1913b):

> *L'unanimité avec laquelle les Beyrouthins ont protesté . . . est d'autant plus significatif, qu'ils ont obéi plutôt à une idée qu'aux ordres de chefs d'une autorité contestable et dont l'inexpérience et le peu de connaissance des choses publiques sont notoires; elle indique que la petite classe elle-même s'intéresse aux reformes, et revendique l'autonomie de son pays, que le mouvement a gagné le peuple et s'y propage; elle indique aussi, et cette consideration n'est pas la moins importante à notre point de vue, qu'une certaine solidarité s'est créée entre chrétiens et musulmans en vue d'atteindre un but commun.*

Naturally, the French Consul General in Beirut, Couget, was not a social scientist or a trained historian, and his sociological observations must be accepted with some reserve. But they are worth recording as contemporary, first-person and expert opinion by a shrewd observer who perceived that the Arabist reform movement had a far broader social base than just a faction of the élite, and that indeed the 'notable' leaders often had little control over their followers.

The evidence adduced relating to the orientation of the majority of Arab members of Parliament, to the election campaigns and their results before 1912, and to the 1913 riots strongly indicates the following: (i) that a populist, mass-oriented dimension had entered Arab politics in the wake of the 1908 Revolution; (ii) that there was apparently broader public participation in at least some aspects of the political process than ever before; (iii) that in some measure, therefore, 'modern politics' had begun to arrive in Syria; and (iv) that in this modern politics, with its broader mass base and appeals to the people, the Arabists – though in many ways similar to their Ottomanist opponents in terms of the social profile of their leadership – were nevertheless far better equipped than the latter to compete for popular favour.

It can perhaps be argued that much of this is based on the observations of British and French consuls who were biased in favour of the Arab movement for autonomy because it promised to weaken central control and thereby indirectly to further the ambitions of their respective countries in Syria. That there was such a bias cannot be denied, although it cannot be accepted that it was of such an extent as to render valueless and without foundation the virtually unanimous observations of trained and experienced observers in every major city in Syria. Perhaps some of their informants told them what they wanted them to hear, or thought they wanted to hear; and perhaps they heard what they wanted to hear from time to time. But it is unlikely that such a phenomenon as the rise of Arabist sentiment, reported in scores of despatches over many years, was entirely the reflection of such bias; or indeed of the Arab nationalist bias of many of its Arab historians (such as Daghir, 1916; Sa'id, 1934; Antonius, 1939; Musa, 1970).

There is, moreover, an important set of independent data which, in spite of other, different possible pitfalls, can serve as a control on what can be gleaned from a careful reading of the foreign consular reports and the standard histories. This is the Syrian press itself, which we have had occasion to cite earlier. The Ottoman Constitutional era witnessed an unprecedented flourishing of the Syrian press, and many of the papers first published in that period are still extant. Although a major, perhaps the most important, source for this question, they have as yet not been fully utilised, or indeed even fully surveyed, as the author has argued in a paper which goes in some detail into the treatment of Arab nationalism and other related themes in one of the main Arabist daily newspapers of the day, *al-Mufid* of Beirut (Khalidi, 1981b, especially pp. 46–60).

Admittedly, the daily political press is prone to be partisan, and it thus must be used as a source with extreme care. However, whenever we attempt to check foreign consular reports or accounts of historians of the period against the press, the latter almost invariably corroborates our other sources. The value of the press, moreover, is enhanced by the fact that during this period there are so many papers to which we can refer, each with its own political orientation.[7]

By and of itself, this would seem to be a finding of some significance in terms of our argument that the Ottoman Constitutional period marked the beginning of the era of 'modern politics' in Syria. More important, however, is the help this massive body of evidence gives us regarding the nature of the political process which was unfolding in Syria, and the nature of the different factions involved. Thus, it is possible to discern the links between local groupings and the political parties in the Empire as a whole, as well as the ties between groups in different cities within Syria. It is even possible, at another, more detailed level, to attempt to determine which officials, notables, intellectuals and others whose names occurred with frequency in the press, were aligned with which faction in the ongoing political conflict in Syrian society.

Such an effort has yet to be made in a systematic fashion, and it is not possible at this stage to propose definitive conclusions. But while awaiting such research and its outcome, we can at least propose some tentative hypotheses regarding the social make-up of the early Arab nationalist movement. These rely primarily on a preliminary study of the press, supported by other secondary sources, and start from the conclusions of Dawn (1973), together with our comments and reservations noted earlier. Building on the evidence already presented here regarding the new form taken by politics after 1912, the most salient of these hypotheses are the following:

1.  It would indeed seem that the Arabist faction attracted dissatisfied members of the Arab élite, that is to say those who had been less successful in gaining public office, as Dawn has shown (1973, pp. 148–179) but alongside such individuals, and perhaps more numerous than they, were members of another group. This was composed of mainly young, educated radicals of a more diverse social background, including some from social strata whose members would in the past have had little access to the Ottoman political process. A cluster of such individuals can be perceived connected with each of the leaders from more traditional élite backgrounds, whether these were Deputies in Parliament or prominent in other ways, and it sometimes seems as if they had as much or more influence than these leaders.[8]

One of the significant things about the opening up of the political process after 1908 was that even where traditional élite figures played a prominent role, this now involved both co-ordination with numerous individuals of different social backgrounds, and appealing to an even greater number of individuals of more diverse social origins. It can of course be argued that to a certain extent the 'politics of the notables' always involved analagous or similar processes. However true this may have been, the significant difference was that with a new kind of politics, new skills and training became necessary, such that teachers, journalists, government officials, military officers and others with similar skills and professional training now played an active and indeed essential role in politics, whatever their social background.

This intelligentsia formed the backbone of the Arab nationalist secret societies, and because of its members' unique combination of skills, access and training, was instrumental in the development and dissemination of the nascent nationalist ideology. While this was clearest and perhaps most significant in the case of the press, as we saw earlier, it was no less the case for teachers, with their enormous impact on educated youth (see for example, Khalidi, 1981b, p. 41, especially note 9; and Salibi, 1976, pp. 203–4). From figures given by Tamimi and Bahjat (1917, pp. 152–3) we can infer that in Beirut *vilayet* alone there were over 600 teachers in state schools at this time.

As was the case of the CUP in the analagous process within the Turkish body politic a few years earlier, an especially important and active part in the growth of nationalist feeling was played by those 'intellectuals in uniform', the Arab military officers. They combined a fairly rigorous professional education, status in society and influence over their colleagues and subordinates, with that indispensable asset for the acquisition and exercise of political power, armed force.

Although it is impossible to prove it, given the limited amount of detail available, an examination of each of these groups, and of the intelligentsia as a whole, gives us ground for asserting that they were more drawn to Arabism than to the ideology of the status quo – Ottomanism. In the case of the press, this is manifest from the larger number of Arabist and anti-CUP papers in Syria than Ottomanist pro-CUP ones. And this fact would seem in turn to be a valuable index of the sentiments of a sizeable, if not predominant, section of the literate population. As for officers, the data on those affiliated to al-'Ahd given by Sa'id (1934, p. 47) at least suggests that a majority was Arabist in sentiment. We simply have no data for teachers and government officials, though it may be postulated that the same was true of them on the basis of clues which can be gleaned from such events as the violent opposition in 1911 of Arab CUP members – most of them officials and teachers – at a secret meeting in Beirut where they were asked to approve anti-Arabist party directives from Istanbul (for details see Khalidi, 1977, pp. 219–20).

It can furthermore be suggested that these generally radical, young and dissatisfied members of the intelligentsia were more likely to be associated with the Arabists than with their rivals, because in the Arab provinces much of the conservative traditional élite tended to attempt to monopolise power locally, and to identify with the ruling party, which for most of the period from 1908 to 1918 was the CUP. The latter thus became identified with the status quo faction of the élite (somewhat paradoxically in view of its radical language and centralisation policies). It is logical that their revisionist rivals, the Arabists – although they too included many members of the élite – would thus be more attractive as political allies to the radical young members of this intelligentsia.

2. Because most traditional means of advancement were blocked, owing to the near-monopoly over high state and religious office held by the partisans of the existing social and political order in Syria who tended to ally themselves with the CUP in the capital, we find both members of the élite faction who had been less successful in the competition for office, and young radicals of diverse social backgrounds, attracted to new careers as a means of upward mobility. These included the officer corps of the expanding modern Ottoman army; teaching positions in the increasing number of government and private, as well as religious and missionary, schools; the burgeoning government service, the press and other allied intellectual pursuits. None of these opportunities were available a century or even fifty years earlier, and with their creation there arose new groups within society with a new potential for political influence. If our preliminary impression from our limited range of sources is correct, a large proportion, if not an absolute majority, of these individuals were more attracted to the Arabists than to their rivals.[9]

It can be noted in passing that individuals from these social and professional groups have since played a prominent role in Arab politics, forming the backbone of many of the movements, parties and regimes which have been active in Syria and other Arab countries in the years between 1908 and the present day. The pre-World War One period marks their first appearance on the Arab political stage.

3. If we are correct in assuming that there was greater adherence to the Arabist cause than to that of the Ottomanists by members of what we have called the new intelligentsia, then their influence in society and their unrivalled ability to shape public opinion (particularly the journalists and teachers among them) in part explain the seeming popular success of this cause in Syria in the years before 1914. We have seen the beginnings of this process from our brief outline of political developments until 1912, but it becomes even more the case in late 1912, in 1913 and in 1914. During these years, the pressure for reform, decentralisation, recognition of the Arabic language in the Arab provinces, and a fair proportion of central and local government positions for Arab officials became so widespread, and popular agitation so intense, that the CUP was forced to make concessions which seemed to strike at the very heart of their original policy in the Arab provinces of the Empire.

The First Arab Congress in Paris in 1913 (organised by many of the most active young Arab nationalist radicals, several of whom were later hanged during the war) and the earlier founding of the influential Beirut Reform Society, mark a high point in the pre-war history of the Arab movement (see, for example, *al-Mu'tamar al-'Arabi, al-Awwal*, 1913; and Sa'doun, 1977). The aftermath of the 1913 Beirut riots, mentioned earlier, is also evidence of the Ottoman Government's perception of the weight and importance of the movement, for the state ultimately backed down, reopening the banned newspaper, *al-Mufid*, as well as the Reform Club, and releasing its arrested leaders. The recognition accorded the latter by the government when it agreed to negotiate with them in mid-1913 is further evidence of the extent to which the Arabist cause in Syria had won, and was perceived to have won, public opinion over to its side.

4. The Arabist trend, which we may seem to have been treating as if it were a homogeneous and coherent political grouping, was in fact extremely diverse and heterogeneous in nature. It included different groups with different objectives and different social backgrounds, and was never as unified as it appears in most of the histories of this period (e.g. Daghir, 1916; Sa'id, 1934; Antonius, 1939; Musa, 1970). In a fluid, fast-changing social order, affected by the impact of the

rapid economic change witnessed in Syria and the rest of the Empire
during this period, it was perhaps natural that this should be the
case, and thus that only a few major points of agreement should
hold the entire movement together.

We know, for example, that there were two major Arab
nationalist secret societies, *al-Fatat* and *al-'Ahd*, mainly made up of
young men, the former largely students and intellectuals, and the
latter Army officers. In some loose connection with these were the
Decentralisation Party based in Cairo (*Hizb al-Lamarkaziyya al-
Idariyya al-'Uthmaniyya*), the Arab parliamentary group (before
most of its Arabist members were defeated in 1912), the Beirut
Reform Society and those in other cities of Syria and Iraq, and
other Arabist groups and organisations. The first two seem to have
been the closest to one another, (and the most ideological in
orientation) and indeed apparently merged during World War One;
but the rest were discrete groups whose aims were by no means
identical, in spite of a certain amount of overlapping of membership.

The corollary of this diversity was the fact that it was in principle
quite easy to divide and thus outmanœuvre such a movement by
satisfaction of some of the grievances of some of its constituent
parts, particularly dissatisfied members of the élite whose main
complaint was that they did not hold an official post. In practice,
this is just what the CUP did in substance in late 1913 and 1914, thus
succeeding in dividing and neutralising the movement, at least
temporarily.

5.  It can be suggested that the political diversity and heterogeneity of
    the Arabist movement in Syria owes something to the development
    in the late nineteenth and early twentieth centuries of certain
    relatively new types of commercial interests, particularly in the
    coastal cities. This was composed of a new and growing group of
    traders many of whom dealt with Egypt or Britain, and thus tended
    to be favourably disposed politically towards the latter; or with
    France and thus tended to sympathise with the power. It seems
    likely that this was one of the main social strata behind the repeated
    private expressions to both British and French Consuls in Syria in
    late 1912 and early 1913 (when it appeared that the Ottoman
    Empire might be about to collapse at the height of the Balkan Wars)
    of a desire for the 'protection' of one or the other power (for a
    detailed discussion see Khalidi, 1980, chap. 5). Such expressions are
    hard to understand except as a reflection, at least in some measure,

of the ambitions, outlook and desires of this group, already closely linked commercially to one of the two great imperial powers of the day, and which formed an important, albeit not the dominant, current in the larger Arabist movement.

Although the approaches to the two powers were apparently made by individuals and groups in many Syrian cities, they seem most frequent and insistent from a segment of the Arabist leadership involved in trade in the coastal cities, and from the predominantly Uniate Lebanese nationalists with whom they were associated in the Beirut reform movement, in the Decentralisation Party in Cairo, and at the Paris Congress. Here, admittedly, we are nearly groping in the dark in the absence of more complete background data on some of the key individuals in this regard, but it seems reasonable to assume that extensive commercial involvement, either with Britain or with France, might dispose such a group towards political co-operation with one of these powers. Naturally, such links would not necessarily be exclusive (a merchant might trade with British, French, Ottoman and other companies simultaneously) and political loyalties would not necessarily follow financial interest: many of these same men bitterly opposed the British and French mandates imposed after World War One. Nevertheless, there is here at least an avenue worth pursuing to help explain one of the important strands of the diverse phenomenon we are discussing.

6.  It is interesting, in view of the large role assigned to religion in most analyses of politics in this region, and in view of the central position assumed by religion in the traditional Ottoman political system, that it appears not to have been a major factor in disposing individuals towards Arabism or Ottomanism. Leaving aside the important exception of the proto-Lebanese nationalism emerging at this time among many Maronites and other Uniates, and more or less restricted to Mount Lebanon, there is apparently a fair sampling of Christians associated with both factions. The Lebanese case is anyway an anomaly, since Mount Lebanon (by its own decision) did not send deputies to the Ottoman Parliament, and in any case had begun to be isolated from the broader political currents of the region since much earlier.

Apart from the Mountain, we find important figures in both of the major blocs who are Christians, from Suleiman Bustani, Deputy of Beirut and later a Senator, or Felix Faris, editor first of a Beirut paper and then of one in Aleppo, and both prominent Unionists; to

Rafiq Rizq Salloum and Jurji Haddad, two of the Arab nationalists hanged in 1916 by the Turks, and both contributors to Arabist papers like *al-Mufid* and *al-Muqtabas*; or As'ad Daghir, one of the earliest historians of Arab nationalism; or Faris al-Khuri, later Speaker of Syria's Parliament and Prime Minister, who was tried in 1916 by Jamal Pasha's *'Aley* Court Martial but found innocent.[10] We find newspaper editors on both sides. Petro Paoli, editor of *al-Watan* in Beirut; Najib Nassar, editor of *al-Karmil* in Haifa; Leon Shawqatly, editor of *al-Sha'b* in Aleppo; Lutfallah Khlat, editor of *al-Hawadith*; Tawfiq al-Yaziji, editor of *al-Ajyal*; and the brothers Jurji and Samwa'il Yanni, owners of the magazine *al-Mabahith*, all three in Tripoli, were all opponents of the CUP and supporters of the Arabist cause; while Felix Faris, Khalil Sarkis, owner of *Lisan al-Hal*, Bishara al-Khuri, later to be President of Lebanon, and editor of *al-Barq* in Beirut, Shukri Knaydir, editor of *al-Taqaddum* in Aleppo, and Yusuf and 'Isa al-'Isa editors of *Falastin* in Jaffa, all were supporters of the CUP and Ottomanists; all were Christians.

Among the Christian-edited papers, as among those edited by Moslems, a larger proportion appear to have been favourable to the Arabists than to the Ottomanists, but this can only be an unverified impression until more research has been done on the more than a hundred papers founded in this period. Another impression, again with little as yet to substantiate it, is that Greek Orthodox Christians tended to be more likely to be Arabists than did non-Orthodox Christians (most, though not all, of the individuals mentioned above are Orthodox or Protestant converts from Greek Orthodoxy). Although this is logical, in view of the 'Arabisation' of the Greek Orthodox church in Palestine and Syria, and what we know of the greater affinity of the Orthodox for Arab nationalism in later years (Hopwood, 1969; Hourani, 1947, pp. 30–1, 82–3; Haddad, 1970), it is not possible to put forth anything more than these suggestions at this stage.

7.  Whatever the precise social configuration of the Arab movement in Syria before 1914, its rise marks a major change in the politics of the region. This is true irrespective of whether or not it was in fact, as our incomplete data indicates, a loose coalition involving, on the one hand, members of élite land-owning and religious-scholar families and merchants in the coastal cities who had prospered in the preceding decades, and on the other hand the intelligentsia, members of new professions from varied social backgrounds whose skills gave them a key place in the new politics. In hindsight, it is

clear that, for all the adeptness shown by the powerful old families of the traditional Syrian upper classes in clinging to power for several decades afterwards, this was the beginning of the transfer of political power in Syria from the 'notables' downwards through the social ladder. In the Ottoman constitutional period we are at the beginning of a path leading to the recent past, when the same professional groups on which we have focused – officers, teachers, junior government officials, intellectuals, in alliance with other social groups – play the dominant role in Arab politics.

## NOTES

1. The differences between our conclusions and those of Dawn are in part due to the restriction of his study to those parts of Syria which were later included in the Syrian Republic, and his examination of only fifty-one individuals as representatives of Arabism. Dawn thereby left out numerous important centres of the Arab movement, such as Beirut, and most other coastal cities as well as all of Palestine. Because of the rapid growth of the coastal cities of Syria, it was here that some of the social factors on which this paper focuses are most apparent.

   As has been pointed out by Hourani (1980, p. 186) relatively little work has yet been done on social and economic history of the region in the nineteenth and early twentieth centuries (with Turkey and Egypt having suffered the least from this neglect). Although this is as true for Syria as for the rest of the Middle East, mention can be made of the writings of Issawi (1966, pp. 205–47; 1977), Chevallier (1960; 1968; 1971) and Buheiri (1980), all of which shed some light on the growing role of the coastal cities.

2. Among those works which deal with this aspect of the politics of the period are Ahmad (1969; 1980), the former based mainly on British diplomatic and Turkish sources; Shorrock (1976), based on the French diplomatic archives, a number of the studies in Buheiri (1981), particularly those based on the use of the press; and Khalidi (1980), which uses primarily British and French archival material, together with some Arabic primary sources.

3. For more on the secret societies see Sa'id (1934); Antonius (1939); Birru (1960); and Musa (1970). They are treated from the point of view of the Ottoman authorities in *La Verité sur la Question Syrienne* (1916) and Djemal (1922). Most Arab officers in the Ottoman Army were of Iraqi origin.

4. In his account of the foundation of *al-'Ahd*, which is the basis of Dawn's list of names (1973, pp. 152–3, note 7), Sa'id explicitly states (1934, p. 46) that the names he cites are those of 'some' of the leaders of the movement. On the other hand, Darwazah, another of the sources cited by Dawn, gives a list (1950, pp. 32–3) which is clearly described as 'the prominent members' of *al-'Ahd*, rather than its entire membership. Similarly with *al-Fatat*, only a small number of whose members are included in Dawn's list, another of the basic

sources declares that the society had over 200 members by 1914 (Antonius 1939, p. 112).

5. The 1908 election results can be found in FO 1908a; 1908b and 1908c; in Turkey, 1328; and in the local press. A table based on these sources and summarising the 1908, 1912 and 1914 election results, as well as by-elections throughout Syria can be found in Khalidi, 1980, pp. 258–9.

6. The description in *al-Mufid* (1912d) of the Beirut speeches by Lutfi Fikri and Shukri al-'Asali runs for three pages, beginning with page 1, and commences as follows: 'Beirut has never before seen an orator with as nimble a tongue, or so eloquent in speech as Lutfi Fikri . . .' The newspapers of the period paint a fascinating picture of the 1912 campaign, the likes of which were not to be seen in Syria for many years afterwards. Some, however, such as *al-Muqtabas*, were closed by the Ottoman authorities for their excessively outspoken opposition to the CUP.

7. As evidence of the variety which can be found in the press of the period, mention can be made of the differences between two papers of broadly similar political orientation, *al-Mufid* and *al-Muqtabas*, the leading Arabist dailies in Syria. While the former had an important Islamic component in its Arab nationalism, the latter was much more secular in tone. On some issues, such as anti-Zionism, however, both papers followed the same line (Khalidi, 1981a). For more on the 1912 elections see the author's 'The 1912 Election Campaign in the Cities of Bilad al-Sham', forthcoming in the *International Journal of Middle East Studies*.

8. As examples of this influence we can cite the secret societies such as *al-Fatat*, many of whose members were not of upper-class backgrounds, and all of whom were young. It can be noted in passing that the individuals who apparently made the crucial decision after the outbreak of the war to contact the Sharif Hussein with a view to launching a revolt against the Turks were not the staid, respected and well-known notables who were the figure-heads of the Arab movement, such as the Arabist members of the Ottoman Parliament, but rather a number of young radical members of *al-Fatat* (Musa, 1970, p. 127).

9. For the Arabist orientation of many Arab officers in the Ottoman Army, see the discussion of *al-'Ahd* above, particularly the statement by Sa'id (1934, p. 47) that 315 of 490 Arab officers in the Istanbul area in 1913 were members of the society. As for the press, no definitive judgement is possible without further research, but it is worth recording the assessment of the French Consul in Haifa in April 1913, who wrote that the majority of the press in Syria was anti-CUP and generally Arabist in its political orientation (MAE, 1913d).

10. For a fascinating discussion of the role of Christians in the Arab movement see the articles by Faris al-Khuri (*al-Muqtabas*, 1910a), and others (*al-Muqtabas* 1910b; 1910c) which deal directly with the subject, stressing the role of Christian Arabs in the Arab nation, and the linguistic ties binding Arab Moslems and Christians together.

# 4 Emergent Trends in Moslem Tribal Society: the *Wazir* Movement of the Mullah of Wana in North-Western Frontier Province of Pakistan

AKBAR AHMED

## AN ANTHROPOLOGICAL APPROACH TO THE RESURGENCE OF ISLAM

This essay[1] is in part an attempt to pose the answers to what is stirring in the Moslem world; in part to learn the causes by elucidating principles of social process in contemporary Moslem society with special reference to Pakistan. The answers may well prove to be the single most important attempt at understanding the dialectics of the exigent forces creating tension in Moslem society between tradition and modernity in these last decades of the twentieth century. The unrest remains largely unstudied and, on the surface, inexplicable. Its complexity, and the diversity of the context within which it appears, defies easy analysis.

Perceptible beneath the ferment are shadowy figures, no more than simulacra, in the shape of religious leaders, *mullah*, *maulvi*, *sheikh* or *ayatollah*. These explicitly challenge the ideological tenets of the modern age. For instance, emphasis is placed on the central role of God and a reversion to fundamental ideology; revulsion is expressed against materialism as philosophy and code of life; and their target is not the king, or president, as symbol of the state but the modern state apparatus

itself. Furthermore, contrary to accepted common thinking the unrest –
or movements – are a result of general economic betterment, not
deprivation. These traditionalist movements are revolutionary in form
and content; death and destruction follow in their wake. Transformation of social and political structure, not merely a change of
government, are desired; not only the kings of Islam are sleeping
uneasily.

Conventional analysis of these movements casts them as revolt
against legitimate authority – translated from notions of state and
nationhood, order and rebellion, the major themes of modern political
discussion. A corollary of this hypothesis is the placing of such
endeavours simplistically within an anti-Western framework. Moslem
revolts, from Sudan to Swat, and their leaders have interested the West
over the last centuries and provided the proto-type of the 'Mad
Mullah'.[2]

During the colonial period, these Islamic traditionalist movements
were explicitly anti-West and anti-colonial. This is not the case today.
The Islamic movements cannot be simplistically analysed as solely or
even primarily anti-West. In fact, the phenomenon is much more
complex than it appears. The target of these movements is primarily
*within* society, and they work through recognisable local ethnic patterns.
The opposition to established authority, whether Islamic or extra-
religious, is a secondary but inter-connected consequence of these
movements.

In the last few years Islamic movements have taken place in widely
different regions, Kano in Nigeria at one end and Wana in Pakistan at
the other end of the Moslem world. In the centre, in Saudi Arabia, a
similar upheaval was reported. The attack on the mosque at Mecca – the
very core of the Islamic world – illustrates the seriousness and
significance of the contemporary Moslem mood. Recent events in Iran
provide dramatic evidence of the revolutionary aspects of Islamic
traditionalist movements.

## THE MULLAH OF WAZIRISTAN

The emergence of mullahs as charismatic leaders of Islamic movements
at times of crisis is not a new phenomenon among the tribes of the
North-West Frontier Province of Pakistan. In the 1860s, in response to
the menacing presence first of the Sikhs and then of the British, the
Akhund of Swat (d. 1877) unified the Pukhtuns of the North-West

Frontier Province under the banner of Islam, selecting a disciple as king with the title of *Amir-e Shari'at*. In 1897–8, the principal remaining followers of the Akhund entered the political scene to lead widespread tribal revolts against the British in the Frontier areas. The bold stand of these mullahs provides a contrast to the quiescent elements in society who preferred to sit on the fence in the struggle against the British. Men such as Adda Mullah, Manki Mullah, Palam Mullah and Mastan Mullah, and in Waziristan, Mullah Powindah and the Fakir of Ipi, seemed to appear from nowhere to mobilise society and lead the struggle. Some like Mastan Mullah of Buner in Swat, known as sartor baba[8] claimed, or were believed to possess, magical powers in the fight for Islam. The struggle, to the *mullahs*, was interpreted as *jihad*, a holy war for Islam to be conducted irrespective of success (Ahmad, 1976). Their extreme devotion to the Islamic cause, as they interpreted it, and consequently its militant expression provided the British with a prototype of what became popular as the 'Mad Mullah' or the 'Mad Fakir' (Churchill 1972, p. 29).

Adda Mullah, perhaps the most famous of these leaders saw the process as *jihad* – a holy war, a fight for salvation and a return to Islam. In a letter to tribal elders and mullahs he explained 'The Kafirs (infidels) have taken possession of all Mussalman countries and, owing to the lack of spirit on the part of the people, are conquering every region.' An extract from a communication of Adda Mullah concludes 'Help from God (awaits us) and victory is at hand. God willing, the time has come when the Kafirs should disappear. Be not idle. What more should I insist on' (Ahmad, 1976, p. 107).

The mullahs of the nineteenth century emerged suddenly and assumed the leadership of tribal mass movements by articulating and expressing an Islamic response to a non-Islamic threat. In the 1970s, when the Mullah of Wana in Southern Waziristan rose to prominence and, in the name of Islam, led the Wazirs in a movement against established authority representing the Government of Pakistan, the situation was no longer clear-cut.

The case in hand is based in South Waziristan Agency, Pakistan. The Agency population, according to the last official census in 1972, was 300 000 divided into two major tribes, the Mahsud and the Wazir. The tribes, segmentary, egalitarian, acephalous and living in low production zones are somewhat similar to other Moslem tribes in North Africa and the Middle East (Ahmed and Hart 1981). The Mahsuds are about 250 000 and Wazirs 50 000 in number. Smaller nomadic groups also live in the Agency (Ahmed 1981b). The Agency is about 3936 square miles in area and is the largest and southern-most Agency in the North-West Frontier Province's seven Federally Administered Tribal Agencies (see Map 4.2, p. 91). The Political Agent heads the administration and represents government. The Political Agent's powers are vast and the tribes call him 'king of Waziristan' (*de Waziristan badshah*). South Waziristan shares borders with Afghanistan in the west and Baluchistan, separated by the Gomal river, in the south. Desolate valleys and barren mountains, for the most part, distinguish the Agency.

Recent colonial history is important to Waziristan. Countless British troops have died here in savage encounters. In the 1930s there were more troops in Waziristan than on the rest of the Indian subcontinent. In 1937 an entire British brigade was wiped out in the Shahur Tangi. The ability of the tribes as fighters is well-recognised; 'the Wazirs and Mahsuds operating in their own country, can be classed among the finest fighters in the world', wrote the British Indian Army General Staff (General Staff 1921, p. 5). To those, like the author John Masters, who fought in Waziristan, the tribes were 'physically the hardest people on earth' (Masters, 1965, p. 161). Some famous British Imperial names are associated with Waziristan, for example, Curzon, Durand, Kitchener and T. E. Lawrence whose note to the South Waziristan Scouts is on exhibition in the Scouts Mess, at Wana, the summer headquarters of the Agency. Tradition, in name and custom, is preserved. The main western gate in the Wana camp is still called the Durand gate and the main picket guarding Wana camp is Gibraltar. Bugles still announce the passage of the day and play at sunset as the Pakistan flag is lowered and the entire camp comes to a halt for those few minutes. Farewells to officers are conducted in traditional and ritualistic manner in the Scouts Mess with the band – kilts and bagpipes – providing music. The romantic aspect of the colonial encounter which created a 'mystification' in British eyes is perhaps most evocative in Waziristan (Ahmed 1978). The participation in the 'Great Game' between Imperial Russia and Imperial Britain further added to the importance of the Waziristan tribes (Ahmed, 1980a).

The attempt to understand these movements and their long-term impact on social structure and organisation is fundamental to Moslems and those dealing with Moslem societies. The present study is one such attempt. It is suggested that the anthropological method, in preference to the more conventional macrosociological method, may provide useful tools for the analysis of traditional and small Moslem groups in situations of change and conflict. More specifically, I suggest it may be heuristically useful to look also *under* the surface of the large configurations of Moslem society and *away* from their main centres of power when examining social structure and process. However, it is suggested we look not too far beneath the surface – not at the typical anthropological village – but at the critical intermediary level, the district[3] or Agency, the study of which remains neglected.[4]

Three broad but distinct spheres of leadership, interacting at various levels, are identified and demarcated at the district or Agency level of society: (i) traditional leaders, usually elders, (ii) official representatives of the established state authority and (iii) religious functionaries. In the case under study in this paper, the last group is the least defined and hence ambiguity in its locus and elasticity in its role are apparent. Each group is symbolically defined in society by their bases situated in uneasy juxtaposition at the district headquarters and which, respectively, are: the house/houses of the chief or elders, district headquarters (flying the Government flag) and/or the central mosque.

Personnel from the three spheres of leadership vie for power, status and legitimacy in society. The competition is further exacerbated as the major participants are Moslems; there are no simple Moslem versus non-Moslem categories to which to fall back as in the recent colonial past. Some form of alliance and collaboration between traditional leaders and district officials are a characteristic of district history. It is the religious leader who must clash with the other two if he is to expand space for himself in society. He can only do so by claiming that he alone speaks for society. In speaking for society, his idiom will inevitably be Islamic.

Once we have identified certain core features in society at the district level we may proceed to construct what may be termed 'the Islamic district – or Agency – paradigm'[5] of socio-cultural process; one that is conceptually precise and empirically based and placed within the regional political framework. The Islamic district paradigm may assist us in discovering meaning and structure beneath the wide range of diversity found in contemporary Muslim society.

What follows is an extensive case-study based on traditional agnatic rivalry in a tribal Agency in Pakistan,[6] the central actor of which is the Mullah of Waziristan.[7] My own role as Political Agent from 1978 to 1980 allows me to comment on the narrative from within the structure, especially with reference to the district paradigm.

The district paradigm, by definition, suggests the perpetuation of one aspect of the colonial encounter. The district structure and personnel, with its official head, the District Commissioner – or the Political Agent in the Agency – were imposed on society by the British. Since colonial times status and authority in the district have rested largely in district officials as representatives of an omnipotent central Government. District officers were the '*mai-baap*' (mother-father) of South Asian rural peasantry.

The continuing importance of the district and its personnel after Independence, in spite of its clear association with the colonial past, heightens tension in society. Although 'native' the administrative personnel reflect ambivalence in their dealing with the other groups in society, and may be viewed as distant and unsympathetic by society. The contemporary power and importance of district officials is further exaggerated as a consequence of suspension of normal political activities (a common phenomenon during periods of Martial Law).

The case-study may be examined in a diachronic perspective, beginning in the late 1960s, when a *mullah* among the Wazirs of South Waziristan Agency used the idiom of Islam to restate a particularistic tribal ideology and to launch a political movement against the cousin tribe, the Mahsuds. He accused the administration of supporting the Mahsud. The mullah of our study first appears after migrating from the neighbouring Bannu District as a builder of a beautiful mosque, unique in the Tribal Areas, at Wana with a complex of schools and dormitories around it. With his emergence in the politics of the Agency the mosque came to symbolise the mullah and his policies. The Wazir mullah defined and identified boundaries within society. His objectives were explicit: the transformation of structure and organisation. His method was ambiguous as he alternated between a secular political paradigm and a religious–charismatic paradigm. The ambiguity allowed him large areas of manœuvre and partly explains his social and political success.

The late years of the 1960s and early years of the 1970s were characterised by new sources of wealth – internal (Ahmed 1977) and external such as remittances from employment in the Arab States (Ahmed, 1980a; 1981a). For the first time the tribesman with initiative could make considerable money. Some of the Wazir money was diverted to the mullah. He appeared as their champion and he needed funds for his organisation. The mullah's religious organisation supported complex economic networks. He invested some of the money in items that confer social prestige among Pukhtuns: Japanese cars, buses, guns and lavish feasts to visiting politicians. Recent Waziristan history may be viewed as a function of the mullah's emergence and politics.

Two important economic developments in the Agency coincided with the construction of the new mosque at Wana. First, a market (*adda*) sprang up between the mosque and the main road. In the late 1950s and early 1960s encroachments resulted in a cluster of small, mud shops. The Scouts protested as this violated rules which prohibit civil construction near their posts and camps. Numerous letters passed and meetings were held between the Commandant of the Scouts, the Political Agent and his senior, the Commissioner. The market, in spite of several setbacks, continued to grow. Because it was on the property of the Mughal Khel Wazirs it came to be known as *Adda Mughal Khel*. Eventually some four hundred shops, not more than a small room or two each, were constructed. The market became a thriving centre for commerce and trade for the Agency. The organisation of the mosque and the market were interlinked by their guiding genius, the mullah. The mosque was popularly called *Adda Mughal Khel Mosque*, that is, the mosque of the Mughal Khel market.

Second, a major dam, the Gomal Zam Project, was started by the Government of Pakistan in Wazir territory. Wazirs provided labour and were given building contracts. Both developments generated local money.

A magnificent mosque costing between 700 and 800 000 rupees,[9] was soon completed. The minarets and dome were resplendent with tiles and glass of many hues. The interior reflected depth and space. A stream passed through the mosque and a variety of coloured fish were kept which fascinated visitors. Indeed no monument as splendid had been seen in that – or other – Agency until then. Elders from other Agencies came to marvel at the mosque and compliment its builder. The mullah basked in his accomplishment and concentrated his energy in further expanding an organisation around the mosque. He built a *madrassah* (religious school) adjacent to the mosque and dormitories for visiting *talibs* (scholars). Most of the *tablibs* were sons of Wazir elders. A set of rooms was built for the mullah on the second floor of the mosque overlooking its courtyard. As a mark of deference people now referred to him as *Maulvi Sahib* and not by his name.

Here I wish to look briefly outside Waziristan. In 1971 after Pakistan's war with India which resulted in the break-up of East Pakistan, Mr Z. A. Bhutto emerged as the political leader of Pakistan, rallying a dispirited nation. In his political style Mr Bhutto appeared to offer a viable model of politics. The mullah watched and learned. Both were relatively young leaders with considerable political skill and organisational ability who relied on their charisma and oratory to secure and stir their followers. Both spoke in the language of hyperbole and poetic populism. Personally their demeanour bordered on arrogance and they brooked no opposition. Their critics accused them of opportunism. The politics of the 1970s in Pakistan were to be cast in the mould of Mr Bhutto. My concern is not with Pakistan politics during the Bhutto era (1971–7) but with their indirect impact on Waziristan.

The Mullah after assessing that the time was ripe in the early 1970s, made a bid for the control of the minds of the Wazir. He was moving from a religious to a political role. For instance, he forbade the use of radios in the *adda*. It was un-Islamic, he announced. Having banned the radio the Mullah listened to the programmes avidly. Selecting information from the radio commentary or news he would 'predict' national events at the Friday congregation in the mosque. His announcement of the National Pay Commission is one such example. The Mullah informed his following that he was praying for increase in pay of the poorly paid Wazir *khassadars* (tribal levies) and Scouts' soldiers (who received between 200 and 250 rupees a month). Increase in officials salaries was being debated nationally during 1972 and 1973 and an announcement on the matter was imminent. The debate was reported in the mass media. Forbidden to hear the radio and generally being illiterate the Wazir tribe was unaware of the national debate. When Government announced an increase in salaries they took it as an example of the Mullah's powers to predict and influence events. The *khassadars* were particularly impressed and committed a monthly contribution of four rupees each for the mosque fund.

At the time the Mullah imitated and developed some of the formalistic aspects of bureaucracy associated with the Political Agent, the official head of the Agency. Armed guards escorted him wherever he went, *mulagats* (meetings) with him were arranged after formal (often written) requests through his supporters. He issued chits to his followers ordering admission to official schools or medical dispensaries and on notes he asked officials to give interviews 'to the bearer of the note'. His requests were honoured and his whims humoured. These were visible symbols of his growing importance in and to society. By appropriating some of the form and content of the Political Agent's function he was setting himself on a collision course with that office.

A sense of destiny now marked his self-assessment. Addressing himself in his diary he noted 'God Almighty has given you status and influence matched by few men in history.' In his diary he referred to himself in the third person, traditionally used by royalty. Indeed, the theme of royalty was not far from his mind. 'When they insisted you address the gathering they introduced you as *the uncrowned king of Wana*' he observed in another place in his diary. The title of king was underlined by the Mullah. But, as we know, there was another claimant to the title in the Agency, the Political Agent. It is a notorious principle of history that no realm can support two kings.

Three economic issues formed the main platform of the Mullah: first, he emphasised the Wazir nature of the market at Wana, the summer headquarters and main settlement of the Agency; second, he challenged Mahsud rights in the timber funds (from Wazir forests in the inaccessible Birmal area) that were distributed among the Agency tribes; and third, he demanded an alternative route for the Wazirs to the Settled Districts along the Gomal river that by-passed the Mahsud area. Each demand had clear social and political implications.

The Mullah, after a steady campaign and increasing tension in the Agency, which resulted in several incidents, damned the Mahsud as *kafirs* (non-believers). Employing religious idiom for tribal rivalry he declared *jihad* (holy war) against the Mahsud. Sure of his power, the Mullah set the Wazirs on a collision course with the political administration, whom he saw as a tool of the Mahsuds. Issuing *fatwahs* (religious instructions) from the mosque, the Mullah declared that the Wazir struggle was an Islamic one. The primary objective, he declared, was to secure the Gomal road. To die in this cause, the cause of Islam, was to gain paradise. If, he declared in his fiery sermons delivered at the mosque, a Wazir killed a Mahsud it would be the equivalent of killing a *kafir*. If, on the other hand, a Wazir was killed by a Mahsud he would become *shaheed* and win paradise as he had been killed by a *kafir*. Wazirs were inflamed by his rhetoric. They were now endowed with an *Islamic* carapace. As a consequence, their particularistic, tribal struggle against the Mahsuds now acquired general, universal significance.

Not being able to dismiss the Mullah as an 'unbeliever' the Mahsuds stepped up their attack on his character (debauch, homosexual, practiser of black magic, etc.) which indirectly reflected on Wazir morality. The Mahsuds impugned the Mullah's 'Pukhtunness' and accused the Wazir of being without shame. Exaggeration of Pukhtun values and virtues was a strategy employed by the Mahsud to balance the accusation of being *kafir* by the Mullah. An ethnic counter-attack was made to a religious attack. Feelings on both sides ran high.

The Mullah opened a new front which would divert attention and keep the Wazir war spirit from flagging. He ordered the main Agency road to be blocked. In late December 1975 a Wazir war-party (*lashkar*), gathered at Dargai in the Maddi Jan area for this purpose. Traffic was entirely suspended and the Agency was cut off from the outside world. The Prime Minister of Pakistan ordered the opening of the road. The Political Agent then, accompanied by a strong Scouts force, moved from

Jandola towards Wana to enforce the opening of the road. Army tanks were moved into the Agency from the settled districts. Simultaneously, a strong Scouts column moved from Wana towards Jandola. Movement on foot or in vehicles for Wazirs was banned by the administration. A fierce and bloody encounter took place at Maddi Jan on that day in which five soldiers were killed and more wounded. It was estimated that 30 Wazirs were killed or wounded. Other clashes also took place on that day causing loss of life.

The Wazirs remained defiant and a few days later once again blocked the Agency road. The sequence of events would be repeated, it appeared. Orders from Islamabad were issued to ensure opening of the road 'at all costs'. The Scouts moved in considerable strength from Jandola but they faced no opposition. The Wazirs had melted into the night and the road was deserted. An abortive attempt to involve Wazirs from outside the Agency was made. The involvement of Wazirs from the North Waziristan Agency or Afghanistan would extend the theatre of conflict beyond the Agency borders and create serious complications for Government. Already Kabul was watching developments in Waziristan with interest. Ideal material was at hand for the Pukhtunistan pro-paganda, which claimed that Pukhtuns in the North-West Frontier Province wished to secede.

The Mullah now ordered a general civil disobedience movement. Wazirs blocked the main roads, shot at the Scouts, and at the climax of the movement imposed a physical boycott of the Wana camp. Major clashes between Wazirs, Mahsuds and the administration took place involving the deaths of tribesmen and Scouts' soldiers. The Agency was in flames. On the Durand line such a situation has international ramifications. After obtaining clearance from the highest authority in the land the administration acted in May 1976. Army tanks were moved into the Agency and the Air Force was alerted. The Scouts took action, the Wana markets of the Wazir were destroyed, and the Mullah's 'cabinet' arrested as was, somewhat later, the Mullah himself. The Mullah and his key-men were tried, found guilty and sent to jail in Hazara, across the river Indus, where they languish. The action, possibly the most severe of its kind in the history of the Tribal Areas, became the centre of controversy.

After the action the Wazirs were in disarray, the Mahsuds jubilant and the administration self-righteous.

The action in Wana and events leading up to it had been followed with interest in Kabul. Propaganda had shaped the conflict as a simple Pukhtun struggle for autonomy against a Punjabi-dominated Central

Government. Indeed, not since the merger of the Frontier States, Swat, Chitral, Dir and Amb, in 1969, had such a live issue presented itself to Kabul. The situation was tense with possibilities. Kabul propaganda underlined the ethnic nature of the Mullah's struggle and pointed out that some of the key-men in the drama – the Central Interior Minister, the Chief Secretary of the Province and the Political Agent of the Agency – were non-pukhtun and hence, they argued, unsympathetic to Pukhtuns.

## ISLAM, ETHNICITY AND LEADERSHIP

We need to know why the Wazir tribe responded affirmatively to the Mullah. Was it clan or lineage pride – which may be termed 'primordial ethnicity' – based on memory of agnatic humiliation at the hands of the Mahsuds? Or was it the promises⁵ of economic betterment? Certainly some of the central issues were economic in nature. Was it the hope of a separate Agency with its political and social implications? Or the Mullah's wealth with which he could patronise the elders and the poor in society? Or the Papa Doc Duvalier syndrome: irrational fear of the evil eye and the immediate fear of thugs who could rough up doubters? Or was it that the Wazirs were performing a religious duty by engaging in *jihad*? The Wazirs thought they were using the Mullah to say and do things that they could not themselves. In the end, did the Wazirs use the Mullah or did he use them?

Here it is only relevant to point out the intensely democratic and egalitarian nature of ideal Pukhtun society. Is the Mullah's emergence and success in peace time an aberration from the Pukhtun model? What are the social factors that caused it? Such questions are important for the study of leadership, social structure and organisation among Pukhtun tribesmen.

The advent and activities of the Mullah created tension and dilemmas in society on three levels: (i) social – women visiting the Mullah with various personal requests provided the enemies of the Wazirs ammunition to talk of deviant Pukhtun behaviour and hint at immorality; (ii) political, as the Mullah challenged the established authority of the State by leading what assumed the form of a rebellion; and (iii) religious – the cousin tribe, the Mahsud, were condemned as *kafir* and a *jihad* declared against them. Tension is implicit in the three levels on which the Mullah worked. To agree with the Mullah posed as many dilemmas to the Wazir as to disagree.

The presence and interaction of the administrative structure is minimised in studies of tribal societies which has raised criticism and even doubts in the literature (Asad, 1973). I have illustrated how administrative interaction can affect tribal policy and strategy. Indeed, for purposes of this study, the administrative organisation may be viewed as the third 'tribe' of the Agency with its own sets of symbols, ritualised behaviour and defined boundaries. Formal interaction with the other two tribes is characterised by ritualistic behaviour. This third 'tribe' has its own esoteric written and spoken language not understood by the other tribes – English. The Political Agent may be seen as the 'chief' of the tribe and the South Waziristan Scouts its 'warriors'. As we have seen, the Mullah was aware of the administrative model and created around himself a highly centralised organisation with a defined hierarchy.

To the Wazir the Mullah appeared to be a rational and sympathetic religious leader determined to establish their honour and rights. To his followers the gross and blatant leaning of administration toward the Mahsuds, the arrest of the Mullah and the 'capture' of the mosque are tantamount to heresy. They argue that the house of God was desecrated and His faithful servant, the Mullah, arrested. Their continuing boycott of the mosque is explained as an Islamic response to a captured house of worship. Religion is not merely metaphysics. For all peoples the forms, vehicles and objects of worship are suffused with an aura of deep moral seriousness. It bears within it a sense of intrinsic social obligation; it not only induces intellectual conformity, it enforces emotional commitment. The Mullah's *jihad* not only induced intellectual conformity, it enforced emotional commitment. The commitment is still explicitly expressed in society.

The Mullah relied largely on his charisma composed of his powerful rhetoric, personality and organisational skills to win the hearts of his followers. Above all he gave them group pride and identity. He was palpably neither a *qazi* (judge) learned in *sharia* (holy law) nor saint nor *Sufi* with a reputation derived from lifelong abstinence, meditation or scholarship. None of this mattered to the Wazir. There are well-known Pukhto proverbs which sum up the relationship of the believing followers to their *pir* such as: 'through the *pir* (saint) himself does not fly his disciples would have him fly' (Ahmed, 1973, p. 19). The Wazirs saw their *pir* in miraculous flight. They entertained high hopes partly due to their need for a saviour figure who could deliver them from their enemies. This need was activated by a prolonged period of frustration stemming from the inability to influence the administration which they saw as allied to the Mahsud. The ground was thus ripe for the emergence of a leader who at one and the same time could organise cultural and religious forces on behalf of his followers. 'Now, it is at such times – when a genuine sense of injustice, or danger, etc., reaches a certain point that a closed cultural complex opens up to the transcendent religious' (F. Rahman, personal communication).

However, in certain actions, for instance by encouraging their children and women to pay him homage, the Wazirs violated a cardinal principle of Pukhtunwali and left themselves open to charges of *beghairat* (shameless) by the Mahsuds. It became fashionable to ask Wazirs 'are you first Moslem?' – implying the laws of Islam – 'or Wazirs?' – those of the Mullah. Either way, the answer posed dilemmas for the Wazir. It also put loyalty for the Mullah to a severe test. To answer 'Moslem' would negate Wazir 'primordial ethnicity' and its aspects in society and the movement and the Mullah. Such jibes, common among the administration and Mahsuds, further embittered the Wazirs and reinforced loyalty to the leader. Such commentary however, encouraged discussion of religious groups and the role of the *mullah* in society. Let us briefly summarise the broad categories of Islamic religious groups in society.

Islamic religious groups providing leadership in society may be broadly divided into three overlapping categories. The first two are defined by their function in society and the third by genealogical links with holy ancestors. The first, the *'ulama*, defined by religious and legal learning, include *mufti*, *qazi*, *maulana* and *maulvi*; the second category defined by esoteric, sometimes unorthodox practice, groups such as the *Sufis*; and the third defined by religious genealogy and descent and thus claiming superior social status, *sherif* or *sayyed* (from the Prophet) and *mian* (from holy men). The *'ulama* represent the orthodox, bureaucratic, formal and legalistic tradition in Islam. They interact with the state even at the highest level and advise the kings, captains and commanders of Islam. In contrast, the mystical orders largely restrict themselves to rural areas shunning worldly pursuits and avoid formal interaction with administration. Such orders command the hearts as well as the minds of their followers. The holy lineages and the members, *sayyed*, *sherif*, *mian*, are accepted in society as associated with holy ancestors. They command a vague and generalised respect especially if they live up to idealised behaviour which is pacific, dignified and neutral between warring groups and clans. What is of interest to our argument is the difficulty in placing the *mullah* easily in any one category. The difficulty is not simply taxonomic but related to the ambiguity and elasticity surrounding his social role. Not quite the learned mufti, sure of his orthodox Islamic knowledge, nor the Sufi, sure of his inner Islamic faith, the *mullah* is forced to define and create his own role. He may, indeed borrow from all three categories elevating himself to Maulvi in one place (as in this study) and *mian* in another (Ahmed 1980a, p. 167). In general the *mullah* occupies a junior position in the religious hierarchy and is defined as 'a lesser member of the religious classes' (Algar, 1969, p. 264). In the North-West Frontier Province, the *mullah* restricts himself largely to the village level of social and political life except in extraordinary circumstances. He appears to thrive in crises.

The Mullah of Wana was a Wazir, that is, a Pukhtun, from Bannu. He was not a *sayyed* or *mian*. The distinction is important in the Pukhtun universe. *Sayyed* and *mian* are traditionally accepted as embodying superior lineage because of their links to the Holy Prophet and holy men. Their claims to superiority are backed by marriage rules and idealised behaviour patterns. Pukhtuns are notoriously endogamous and reluctant to give their women to non-Pukhtuns are prepared to waive the prejudice for sayyeds (Ahmed 1980a; Barth 1972). They are settled between Pukhtun clans, a placement which is symbolic of their role as mediators between warring groups (ibid.). The *mullah* is more often than not a poor Pukhtun of a junior or depressed lineage. Translation of role from religious to political spokesman *within* the boundaries of society was thus inevitable once the Mullah's following grew. No lineage structure constrained him; as the son of a migrant member of a junior lineage he remained outside the local lineage charter yet part of the larger Wazir tribe. From a *mullah* supervising religious function he became a leader promising specific political goals. Lacking charisma of lineage, the Mullah turned into an Islamic ideologue, using his presumed knowledge of Islamic law and doctrine to buttress his authority.

Let us take a closer look at the role of the *mullah* in society. Among Pukhtuns the *mullah* remains subordinate to the lineage elders and usually does not feature on the genealogical charter (Ahmed 1980a). The observation is confirmed by archival material based on contemporary records for Waziristan (Bruce 1929; Curtis 1946; General Staff, 1921, p. 4; 1932; 1935; Howell 1925; Johnson 1934a, and b; Johnston 1903). As I illustrated in *Pukhtun Economy and Society* (Ahmed 1980a) Pukhtun elders saw political activity as their preserve and restricted the role of the *mian* or *mullah* ('*mian-mullah saray* – a *mian* or *mullah* man' (Ahmed 1980a, p. 162) to specified pacific religious functions. The important function of the *mullah* is to organise and supervise *rites de passage* based on Islamic tradition. Among *nang* Pukhtuns, social leadership is firmly lodged in the lineage charter (Ahmed 1980a). In any case, the *mullah* in society has no proselytising function. He must, perforce, explore other areas if he is to enhance his role and authority in society. The *mullah* may rise to power in extraordinary times rallying Moslems against invading non-Moslems. As was pointed out, in the Tribal Areas and *nang* society *mullahs* have led widespread revolts with singular courage and conviction against the British as they did in 1897.

The role of the *mullah* is negligible in cases where the invading army is Moslem. In such a situation an ambiguity is inherent in the conflict. *Jihad* cannot be invoked against Moslem brothers in the faith. When the Pukhtun tribes fought Mughal armies representing a Moslem dynasty they were led by traditional tribal leaders. The Mullah of Wana provides an interesting example of a *mullah* who mobilised an entire tribe by creating a religious battle hysteria against kin groups, belonging to the same sect and local administration in peacetime. The Waziristan study may be interpreted as the rejection of the traditional pattern. This rejection creates problems in society, as it affords possibilities for the Mullah. The Mahsuds neither fitted the non-believer nor the heretic categories. To condemn them as *kafir* was in itself an act of considerable audacity. The Mullah's *jihad* clearly rested on a weak theological but a strong sociological base.

It is usual for the Mullahs to employ transparent tricks and clever devices in order to convince people of their special powers. The Sayyed or *mian* assured of their position, do not need to resort to such tricks and devices to further their claim for leadership. The Wazir Mullah had installed a 'wide-angle door-viewer' sent by a follower from the Arab Gulf States in his door. He could thus 'foresee' and predict who his visitor was, looked like or what he wore. His capacity for seeing through opaque doors was further evidence of his power. Wazirs believed he possessed 'the magic eye' – *de jado starga*. Even educated people believed the door-viewer was a magic device. Another Mullah, Nalkot Pacha of Swat, explained to me the devices he employed as part of his strategem. His favourite was to stitch a thin piece of wire under the skin on his stomach and then in front of a selected gathering to 'eat' another bit of wire. As the audience watched in amazement he would slowly pull out the first wire. This and other such tricks were explained at Nalkot, his village, in 1976 before some friends.[10] 'Am I to blame?' he repeated twice 'if people are so simple and believe everything?' People not only believed in his powers but some elevated him to the role of 'saint'. In anthropological literature the Swat village quack has been elevated to the rank of a prototype saint (Bailey, 1972; Barth, 1972), although blatantly manipulating people around him with mumbo-jumbo and chicanery.[11] Similar stories are told about the Mullah Powindah, the better known and more historical religious leader of Waziristan.[12]

The problem of ambiguity is directly related to the problems of definition. Was the Wazir movement an outright rebellion, a struggle for legitimate political rights, or an attempt at transforming social structure or defining ethnic boundaries? A common answer suggests itself for the questions: it was all of these things to different men at different times. The ambiguity of the answer, and what it meant for the Wazirs, reflects the range of interpretations open to us. The ambiguity is compounded by the ambiguity surrounding the Mullah himself.

A question that arises from the above discussion is: 'how Islamic are these tribes?' In a sociological and cultural sense they may be defined as Islamic. The local tribesman equates his Pukhtun lineage with Islam. To him the two are inextricably bound and interrelated. Concepts such as *jihad* are therefore potent and meaningful to him. Although he is aware of certain deviant behaviour from Islamic theological tradition, especially regarding women's rights, he is never in doubt about his Moslemness. Anthropologists studying Moslem tribal groups such as Fredrik Barth (1972) have been criticised for omitting the framework of Islam and its symbols as a feature in understanding society (Ahmed, 1976).[14] It is misleading to study Islamic tribal groups without reference to a larger framework. The tradition in anthropology derives in the main from the study of non-Islamic African tribes (Fortes and Evans-Pritchard, 1970; Gluckman, 1971; Middleton and Tait, 1970).

The question of relating religious to tribal identity, Islam and Pukhtunness in this case, has engaged anthropologists studying tribal groups both Pukhtun (Anderson, 1980; Beattie, 1980; Canfield, 1980; Ghani, 1978 and forthcoming; Tavakolian, 1980) and others (Geertz, 1968, 1979; Gellner, 1969a and b; Vatin, 1980). The exercise in itself serves little purpose. The debate generated could be misleading. We may more usefully pose the problem, as the tribesman himself views it, by examining the relationship between Islam *and* Pukhtunness, and not as Islam *versus* Pukhtunness. To the tribesman Islam provides political and socio-religious formations within which his Pukhtunness operates. The two are in harmony and he sees them as a logical construct. The two are deeply interrelated; to suggest a dichotomy is false. Rather, the understanding of religion as confined *outside* structure is to be viewed as a European one. The differentiation of religion and political systems into discrete categories is orthodox methodology in Western thought.

As I have illustrated in this paper Islam and Pukhtunness coalesce and overlap. The interiority of the Pukhtunness in Islam is seen as axiomatic in society. Therefore, any dichotomy separating Islam and Pukhtun is palpably sterile. Whether embarking on a religious war or cattle lifting,[15] the Pukhtun invokes his God. His objectives may be at fault but not his sincerity and correctness in invoking assistance from heaven. Perhaps a rephrasing from Islam versus Pukhtunness to bringing Pukhtun custom and tradition into accordance with Islamic tradition, that is, Islam *and* Pukhtunness, may be a more useful method for studying the problem. Indeed, the success of the mullah is partly explained by his recognition of this equation. Once Islam was equated to kinship and Islamic idiom employed, his success in leading and consolidating the Wazirs was ensured. The criteria used to maintain and harden Wazir ethnic boundaries were drawn from an Islamic frame. The mosque, as we know, remained the base of the Mullah's operations and key symbol of Wazir identity.

Earlier in the study I incautiously promised that the study would consider the question 'who speaks for Moslem society?' At the end of the study I appear to have no definite answer. It is the same question, perhaps differently worded which teases the minds of men and causes problems in the resolution of social and political issues in Waziristan. The definition and location of spokesmen and chiefs reflects a crisis within society. The very title *badshah*, king, has been applied to each major actor, Malik (the word itself means king), the Political Agent and the Mullah. Does the Malik speak for society? Although he is from within society, unlike the other two, the *teeman*, tribe-at-large, do not reflect much confidence in him. The Political Agent speaks more *to* society than *for* society. It is the Mullah alone who appears at one stage of his career to have won a following which cut across boundaries of lineage, hierarchy and age. For a while he spoke for society. But in his heart, he too wished to speak to them not for them. And it was not long before the Political Agent wrested the title of spokesman – *Badshah*, if we will – back from the Mullah. It is precisely the method by which the Political Agent won back his title which underlines the structural weakness of his position in society.

The internal tension between the main groups these men represent is not resolved. The disparate nature of the three groups – the first characterised by tribal code, lineage identity, cousin rivalry; the second, Indo-British secular, liberal service traditions; the third, Islamic lore as locally understood – suggests the problem may be irresolvable. It may be irresolvable because the major actors are all Moslem; each one claims to know and speak for society. The strength of this conviction, rooted in the characteristic traditions of their group, ensures each leader perceives society and its fundamental issues in a different perspective from the other.

Do the events that took place in a remote part of Pakistan predict future political patterns in Moslem society? Is the Mullah of Wana to be seen as a modern revolutionary leader or as a traditional product of traditional Moslem structure and organisation? Are we witnessing a shift in style and loci of leadership away from urban, westernised bureaucratic élites? May we relate this movement conceptually to the current waves of fundamental revivalism surging in many Moslem countries, and finally, can universal principles of behaviour, suggesting models which predict and forecast, be adduced from this case study? Although tentative answers may be suggested in the affirmative it is too early to provide long-term and clear answers. To make matters worse there is almost no literature nor information on such leaders and movements in the contemporary Moslem world. Yet, the Wana example foretells what may well be in store for Islamic Governments and societies in the coming decades.

## NOTE ON TRIBAL AND POLITICAL BOUNDARIES IN WAZIRISTAN

When conceptualising the tribe as a political unit in holistic argument, it would be well to keep in mind the present administrative boundaries which do not always correspond to tribal boundaries. The continuing legacy of the colonial period is illustrated with reference to these boundaries. Districts and Agencies – indeed, as also the international Durand line, were created at the turn of the century by the British, often with a disregard for tribal boundaries. Major tribes such as the Mohmand or, as in our case, the Wazirs, were divided in two by the international border, and others untidily distributed between district and Agency (the Afridis, for example are in Kohat District and Khyber Agency). The Ahmedzai Wazirs were separated from their Utmanzai Wazir cousins, confined to North Waziristan Agency, and placed with their traditional rivals the Mahsuds in South Waziristan Agency. Like other tribes in the region the Ahmedzai Wazirs for three generations have confronted the fact of the British-created borders. On either side of the Durand line differing political, educational and economic factors have widened the gap between Wazir and Wazir. New political realities have enforced the creation of new social boundaries which take precedence over traditional alignments. We may thus conceptualise the Wazir tribe as a unit but must keep in mind administrative realities on the ground. Figure 4.1 depicts, in encapsulated form, the Wazir-Mahsud genealogy. In the ideal, segmentary theory suggests that the Ahmedzai would be assisted by their Wazir kin when in conflict with the Mahsud.

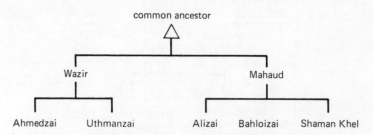

FIGURE 4.1    *Wazir-Mahsud lineage*

Map 4.1 reminds us that while Wazirs live in Afghanistan and North Waziristan Agency also, the Mahsuds are restricted to South Waziristan Agency.

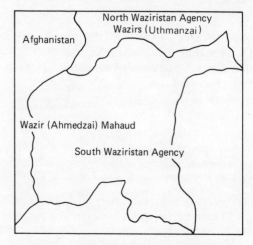

MAP 4.1    *The South Waziristan Agency*

Not only are the Uthmanzai Wazirs separated by administrative boundaries from their Ahmedzai cousins but the Ahmedzai themselves are divided by the international boundary. If we superimpose Map 4.1 on to Figure 4.2, the importance of administrative boundaries in affecting tribal life is made clear.

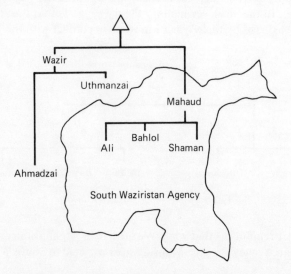

FIGURE 4.2    *Wazir-Mahsud lineage and the Agency*

The Wazirs find themselves restricted by the Agency borders. The impotence of their near kin to assist the Ahmedzais of South Waziristan Agency in times of crises was clearly brought out in the extended case-study described.

## NOTES

1. Themes in this paper are explored at greater length in *Religion and Politics in Muslim Society: Order and Conflict in Pakistan*, Cambridge University Press, 1983.
2. See Talhami (1981) and Voll (1981). The apprehensions which have revived as a result of recent developments are expressed by one of the leading Western authorities on Islam: 'The Iranian revolution and the (already disquieting) Muslim fundamentalist movements whose hopes it nurtured, changed all that, helped by the rising price of that petroleum with which Allah endowed his followers in such ample quantities. Once again the Muslim world became an entity jealously guarding its uniqueness, its own culture, comprising much more than just spirituality. And might not this entity again become a threat, as it had only three centuries ago when the

MAP 4.2 *North-West Frontier Province of Pakistan*

Ottoman armies laid siege to Vienna? Might the way of life so valued by the West be in serious danger?' (Rodinson, 1980, xlvii).

3. The district was the basic and key unit of administration in British India (Woodruff, 1965). The district was further subdivided into sub-division and *thana*. In turn, the district formed part of a division which was part of a

province. The Agency in the Tribal Areas corresponded to the district in the administrative universe. Although I call this intermediary level district to help conceptualise the unit of analysis, district (or Agency) boundaries do not always correspond with ethnic ones, a fact which continues to create political problems. In some cases new ethnicity was formed as a result of new districts, such as Hazarwal in Hazara District (the problem is discussed in *The Forest Dwellers of Hazara: Problems in Ethnicity and the Sociology of Development*, Ahmed, forthcoming book). An understanding of the district structure and its personnel is therefore necessary in order to understand, what I call in this study, the Islamic district paradigm. Pakistan, like India, retains the administrative structure it inherited after Independence in 1947. Most districts and Agencies remain profoundly rural in character and somewhat isolated from national developments. There is a vast literature on the subject, much of it written by British district officers themselves. For a fresh contribution see Hunt and Harrison (1980); the latter was once a member of the élite Indian Civil Service. The fact that I have been a district officer perhaps assists me in viewing the problem from inside the structure and thereby making some contribution.

4. The academic neglect may be partly due to methodological considerations, for the district does not correspond either to the larger subject-matter – state, nation or region – traditionally studied by political scientists, sociologists and historians or the smaller micro-village-society studied by anthropologists. However, as mentioned in the previous footnote, there is no dearth of general writing on district life in the form of memoirs.

5. I shall refer to the district rather than the Agency as paradigm because the former is older in history, indeed it is the forerunner of the Agency, and more widely known.

6. In place of the technical anthropological term 'Father's Brother's Son's I shall employ the lesser jargon, agnatic rivalry, which I define as rivalry between males descended in the patrilineage from a common ancestor.

7. Waziristan, when used generally, refers to the area of North and South Waziristan Agencies. The name derives from the Wazir tribe. Wazir in Arabic and Urdu means 'minister'.

8. *Sartor* is literally 'black head', the name implies one whose head is uncovered as a result of poverty, grief or some personal obsession, here it would signify an obsession for the cause of Islam; *baba* is a term of respect for an elder.

9. About ten rupees equal one US dollar.

10. Among the friends was a Director of Routledge & Kegan Paul who was visiting me.

11. I have discussed Nalkot in relation to certain methodological assumptions of anthropological fieldwork elsewhere (Ahmed, forthcoming).

12. The Mullah's grand-nephew, Ahmedo Jan, one of the leading elders of the Agency, recounted various devices his ancestor employed to illustrate his powers. A favourite was to predict that the *niswar* (snuff) to which his followers were addicted would turn to faeces if they did not give up the habit. At night his selected campanions would place dog faeces in the *niswar* containers, and on rising in the morning his followers would marvel at the Mullah's powers. Such tricks win some following which can be manipulated to consolidate leadership.

13. For the orthodox Moslem the crime of Akbar the Mughal, the most famous case of Imperial heresy in South Asian Islam, lay in his attempt at redefining Islam; for the majority Moslems of the Agency the crime of the Mullah lay in his redefinition of *jihad*. The Mullah, however, is not alone in reinterpreting *jihad*. *Jihad* has been translated in the contemporary world in dramatically non-traditional ways. For instance in April 1981 an Indonesian Moslem group, calling itself Komando Jihad or Holy War Command, hijacked a DC-9 passenger aeroplane belonging to the Garuda Indonesian Airways. Indonesian commandoes successfully foiled the attempt at Bankok airport killing all five hijackers. Although the idiom of *Jihad* was employed during the hijack the case remains clouded in obscurity. *Jihad* is also used for other daily even secular activity. As we know there is at least one daily newspaper called *Jihad* in Pakistan.

14. Professor Barth, perhaps acknowledging the criticism, has recently re-examined his earlier work (1972) in 'Swat Pathans reconsidered' (in Barth, 1981). See also Meeker (1980).

15. A revealing and delightful anecdote is recounted by Minhajudin Mahsud illustrating the point I have made. It also reflects the attitudes of Mahsud tribesmen to dacoity (non-Mahsud cattle from the settled district are fair game), prayer (rigidly observed) and invocation of saints and God (constant and fervent appeals in endeavour, however dubious or illegal its content): Mr Mattak Khan is an ideal man I can quote. In his youth he has been a famous dacoit having a gang of daring and skilful fighters and artful thieves. He has a notorious record in this regard. But he has all along been very religious-minded. He prays regularly, observes fasts, pays *zakat* (compulsory alms) – even from his stolen things. He serves religious leaders with great zeal and honesty. One of his stories goes thus: he and his gang came out on an expedition of stealing cattle from a village in Jandola. He was telling me that they prayed their later afternoon (third) prayer at such and such place and started for the destination: prayed their evening prayer at such and such place and again moved ahead. At midnight after the night prayer they reached the spot.

Like in the rest prayers of this day, they humbly prayed to Allah, besought great *pirs* and vowed to shrines to bless them with success. They held positions and started breaking through into the cattle band. After having successfully stolen the cattles, they made for their homes. Soon a group of armed villagers followed them. It was the morning prayer time; they prayed to Allah to save them and help them carry the cattle safely. They vowed that out of these cattle so many will be sacrificed and given in charity in the name of Allah and they called upon *pirs*; through their tactics they were successful in bringing the cattle to their homes. Honest to their promises, they slaughtered some sheep and goats at shrines, gave some of them to Maulvis in charity – Maulvis have established that they are the most rightful receivers of charity. The Maulvis well in the know about these cattle, accepted these under the pretence that these were *halal* (pure) for them as they did not steal these and were given to them in the name of Allah and holy persons (Mahsud, 1970, p. 92).

# 5 National Integration and Traditional Rural Organisation in Algeria, 1970–80: Background for Islamic Traditionalism?

## PETER VON SIVERS

Algeria marches as the rearguard of contemporary Middle Eastern and North African countries in terms of popular social movements springing up at the grassroots level. The lonely student-protests of 1975 against the Agricultural Revolution and of 1979 against the absence of career chances for Arabic-educated graduates would seem to be a rather narrow cone on top of the Arab Islamic traditionalist volcano, if such a volcano indeed exists in Algeria. Furthermore, the protests of Berber students in Tizi-Ouzou in 1980 against forced Arabisation serve as a reminder that not every young Algerian is a potential recruit for the Arab Islamic traditionalist movement. Thus, while associations of Arab traditionalist Moslems have spontaneously erupted on the political scene, for instance in Iran, Egypt and Tunisia, in Algeria they have yet to appear.

It is possible to explain the relative absence of social movements of the traditionalist type in Algeria by the specific historical past of the country. Exposure to colonial settlers, the small size of a traditional urban class, the decline of Arabic literacy and the proletarisation of a portion of rural labour during more than a century of French domination can all be cited as partial causes for the absence of traditionalist movements. One might also mention the mandate of Arabisation and Islamisation bestowed upon the Algerian government by the coalition of small to medium landowners and small-town shopkeepers who fought the war of national liberation and constituted perhaps the most traditional groups of colonial Algeria. Since the present members of the government and administration are still partially recruited from this coalition, it is not easy to challenge their commitment to Islam, no matter how thin this commitment has worn in the nearly two decades of socialist-etatist planning. Furthermore, Algerian government planning has been more systematic and rigorous than in most other Middle Eastern or North African countries and the government has allowed little liberty for spontaneous grassroots movements to spread. These are some of the principal reasons with which it is possible to explain the tardiness of traditionalist social movements in Algeria.

Of course, these reasons might ultimately not be weighty enough to keep traditionalist movements from springing up in the country, but this is a matter of the future. In spite of all disruptions brought about by colonialism as well as by post-independence urbanisation and industrialisation there is certainly enough tradition left to feed a potential future traditionalist movement. Unfortunately the existence of tradition in Algeria is usually recognised only in a negative fashion: the persistence of pernicious 'archaic mentalities' is seen as hampering the full impact of the benefits of urbanisation and industrialisation. The reverse possibility, according to which 'archaic mentalities' survive because of the unwillingness or inability of the government planners to recognise flaws in their urbanisation and industrialisation programmes is rarely seen. To my knowledge no systematic analysis exists in which tradition is viewed as an instrument of self-protection against the inevitable shortcomings of government planning. In this paper an attempt is made to provide such a systematic analysis of 'archaic mentalities' clinging or returning to tradition in order to cope with the insufficiencies of the government. With the help of this analysis it should then be possible, at the end of the paper, to return to the question of why in Algeria the practice of tradition has remained a more or less silent affair and so far has not erupted into a vociferous militant tradition- alism, as is the case in Iran.

'Tradition' is defined in this paper primarily in economic terms and as agricultural self-sufficiency, that is, avoidance of productive specialis- ation and preference for auto-consumption. In a wider sense 'tradition' is taken to signify non-involvement with the government and paroch- ialism in religion. If, then, 'tradition' is understood here as the quiet practice of economic self-sufficiency, political non-involvement and religious parochialism, as such it is to be distinguished from the articulated ideology of traditionalism which calls for the activist maintenance or revival of all or some of these traditions. These definitions resemble those proffered by the important paper of Said Arjomand on Iran published in this volume (Chapter 10) and thus invite direct comparisons between the Algerian and Iranian cases of tradition and traditionalism.

By contrast, government planning in support of urbanisation and industrialisation is defined as an effort at integration. The government seeks to replace self-sufficiency with market interdependence, non-involvement in politics with popular assemblies, and religious parochialism with a state-controlled Islam emphasising ecumenical or secular tendencies and reducing parochial doctrines offensive to non-religious or religious minorities to a minimum. Of course, in the governmental process the contrast between self-sufficiency and integration, or as it is usually called, tradition and modernity, is rarely sustained. Compromises are established daily and as a result self-sufficiency takes on integrative features and integration is fragmented into parochial arrangements. For the historian it is a commonplace that tradition is constantly modernised and modernity continually traditionalised. Nevertheless, the tension between self-sufficiency and integration never disappears completely. In the following sections of this paper I shall address myself to a number of topics which exemplify the current interplay between tradition and modernity as well as the underlying irreducible tension between the two, that is, first, self-sufficiency farming; second, specialisation, cooperatives and markets, and third, the Agricultural Revolution and tradition.

## SELF-SUFFICIENCY FARMING

In Algeria about 40 per cent of the active male population or 1.5 million persons are employed in agriculture[1] (Schnetzler, 1980, pp. 451–71, esp. p. 460; Jönsson, 1978, p. 21; Bessaoud, 1980, pp. 605–25, esp. p. 615; Palloix, 1980, pp. 557–76, esp. p. 558). Of these, about one million persons either possess no land at all (approximately 420 000) or less than is necessary for feeding a family of five under traditional agricultural methods (approximately 578 000 with 1 to 10 hectares) (Dahmani, 1979, pp. 150, 152; Ait-Amara, 1974, pp. 35–62, esp. p. 46; Ollivier, 1975, pp. 91–114, esp. pp. 95–97). The Agricultural Revolution of 1971–6 has provided some 90 000 formerly landless farmers with sufficient land in co-operatives to guarantee the agricultural minimum income (Guichaoua, 1977, pp. 583–601, esp. p. 593; Smith, 1975, pp. 259–78, esp. p. 274; Elaidi, 1980, pp. 627–47, esp. p. 627; Bessaoud, 1980, pp. 615–16). About 250 000 men work in the public sector farms known by the name '*autogestion*' (Abdi, 1975, p. 33). Another 138 000 farmers own and for the most part operate private farms of 10 to 50 hectares and are considered as receiving sufficient incomes; they are referred to in this paper as the 'middle peasantry' (Bessaoud, 1980, pp. 613–14; Ollivier, 1973, pp. 33–140, esp. pp. 96–110). Finally, 10 000 Algerians with large units between 50 and 100 hectares and 3400 Algerians with estates in excess of 100 hectares, who both can be described as large landowners, fell victim to the expropriations of the Agricultural Revolution and lost their land for the most part to the co-operatives mentioned above[2] (Abdi, 1975, pp. 33–41). Officially, only 'small and non-exploitative' properties are tolerated.[3] Quite clearly the Agricultural Revolution made barely a dent in the monumental problems engulfing Algerian agriculture where nine out of ten farmers or nearly one-third of the active male population lives under highly precarious circumstances.

How precarious these circumstances are becomes clear when one takes a look at one of the few concrete studies of the traditional peasantry which are available. In an important article Djilali Sari investigates the circumstances of farming in the Ouarsenis mountains 150km southwest of Algiers during the 1970s (Sari, 1972, pp. 39–72; Guillermou, 1977, pp. 603–13; Lacoste-Dujardin, 1976; Etienne, 1975, pp. 3–44). The main point of the article is that as a result of a continuous demographic increase since the end of the nineteenth century the population density has doubled, to forty to fifty persons per square kilometre. At the same time, however, a formerly diversified self-sufficiency agriculture has been reduced to its bare essentials. As the population grew, the need to concentrate on the basic food staples became more pronounced.

Those who possess land engage in nearly nothing but cereal agriculture, while those who are landless raise little more than goats and a few sheep. The formerly rich cultivation of trees bearing figs, chestnuts, olives, pears, plums, apples, pomegranates and almonds has regressed catastrophically. Few trees are still pruned, quality and quantity of the fruits are low and agricultural pests are rampant. Most fruits are consumed on the spot and little is preserved for the winter. The little that is left over is marketed, but only if the markets are close, since the slowness of what is still predominantly animal transportation causes most fruit coming from the mountains to spoil. Olives can no longer be processed into oil because of the absence of oil-presses. Gardens have shrunk for the lack of water and their products are almost entirely destined for domestic consumption. The markets offer a few kilograms of onions and green peppers, while potatoes and beans appear only intermittently. The only fruits available in abundance are Barbary figs produced by hardy cactuses which alone are adapted to the declining, rocky soils. Altogether Sari estimates that aboriculture generates, at best, income for a month and a half per person during the year.

With arboriculture almost completely gone and horticulture severely restricted, wheat has become the crucial staple. In order to satisfy the minimum annual requirement of 4000kg per family, on the poor mountain slopes of the Ouarsenis 10 to 20 hectares are needed, including fallow lands. But a full third of all farmers owning land do not possess this surface. These micro-farmers are forced to keep fallow as small as possible, thereby increasing the danger of soil-exhaustion and erosion, and reap diminishing harvests from soils which they are unable to fertilise for lack of cattle or money for chemical fertilisers. Harvests as a rule now are barely above the amount of seed sown. In addition, a few goats and sheep are kept, but since fallow land is minimal, these animals have to be sent more or less illegally on to private and public brush lands and forests. What is not gained through farming and grazing has to be earned in the form of irregular wages for work on the larger farms. Micro-farmers live from a mixed self-sufficiency and wage economy.

About half of the population of the Ouarsenis is landless and earns its income primarily through the breeding of goats which are grazed on the brush lands and in the forests. The goats provide two or three offspring per year as well as milk, hair, skin and meat to their owners. While the forests yield wild foods. Beehives have disappeared completely from the landscape and the number and size of chicken coops is greatly reduced. In order to make up for the absence of wheat, some of the animals are sold or work for wages is sought on the larger farms, in the local iron-mine or (ironically, perhaps in order to gain a cover) in the Soil Conservation Service, which controls the forests. Thus with the traditional diversified and balanced agriculture gone, a stripped-down system of self-sufficiency has sprung up.

In some typical budgets of these micro-farmers and micro-pastoralists self-sufficiency, that is, production for auto-consumption and for supplementary sales on the market, comprises 57 and 48 per cent of the annual income respectively. Grain for the two food staples, bread and couscous, is processed at home and fuel is collected in the forests. The self-built dwelling (*gourbi*) consisting of two miniscule rooms of $2 \times 1.5$ and $2 \times 1$m is made of pinewood and baked earth. It contains home-made mattresses, mats, wooden chests, earthen jars, pottery, kitchen utensils, axes and hoes. Cloth, used cloth (the so-called *friperie*), shoes and plastic sandals are bought in the market. Nineteenth century diversification, involving the manufacture of textiles at home, has fallen largely by the wayside, in favour of basic food production. Nevertheless, the percentages of self-sufficiency are still surprisingly high, particularly if one takes self-reliance not only for a portion of the food but also for the procurement of fuel, the processing of food and the construction of shelter into account.

By contrast, farmers with properties of at least 15 hectares produce enough for basic self-sufficiency and supplementary market exchange and do not have to take recourse to income from wages. Goods purchased on the market include bottled gas for fuel, fresh meat on a regular basis and new clothes. In addition, a portion of the production is exchanged for money to be paid in the form of taxes. [Micro-farmers and micro-pastoralists with incomes of less than 500.00 Dinars (DA) (DA) 4.00 = \$1.00) monthly are tax exempt (Dahmani, 1979, pp. 161).] Farmers in the range of 30 hectares produce profits equal to or larger than the household expenditures, although they basically are also limited to cereal agriculture and small animal breeding. Annual incomes in the Ouarsenis range from DA1600.00 (\$400) per month in the wealthiest families to DA200.00 (\$50) per month in the poorest households. Few profits are invested in either re-diversification or in agricultural improvements, partly because of infrastructural insufficiencies, such as lack of electricity, irrigation, roads, soil conservation and a slow and inefficient market system; partly because of low agricultural prices.

What springs to the eye from this sketch of Ouarsenis agriculture by Sari is the remarkably high degree of self-sufficiency even on the most disadvantaged income levels. Admittedly, self-sufficiency is largely stripped of the seeming non-essentials, such as traditional horticulture and arboriculture. Nevertheless, even in its undiversified state, self-sufficiency still provides for much of the food and shelter requirements as well as for the supplements to be acquired through the sale of small surpluses on the market. In fact, in spite of their small size, the surpluses are not unimportant, comprising, as they do, 27 per cent of the overall annual rural incomes, wages included, or 63 per cent if micro-pastoralism is taken alone. Viewed from the angle of self-sufficiency, micro-pastoralism and micro-farming do not look quite as miserable as one would expect in an ill-managed agricultural system such as that of Algeria.

Of course, such high degrees of self-sufficiency can be maintained only as long as brush and forest lands are still available and the government tolerates its use. In 1965 public uncultivated and uncultivable land in northern Algeria amounted to 10 155 500 hectares, forests to 2 419 320 hectares. Together they represented 43 per cent of the total land surfaces of the North (Smith, 1975, p. 260; Abdi, 1973, pp. 223–37; Cecconi, 1974, pp. 89–110, esp. p. 95). In spite of their large size, however, these lands and forests do not contain unlimited resources. Erosion resulting from over-grazing and forest destruction diminishes the available resources at alarming rates.

The mixture of self-sufficiency and recourse to the market in the present day Ouarsenis represent an interesting combination of tradition and modernity. Inherited tradition prescribed a diversified self-sufficiency agriculture in which the basic growing of wheat and pasturing of animals were supplemented with arboriculture, horticulture, apiculture and the raising of poultry, not to mention cloth-manufacture and the construction of shelter. This tradition is being 'modernised' (if such a false euphemism is acceptable) through the stripping away of diversification and an over-emphasis on cereal agriculture and livestock-raising. Modernity is also making itself felt, albeit hesitatingly, with the need for increased market frequentation and wage labour. The force pushing ineluctably in the direction of modernity is demographic increase. So far the emphasis in the Ouarsenis is more on the 'modernisation' of self-sufficiency farming than on the appearance of modernity through the market system. The one, possibly major, factor which has favoured the maintenance of self-sufficiency, at the expense of an enlarged market system, is the availability of public land. This land acts as a buffer shielding the Ouarsenis from modernity – ironically, since the Algerian government, administrator of this land, is otherwise known as an ardent proponent of modernity.

## SPECIALISATION, CO-OPERATIVES AND MARKETS

The optimal path of agricultural evolution in a situation of rising demographic density is away from self-sufficient diversification and towards intensification, specialisation and urbanisation, so as to increase food production and create more jobs (Boserup, 1975, pp. 257–70; Darity, 1980, pp. 137–57; Grigg, 1979, pp. 64–84). Under Algerian conditions, arboriculture, horticulture as well as poultry and dairy farming can be employed to result in more intensified labour and product specialisation, whereby entire regions concentrate on specific crops or products and use market exchange for diversification. However, as shown in the foregoing section, in areas of Algeria such as the Ouarsenis, agricultural evolution under population pressure follows quite a different path. On the one hand, farmers are clearly turning away from self-sufficiency diversification and are intensifying their efforts in favour of a few basic products. They also participate eagerly in urbanisation since they are leaving the countryside in droves. But on the other hand they are not engaged in specialisation, working as they are in the unspecialised occupations of cereal-growing and livestock-raising. Thus one of the essential steps on the optimal path towards adjustment to the demographic rise has been neglected.

What is going wrong in the Ouarsenis and other inland regions which contain the majority of Algeria's population engaged in self-sufficiency farming? At the centre of the problem are the unequal relations between the rural and urban areas of the country. As throughout much of the past, the countryside today is still forced to invest more in the cities than it receives: it is the recipient of less than half the governmental investments going into industry (Abdi, 1976, pp. 663–74, esp. p. 671; Karsenty, 1975, pp. 115–42). It loses a good portion of its prime labour force to the cities, in the form of rural–urban migrants, retaining mostly the middle and older generations (Bessaoud, 1980, p. 621; Ollivier, 1973, p. 96). It likewise loses a good portion of its production to urban-based merchants or government-controlled marketing co-operatives at prices dictated by the latter. There is little question that Algeria's urban population today still lives off the countryside in time-honoured fashion (Guichaoua, 1977, pp. 598, 601).

The governmental effort at collecting the available rural food production for distribution in the cities is a particularly illuminating case of rural inequality. In a series of nationalisations the Algerian government has sought to eliminate private wholesalers from the food collection and distribution circuits, in order to remove speculative profit-making and exaggerated urban prices, and to shift collection and distribution entirely to the government sector, which however is no less urban-based. In 1968 the market of grains and dry legumes was nationalised. Then in 1974 the same was done for all remaining food items as well as for exports, which subsequently were drastically curtailed in favour of national distribution (Bouzidi, 1977, pp. 502–39). Today the government determines all food prices (Jönsson, 1978, p. 58). It has tended so far to keep these prices well below the world-market level, obviously with greater concern about urban food riots than for rural sentiments about exploitation (Jönsson, 1978, pp. 57–8; Dahmani,

1979, pp. 91–2; Ait-Amara, 1973, pp. 161–76; Antoine and Labbé, 1976, pp. 505–56; Benissad, 1978, pp. 11–34; Benissad, 1979). The lag in rural production is balanced by wheat imports at world market prices – to the tune of one-third of the foreign-currency earnings from oil and gas sales – to be retailed in the cities at local prices (Dahmani, 1979, pp. 59, 64; Malder, 1975, pp. 251–71, esp. pp. 254–5). With one exception, to be discussed below, the government has chosen to maintain the time-honoured system of urban control over the food market, the only difference being that the appropriation of the middleman's margin has been shifted from urban-based private merchants to urban-based public agencies.

The exception concerns the creation in 1974 of marketing co-operatives in order to mobilise all members of the farming co-operatives and any private farmers desirous to join for market production. These marketing co-operatives are entitled to a 30 per cent price mark-up in return for the collection of the rural production from the farming co-operatives and its distribution to the urban retailers. Whatever profits remain from this mark-up are disbursed to the constituent farming co-operatives and private farmer members (Dahmani, 1979, pp. 171–2; Jönsson, 1978, pp. 37–8). In a seemingly sensational revolutionary move the Algerian government redressed the age-old disparity between countryside and city and finally offered a workable model of producer-controlled market organisations.

Unfortunately, however, cumbersome governmental controls, low prices, participation of urban dealers and bureaucratisation of the executive positions have tended to urbanise the marketing co-operatives almost as soon as they were created (Bouzidi, 1977, pp. 522–32; Jönsson, 1978, pp. 56–8). Directors are nominated and installed by the Ministry of Agriculture and the price commissions are run by the political officials and co-operative directors of each country (*wilāya*), without the representation of the farmers (Jönsson, 1978, pp. 56–8). (Although at least some of these officials and directors are local landowners [Lepoul, 1977].) Distribution problems are endemic and huge deficits often pile up, depriving the producers of much of the middleman's margin which they appear to have taken away from the cities (Cecconi, 1974, pp. 101–4; Elaidi, 1980, p. 595; Dahmani, 1979, p. 171; Bessaoud, 1980, p. 613; Jönsson, 1978, pp. 57–60; Guichaoua, 1977, pp. 595, 601; Ait-Amara, 1973, p. 170; Fielder, 1976, pp. 126–48, esp. p. 128). While the idea of bringing production and marketing organisations closer together is salutary, a full unification under the control of the rural producers is required, if Algerian agriculture is to become productive again.

In the absence of fully producer-controlled marketing co-operatives a muddled system of at least three parallel distribution organisations exists. First, there is the sector of nationalised distribution (at best only marginally profitable) hampered by insufficient quantities and a low quality of goods as well as by bureaucratic inefficiency (Nellis, 1980, pp. 407–22). Second, there is the unofficial private market dominated by urban wholesalers who buy directly from the producers and maintain an efficient distribution system, albeit at inflated prices (Karsenty, 1977, pp. 31–9). Third, there are the small farmers' markets which continue to exist, particularly in the small towns and rural areas, even if they have little to sell, as we have already seen (Coutsinas, 1975, pp. 773–81). The latter actually constitute the only true farmer-controlled markets, although so far they have lingered more than prospered. Weekly donkey trips with a few mediocre onions and green peppers to the nearest town do not do enough to make the more prosperous farmers come nor to build better homes and gardens. The three market circuits check each other and their cumulative impact does little to stimulate an overall agricultural improvement.

Faced with a market dominated by urban bureaucrats and whole-salers, farmers have no choice but to stay with one leg in self-sufficiency farming. Of course, farmers at some distance from the market encounter the additional problem of slow communications. Algeria still has only half the length of road and railroad network per head as compared with that of France and electricity has yet to arrive in 40 per cent of the households (Gauthier, 1978, pp. 72–101; Dahmani, 1979, p. 64). Whether close to the market or far removed, farmers remain the closest to self-sufficiency if they live on farms, co-operatives or public *autogestion* domains with relatively high land/farmer ratios. On these generally large landholdings a strong resistance exists against sub-division either by inheritance or governmental redistribution campaigns, since the resulting higher population density renders self-sufficiency more difficult. On the already subdivided small plots and in the absence of any chances of market domination, the farmers have no choice but to hold on to as much self-sufficiency as possible, even while slowly sinking to the absolute minimum of rural work, and to micro-pastoralism on mostly public brush and forest land.

In answer to the question of why agriculture is disintegrating in the Ouarsenis and other areas of the Algerian hinterland it can thus be concluded that the lack of opportunities for market control by farmers is the main culprit. Even though the optimal path of farming in circumstances of rapidly rising population densities is away from self-sufficiency diversification and towards greater labour intensity and product specialisation, this path leads nowhere if direct marketing to the cities does not become a reality, and consequently peasants still find it more advantageous to produce for their own needs first before going to the market.

The pressure on the peasants to stay in self-sufficiency agriculture rather than to seek full product specialisation is superbly illustrated in an article by Cyrille Megdiche and C. Doret. This article provides a vivid description of daily life in the newly created village of Tessala el Merdja, established within the Agricultural Revolution for the purpose of increasing the population density on some of the hitherto overly self-sufficiency-oriented large public and private landholdings (Megdiche and Doret, 1977, pp. 255–96; cf. Cote, 1975, pp. 173–84; Benguergoura, 1976, pp. 241–9). The villagers are supposed to engage in intensive labour for the production of specialised crops and products, but in the absence of a directly accessible market find themselves pushed towards the maintenance of self-sufficiency farming.

Originally, in 1975, Tessala el Merdja on the Mitidja plain near Algiers was built with high hopes for an integration of the farmers into the market as well as into national life in general, although under the mistaken idea, as we have seen, of turning the farmers into specialised producers under government tutelage rather than their own market initiative. The government provided the villagers with standardised, urban-conceived housing consisting of a closed courtyard, a kitchen (with a sink, running water and a small gas-heated stove), three rooms, a toilet, a bath and a stable. In the centre of the village is a mosque, with an annexe of two rooms for religious instruction (*zawiya*) and an upstairs hall for the women's prayers. Adjacent to the mosque are a commercial centre, primary school, medical dispensary, municipal bureau, post office and assembly hall (*nadi*) with a youth centre. However, the commercial centre did not open until 1976 and then with only two stores for vegetables and groceries. Five of its remaining stores are still empty. The localities foreseen for the bakery and the coffee house are currently occupied by youth groups. Obviously the government technocrats were a little too optimistic about their ability to integrate the farmers into the economic life of the nation.

In addition, the planners were apparently also a bit hasty. There are cracks as well as unfinished places in the roofs and walls, for which state-run construction firms are responsible. Sanitation, electricity and carpentry installed by private firms seem to function better. Very little running water is available and children with buckets are a common sight in the village. Many families have covered the windows which open into the streets (they were obviously built too large for the villagers' taste) and there are complaints that women cannot use the rooftops without being seen by neighbours. The lack of street lighting and the absence of a bakery are felt severely.

Initially no stables were planned, but without them few families signed up for settlement. Planners then built stables for eight cows each, so as to continue to encourage specialisation and wean the farmers away from self-sufficiency. But it was apparently forgotten that dairy farming requires an intricate production system involving fresh and dry fodder, straw, natural and chemical fertiliser and transportation. Since nothing of this sort was foreseen for the villagers, the stables were transformed for self-sufficiency and are now populated with cattle, mules, sheep, goats, chickens and geese. Frontyards, courtyards and a few other small plts in and around the village are no longer devoted to the surburban dreams of the technocrats responsible for the planning, which one assumes tended towards neatly trimmed lawns. Instead these plots are used for the growing of vegetables for household consumption and for sale on farmers' markets. Additional free vegetables and fruits come from the co-operatives where most men of the village work, although this produce is only a reluctantly given gift from the government which would prefer to collect the entire crops and force the villagers to become market consumers. Obviously not everything works as planned in Tessala el Merdja and national integration seems to be of scant concern to the villagers.

Some 60 per cent of the men in the village work on the eleven agricultural co-operatives in the vicinity, where their land shares total 280 hectares. They receive salaries of DA350.00 ($87.50) per month plus DA900–1000 ($225–50) for the feast of *al-'id* – salaries which are among the most modest in Algeria. The co-operatives average 27 hectares and each farmer holds a share of 2 hectares. Such a share is extremely low for Algeria, particularly if compared to the 10–20 hectares needed for self-sufficiency in the Ouarsenis and other mountain regions. It demonstrates how, through labour intensification and product specialisation, the land/farmer ratio can be decreased quite dramatically. Products are indeed specialised in Tessala el Merdja: the main goods are citrus and other fruits, vegetables, wheat on non-irrigated land and dairy products to a limited extent on some co-operatives. Four commercial co-operatives in the area around the village are in charge of the marketing of the agricultural production. These co-operatives deliver to the two stores in the village and pay the salaries of their managers who are also co-operators. Members of eighteen families work in dual agricultural and industrial jobs; nine are in industry alone, thereby technically forfeiting their right to live in the village. At least officially, intensive labour and product specialisation are geared towards complete market distribution, contrary to the self-sufficiency tendencies noted above.

National integration is intended to be further enhanced by the presence of national services. Two doctors of the national health system alternate in weekly two-hour consultations in the village. Two nurses are present daily during the week but do not live in the village. The postmaster is a permanent resident and also serves as scribe, impresario of the local band, and soccer player. Villagers assemble before his office well before the 11 o'clock mail distribution and, in general, the post office functions as the main meeting place for gossip and news.

The primary school employs twenty-one members of staff on three levels of qualification. A majority of the teachers are younger than 25, six teachers are women and four of the twenty-one teach French. There is a high turnover of almost half of the teachers every year and most are not of local origin. Student failure rates are high, particularly in the upper classes. Only 30 per cent make it to the sixth class (age 12) on first try. Religious instruction in the *Qur'an* and the prayer ritual are given in the *zawiya* by the local *imam* to about 25 per cent of the children, each paying a fee of DA15.00 ($3.75) a month. Practical courses in typewriting, agricultural mechanics and bookkeeping as well as adult education are offered in the youth centre by eight instructors. But these courses languish because of a lack of equipment and supplies, the requirement of fees and parental fear of the mixing of sexes. It is clear that of all services only the post office is a truly comfortable place for both young and adult villages to congregate in, whereas the other services are considered more or less alien.

The villagers have an acute sense of the alien 'outside'. In 1976 a dispute broke out between the villagers and the school over a teacher who allegedly wore a mini-skirt, hitch-hiked and held forth on controversial topics. The school director eventually had to have her transferred. In 1977 a group of young people spontaneously moved out of the assembly hall with its official youth centre and took over the empty stores in the commercial centre for the establishment of an alternative youth centre. Scout and soccer groups were formed as well as a club to organise a vacation colony for children. At the same time a local band assembled, rehearsing in the new youth centre with the justification that it is better for each of the two youth groups 'to be among themselves. Here one is left alone and can rehearse whenever one wants'. Grudgingly, the mayor of Boufarik, the nearby town on which Tessala el Merdja depends, has begun to allocate small subsidies to the alternative youth group.

The dislike between the villagers and the 'outsiders' is mutual. One instructor complains that the villagers purposely cut the assembly hall off from water supplies. The villagers are viewed as narrow-minded mountaineers who expect the directors of the assembly hall and the school to do everything, while themselves contributing nothing, as both directors state in unison. All schoolteachers are in agreement that the villagers are unsociable, stay at home as much as possible and take advantage only of their new living quarters. Children are sent to school, but, in the eyes of the teachers, the parents do not show the slightest interest in parent–schoolteacher meetings or in the progress of their children altogether.

On the other hand, according to both the municipal administrator and the *imam* the villagers appreciate both the schools and the less back-breaking labour in the fields, compared with their pre-village occupations. The villagers are described as open, politically interested through radio and television (half of them own sets). They travel with increasing regularity to outside markets (two or three own cars; a dozen, mopeds) in spite of an irregular bus system and regular visits by ambulatory traders to the village. The villagers' horizon clearly extends beyond the village confines, but they maintain a strict distance between themselves and 'outside' officials.

From this most instructive account of basic life in a socialist village by Megdiche and Doret a number of conclusions can be drawn. On first sight the problem of changeover from self-sufficiency diversification to intensive product specialisation has been solved. Except for small gratuities all agricultural products are sent to the market and the co-operators receive regular salaries. Although self-sufficiency vegetable and animal production in the village is quite high, in relation to the low salaries, the existence of two food-stores indicates the definite presence at least of a basic market orientation in the households. Unfortunately no budgets are available and so one can only tentatively conclude that self-sufficiency is less significant than market dependency. Even though the village does not go the entire way along the road to integration which the planners had charted for it, nevertheless it seems to have gone a good portion of the way.

However, upon closer investigation it becomes clear that integration is pretty much a dead issue for the villagers, both in its narrow market and wider national meanings. As far as the market is concerned, a strict separation is made between work on the co-operatives and in the village. It is mostly through self-sufficiency diversification in the village that additional income is generated. Efforts at product specialisation and direct marketing are less pronounced. Only in the case of one or two varieties of vegetables do we find the market mentioned, unfortunately without any reference as to the marketing method. Do the villagers travel to farmers' markets or are they visited by urban wholesalers or administrative agents? Altogether there is little question, however, that the villagers care less about product specialisation on the co-operatives than about product diversification at home. Integration ranks manifestly lower than autonomy.

Reluctance towards integration and preference for autonomy also emerges if one turns to the more general issue of the insertion of the villagers into the national life. The villagers participate with reluctance or indifference in both the religious and secular schools offered by the government. They take advantage of the health services, such as they are. They feel fully comfortable only in and around the post office, which of course is the fountainhead of good tidings by disbursing annually some DA237 500 ($59 375) in paychecks and money orders coming from the National Bank and from overseas relatives. Doctors, nurses and teachers are regarded as outsiders and since they prefer to commute from the outside rather than take up residence among the villagers, if they can help it, they are perceived in the same manner as urban wholesalers and government agents, that is, as intruders into domains that should legitimately be under the control of the villagers. A government that takes away food from the village for distribution in the city rather than allowing farmers to bring it voluntarily to the city deserves to be eyed suspiciously for its efforts in housing, health and education as well.[4]

## THE AGRICULTURAL REVOLUTION AND TRADITION

There are about 100 socialist villages of the type of Tessala el Merdja in Algeria at present (Guichaoua, 1977, p. 596; Elaidi, 1980, p. 627; Lepoul, 1977, pp. 40–7). These villages, together with the co-operatives in existing villages and the *autogestion* domains form the public sector of Algeria's agriculture. This sector employs about 250 000 men or 17 per cent of the total active agricultural work force on about 2.5 million hectares or 30 per cent of the cultivable land (Guichaoua, 1977, p. 591;

Schnetzler, 1980, p. 460; Cecconi, 1974, p. 108; Ollivier, 1973, p. 97; Abdi, 1975, p. 33). These figures amount to a ratio of one worker for every 12 hectares in the public sector (Abdi, 1975, p. 33). The corresponding ratio in the private sector is 1:24 if owners with at least the self-sufficiency minimum of 10 hectares are taken into account.[5] The public sector thus appears to be solidly anchored in intensive labour and product specialisation.

However, a closer look reveals that the public sector is by no means all that much ahead in intensification and specialisation compared with medium and large private farms. Admittedly, it produces 87 per cent of all citrus fruits, 68 per cent of all industrial crops and 67 per cent of all fodder plants. But the private sector, taken as a whole, produces 71 per cent of all olives and 58 per cent of all vegetables. Grains and dry legumes are shared more or less evenly (Dahmani, 1979, p. 166; Karsenty, 1977, p. 33). Only about one-quarter of the cultivable public land with three-quarters of the active labour force in the public sector is devoted to anything resembling intensive specialisation. The rest of the public sector work force is distributed sparsely (one worker per 30 hectares) over gigantic domains averaging more than 1000 hectares each (Ait-Amara, 1973, p. 175; Guichaoua, 1977, pp. 591–2; Trautmann, 1979, pp. 215–26; Sari, 1977, pp. 11–24). A good portion of the public sector land is cultivated as extensively, if not more so, than the private land.

Of course, on many of these gigantic public domains annual precipitation allows at best the cultivation of barley and wheat, unless enormous efforts at irrigation are undertaken. However, the 1:30 ratio indicates that with the employment of a more modest machinery a considerable number of additional farmers could be settled (Ait-Amara, 1973, pp. 163–9; van Malder, 1975, pp. 261–2; Etienne, 1977, p. 216; Vassilis, 1976, pp. 985–94). If chemical fertilisers were employed more systematically, the fallow of currently 30.5 per cent of the cultivated area could be substantially reduced, allowing for further settlements (Trautmann, 1979, p. 219; Fielder, 1976, p. 127). Although a large area of Algeria can be devoted at present only to relatively labour-extensive and unspecialised cereal agriculture, the public sector can still benefit from greater intensification efforts.

Even on relatively highly intensive and specialised public sector farms backsliding into self-sufficient extensiveness is not uncommon. Typically the Mitidja plain near Algiers shows such signs of backsliding. Tessala el Merdja, which is on this plain, possesses a flourishing self-sufficiency economy, as we have seen in the previous section. More generally, in the Mitidja one-third of the citrus trees are aging and have not been replaced in time by new trees reaching maturity. More than half of the citrus production is therefore of low quality and overall only 50 per cent of what once grew during colonial times is now harvested. Wine from the highly labour-intensive vineyards is no longer profitably marketable in Islamic Algeria or on the selective world market and hence vineyards had to be replaced with fruit trees or dairy farming. But a portion of the former vineyards has also been planted with wheat, even though only one-tenth of the former labour for the production of only one-third of the former value is required. Altogether work hours have shrunk by one-third during independence (Mutin, 1975, pp. 143–71; Mutin, 1977; Koulytchizky, 1974; Miyaji, 1976). Thus there is a tendency on the intensive and specialised public sector farms to slip towards a lower population density and self-sufficiency while private micro-farms and micro-pastures continue to exist in large numbers.

The primary reason for the backsliding into extensiveness is the attraction of the cities. Most of the supposedly intensive and specialised agriculture in the public sector is located near Algeria's large industrial centres. Every year valuable land and water are lost to these rapidly expanding centres, making agriculture more difficult on the remaining farms (Couderc and Desiré, 1975, pp. 17–30). Labour on these farms with their high requirements or discipline, regularity and technical expertise makes the workers ideal candidates for defection to nearby industrial jobs. Every year 20 per cent of the *autogestion* workers and 30 per cent of the co-operative farmers leave for better paying urban employment. Their replacements are usually less qualified (Jönsson, 1978, pp. 68–70). Public sector farms based on intensive labour and product specialisation function as way-stations to the cities, not as goals for failed self-sufficiency farmers.

In view of the high capacity of the public agriculture sector to absorb additional labour, the much touted Agricultural Revolution of 1971–7 already mentioned several times in the paper, looks like a rather timid event. Just like the public sector with its gigantic domains, so also the private agricultural sector has a number of large and thinly populated estates. Prior to the Agricultural Revolution there were about 13 000 large landlords with farms of 50 hectares or more who owned 22 per cent of the private land, while 578 000 micro-farmers subsisting on farms of 10 hectares or less owned only 29 per cent of the private land, not to mention the at least 420 000 landless pastoralists living from brush and forest lands (Gauthier, 1978, pp. 75–6; Smith, 1975, p. 270; Fiedler, 1976, p. 129; Guichaoua, 1977, p. 591). In order to make this grotesque unevenness of land distribution more tolerable, the government confiscated some 600 000 hectares from the large as well as a good number of the medium landowners (on the latter see next paragraphs) in return for compensation through government bonds (Cecconi, 1974, pp. 107–9; Etienne, 1977, p. 58; Leca and Vatin, 1975, p. 434; Sutton, 1974, pp. 50–68). This by no means negligible chunk of confiscated land, comprising about half of all large holdings, was then redistributed in the form of co-operatives to the landless and we have seen Tessala el Merdja in the previous section as a typical example of these co-operatives.

Overall, the Agricultural Revolution, beneficial as it was, has been at best only a half step towards an overall more even distribution of the agricultural population over the cultivable land – a step which would have to be completed with a denser settlement of the *autogestion* domains. If any further backsliding of these domains into self-sufficiency extensiveness is to be avoided, a portion of their lands will have to be turned over to some of the remaining landless people. It is probably not necessary to employ the same high-pitched revolutionary propaganda to mobilise these landless, as in the case of the confiscation of the private lands, but some redistribution is indispensable. It seems the best way would be to increase the population density on the domains by quietly cutting them up into smaller units and settling landless farmers on unpopulated sections (Ollivier, 1973, p. 111; Karsenty, 1977, p. 36; Trautmann, 1979, pp. 224–5; Raffinot and Jacquemot, 1977, p. 338). This way the socialist ideology of *autogestion* would not have to be sacrificed.

Not surprisingly, the Agricultural Revolution has met with stiff resistance from the 13 000 large landowners. Why should they be required to give up land while *autogestion* domains continue to exist in gigantic splendour with high land/farmer ratios? In addition, a good number of medium landowners were affected by the Agricultural Revolution. Medium landowners with 10–50 hectares form a large group of about 138 000 members controlling about 48 per cent of the private land (Jönsson, 1978, p. 21; Ait-Amara, 1974, pp. 47–8). Of all large and medium landowners, some 40 000 were subject to confiscations, but the government dared touch only 28 000 (Dahmani, 1979, p. 43; Elaidi, 1980, p. 627; Jönsson, 1978, pp. 24–9; Fiedler, 1976, p. 133; Karsenty, 1977, p. 35). It was relatively easy to coax some 900 government functionaries with big landholdings into donating their lands, in the face of more or less subtle threats against their positions in the administration. But donations in the end made up only about 5 per cent of all lands allocated in the Agricultural Revolution. A much more difficult job was the expropriation of medium landholders who used a whole array of ruses to get around the laws. Some declared their lands as gifts, urban real estate or put up dummy owners, so as to evade the Revolution (Fiedler, 1976, p. 131). Others leased their expropriated lands back or continued to control their former properties via the new co-operatives (Fiedler, 1976, p. 133; Bessaoud, 1980, p. 609). Thus the already modest scope of the Agricultural Revolution, which did not touch the *autogestion* domains, was reduced even more because of the resistance put up by the large and medium landowners.

The attack against the block of medium farmers is all the more remarkable since private farms of 10–50 hectares probably constitute the healthiest agricultural enterprises in Algeria, responsible for much of the badly needed wheat production. In the first section on the Ouarsenis we have had a glimpse of this middle peasantry. To be sure, many medium farmers are still deeply moored in self-sufficiency agriculture, but since they are also frequently located in the hinterland and do not enjoy a good infrastructure for easy market access, they cannot really be blamed for their weak integration into national economic circuits. Under the present conditions prevailing in many rural areas of Algeria outside the plains and valleys of the North it is hard to imagine, who, in the place of the middle landholders, could provide for more productive forms of agricultural labour.

## THE STRUGGLE OF THE MIDDLE PEASANTRY AND PAROCHIAL TRADITIONALISM

The conclusion is inescapable that the Agricultural Revolution bears all the signs of an intra-governmental struggle between the local/regional administrators coming from the middle peasantry and the national/urban technocrats forming the middle class (Durand, 1977, pp. 123–40). The total of administrators, officials, functionaries and technocrats in Algeria was estimated to be about 400 000 individuals in 1977.[6] The middle peasantry has a long tradition of administrative involvement, reaching back at least to the mid-nineteenth century (von Sivers, 1980, pp. 679–99). Therefore it can be assumed that probably a good portion of its 138 000 members hold various local and regional, if not also a few national, positions. It is, however, outnumbered now by the urban commercial, entrepreneurial and professional middle class, which is estimated to consist at present of about 200 000 members (Benachenhou, 1975, p. 79). This class contributes increasingly to the recruitment of national technocrats and it is quite obvious that the Agricultural Revolution of 1971–7 was intended to be its first show of strength.

The stakes in this show of strength are by no means negligible. The middle peasantry is well-entrenched, numerically strong and economically sound. It controls only a small fraction of Algeria's capital assets, as opposed to the billions of dinars which the technocrats dispose of for investment, but it controls the micro-farmers and micro-pastoralists through the wage labour it offers and thus possesses a preponderant influence among nearly one-third of Algeria's active male population. The micro-farmers and micro-pastoralists have no choice but to invade the uncultivated brush and forest lands, as we have seen in the first section, since nothing of the nearly 80 per cent of all cultivable land in the hands of the middle peasantry can be spared for their use. It is quite illusory for the urban technocrats to dream of an alliance with the landless, forged through the Agricultural Revolution, with the help of which the middle peasantry could be swept out. The landless masses on brush and forest lands prefer the meagre seasonal wages from middle farmers as supplements for their self-sufficiency incomes over transplantation into a few far-away socialist villages offered by the technocrats. As is well-known, the once great dream of 'A Thousand Socialist Villages' by 1980 has now shrunk to a modest programme of about 100 villages barely capable of attracting enough applicants amidst turnover rates of up to one-third of their annual population (Lepoul, 1977).

Similarly, the middle peasantry controls a major share of the production of wheat and legumes. If the government controls over the marketing co-operatives were lifted, it is likely that the middle farmers would step in and organise the food distribution to the cities. By refusing to lift these controls the technocrats prevent the middle farmers from strengthening their influence, but the price paid for the continuation of urban-governmental controls is the stagnation of labour intensification and product specialisation on the farms. Co-operatives probably are the optimal form of agricultural organisation under strong demographic pressure through which a viable group of small farmer collectives could be created. But because of lack of encouragement in the public sector of agriculture this group languishes, as we have seen in the second section in the case of Tessala el Merdja and has yet to develop into a counterweight to the middle peasantry in the private sector. Algeria's technocrats have not yet found the right formula for neutralising the influence of the middle peasantry.

Nevertheless, in the struggle between the urban technocrats and the middle peasantry the former have one important advantage. The rural–urban mass migration constantly deprives local and regional administrators of a portion of their constituency. A good percentage of every new generation in the villages unfailingly departs every year for the cities. Middle farmers themselves cannot help but send some of their children to the cities, if they do not want to risk an impoverishment of their self-sufficiency farms and have no opportunity to intensify and specialise. An essentially stagnant rural population, in which high birth-rates are offset by high rural–urban migration rates, is politically more defensive than aggressive.

However, even though the middle peasantry loses a number of its children to the cities, these children do not necessarily succumb to the technocrats' version of urban ideology with its modernist emphasis on technology, management and accounting. In the past, Middle Eastern and North African cities have often maintained their dominance over the countryside with the help of a learned, urban Islam which claimed to be superior to the allegedly superstitious village Islam. With the growth of the cities and the inevitable rise of the service sector, in which demands on technical, managerial and accounting skills are less rigorous, it is not surprising that the older Islamic ideology is making a comeback (Souriau, 1975, pp. 359–74; Grandgouillaume, 1980, pp. 51–62; Haddab, 1976, pp. 957–70). With the participation, if not under the leadership, of the comparatively well-educated and highly motivated children of middle peasants this Islamic ideology might very well replace that of technocracy. In this respect it is not the middle peasantry directly but rather its urbanised children who constitute a potential threat to the dominant technocrats of Algeria.

For the moment there is not much evidence for the sons and daughters of the middle peasantry, coming to the cities for jobs or education, to spearhead a traditionalist urban Islamic ideology. In 1975 clashes occurred in Algiers between students attacking and others defending the Agricultural Revolution (Abdi, 1975, p. 37). In 1979 students in the Arabic-taught section of the University of Algiers rioted, protesting the lack of jobs available to them in comparison to those open to French-educated graduates.[7] But these spontaneous outbreaks have not solidified themselves into a more durable organisation and to speak of a social movement of traditionalist Algerian Moslems with ties to the countryside, particularly the middle peasantry, is premature.

Nevertheless, since the record of the technocrats in providing urban jobs for the rural–urban migrants is not overly impressive, there are ample opportunities for the Arabic-educated students to link up forces with less privileged rural immigrants in the cities. In 1975 nearly 20 per cent of the active male population in the thirteen largest cities were unemployed and in 1977 there were 650 000 job-seekers as compared with an urban labour force of a little over two million. Half the unemployed were new on the job-market (Schnetzler, 1980, p. 469; Leca and Vatin, 1977, pp. 63–7; Grimaud, 1976, p. 72; Ecrement, 1979, pp. 821–32; Sari, 1975, pp. 42–50). The foot-soldiers for a potential traditionalist movement are certainly there.

Furthermore, a substantial number of the employed workforce in the cities are potential recruits for a traditionalist movement. The urban workforce in 1977 numbered slightly over two million (as compared with the one and a half million in agriculture discussed earlier). In this workforce the following branches and percentages can be distinguished: industry 17.5, handicrafts 2.3, construction 15, transportation 5.5, commerce 14.1, services 13, administration 19.5, students and others 14.5. Handicrafts, construction and commerce, comprising together 31.4 per cent of the urban work force are perhaps the most accessible branches for the rural–urban migrants (Palloix, 1980, p. 558). It is in these branches that self-employment is easily possible, hours are highly flexible and can be extended and such modern rigours as specialisation, punctuality and precision do not necessarily have to be learned. Obviously, not all members of these 31.4 per cent can be assumed to be recent arrivals or even first-generation job-holders. Likewise, not everyone is self-employed nor subscribes to the notions of extended or irregular work. Nevertheless, hidden in this percentage are a good number of urban dwellers only marginally integrated into the national economy, committed to traditional forms of making a living and thus accessible to the ideology of traditionalism.

The branches of handicrafts, construction and commerce are, ever since the Iranian revolution commonly referred to as the 'bazaar sector'. Contrary to Iran, however, in Algeria this sector does not have a long historical tradition of its own, except in Constantine and Tlemcen, and thus does not possess a network of traditional commercial families and Islamic scholars. As in the case of the unemployed, there are many potential followers of a putative traditionalist movement in the Algerian bazaar sector, but contrary to Iran there is no recognised leadership. Such a leadership, therefore, could only come from the students who so far have not yet linked forces with the urban jobless and the bazaar sector. Any threat to the technocrats is still theoretical.

The government technocrats with their commitments to market integration, urbanisation and industrialisation (Ammour, Leucate and

Moulin, 1974; Doucy and Monheim, 1971; Elsenhans, 1977; Gauthier, 1976; Lucas, 1978; Mallarde, 1975; Tammar, 1974; Martens, 1973) are thus faced with a determined resistance of middle farmers as well as the less organised scepticism of rural people with small or no landed property and urban dwellers without employment or belonging to the bazaar sector. It is difficult to imagine that anything other than market integration, urbanisation and industrialisation would respond better to the challenges posed by the strong demographic pressure which is characteristic of Algeria. Yet it would be a mistake to view the resistance or scepticism of a strong segment of the rural and urban population as a retrograde attitude. The clinging to the traditions of economic self-sufficiency, political non-involvement and religious parochialism is a quite legitimate posture if the government fails fully to translate its commitments into programmes that work. Tradition then becomes a shield for self-protection, to be activated in the form of an ideologically full-fledged traditionalism if frustrations become too strong.

The central failure in the governmental commitments to market integration, urbanisation and industrialisation is that it is not sufficiently strongly built on agricultural specialisation. It makes little sense to allow the population density on those farms which are most suited to agricultural specialisation to decline. In the long run it will be unavoidable to either reduce the population density in the relatively unspecialised wheat and livestock belt or improve the conditions for specialisation through irrigation and other capital investments. The latter course of action, obviously, requires a considerable outlay in funds, needs time for implementation and can be implemented only in selected spots. As long as the only alternative to demographic pressure in the Algerian wheat/sheep belt is emigration to the cities, tendencies towards self-sufficiency and distrust of the government remain high. The middle peasantry opposes further encroachments on the size of its farms, since only large farms with low population densities are suited for wheat cultivation and stock-breeding under dry-farming conditions. The small farmers and landless rural people remain beholden to the middle peasantry through salaried, mostly seasonal, labour. Only a systematic shift of the rural population from the wheat/sheep areas to the co-operative and *autogestion* farms will reduce self-sufficiency and distrust.

A subsidiary governmental failure consists in the continued belief in the necessity of an urban-controlled market system. Agricultural specialisation on the co-operative and *autogestion* farms has little meaning if the farmers have no influence on distribution and prices.

Accordingly, these farms have suffered; farmers have slipped back into self-sufficiency and avoid involvement with the administration. Recent support price increases have alleviated the situation, but the main problem is still the urban-oriented supervision of the price system by the government. Algeria's market and distribution system does not yet instil trust in the producers.

In the countryside there is thus currently no reason for the traditions of self-sufficiency and non-involvement to diminish. Even in the cities traditions tend to be preserved, particularly among the students in the Arabic-taught fields of university studies and the members of the bazaar sector, both being largely of rural origin. The students and bazaaris are relatively unintegrated and untouched by the challenging requirements of market interdependence, job discipline, commuting or the other ingredients of modern living. Yet peasants, students and bazaaris are under constant challenge by a government which propagandises its commitments to market integration, urbanisation and industrialisation and thus experience a tension between tradition and modernity which is basically unsolvable. The economic and political circumstances of daily life favour the traditions while government propaganda promises (and delivers, albeit only to a portion of the population) the easier and more comfortable elements of modern life. Traditions are definitely modernised, particularly in the urban context, but ultimately they remain worlds apart from the modernity of market interdependence, urban existence and factory or office work.

In this paper I have investigated primarily the traditions of economic self-sufficiency and political non-involvement and have discussed the tradition of religious parochialism only incidentally. Should these traditions evolve into a conscious ideology of traditionalism in Algeria they would be likely to crystallise around the issue of parochial religious duties. The Algerian government is strongly committed to Islam as the dominant religion in the country, but has unofficially steered a course of ecumenism. This ecumenic tendency of keeping the interpretation of Islam as broad and general as possible is typically visible in the unwillingness of the government to commit itself to issuing a reformed family law, regulating marriage, divorce, bridal money, alimony and inheritance. These matters continue to be covered by a patchwork of colonial decrees. As a result, family law practised among the secularised technocrats tends to be more equality-inspired, while it remains parochially discriminatory towards women in the rural population and the bazaar sector. So far no serious conflict has occurred and thus the issue of religious ecumenism versus parochialism has remained in the shadow of the more tangible tensions between integration and self-sufficiency or political participation and abstention.[8]

However, since religion is justice in its most general form, transcending economic and political concerns, it would be religious parochialism which the potential traditionalist militants of Algeria would adopt. As long as the volcano of traditionalism is quiet in Algeria, self-sufficiency and distrust of the government remain the faces of tradition.

## NOTES

1. The numbers are not entirely precise.
2. For general discussions of land distribution and agricultural reform see Romero, 1976; Schliephake, 1972, pp. 44–59; Treydte, 1979.
3. Formula coined in the *Charte nationale*. (Cf. Leca and Vatin, 1975, pp. 255–8.)
4. On peasant interest (or disinterest) in government efforts to improve agriculture see further: Burgat, 1979, pp. 56–62; Zghal, 1975, pp. 295–311; Corrèze, 1976.
5. Calculated from figures in Jönsson, 1978, p. 21; cf. Abdi, 1975, p. 33.
6. The figures are not very precise. (See Benachenhou, 1975, pp. 7–45, esp. pp. 8–9; Etienne, 1977, p. 58; Palloix, 1980, p. 559; Leca and Vatin, 1975, p. 434; Leca and Vatin, 1977, pp. 15–18; Grimaud, 1976, pp. 70–7; Michel, 1973, pp. 87–122; cf. Michel, 1975, pp. 98–106.)
7. *Jeune Afrique* 1008 (30 April 1980) and 1012 (28 May 1980).
8. I have investigated the question of traditionalism and religion further in von Sivers, 1981; summary by Clement, 1980, pp. 25–7.

# 6 Politicisation of Islam in a Secular State: The National Salvation Party in Turkey

## BINNAZ TOPRAK

One of the many witticisms of Necmettin Erbakan, the leader of the National Salvation Party (NSP) (*Milli Selamet Partisi*) is a term he often used to describe his opponents. He labelled them as members of the 'Western Club': a club for people of short memory who have forgotten their past in the whirlwind of a misdirected quest to embrace Western culture and civilisation. According to Erbakan and the NSP, the rejection of Islamic in favour of Western civilisation has stripped Turkish intellectuals and statesmen of a political vision. Politicians of the 'Western Club', insofar as they lack a sense of history, are doomed to failure in their efforts to lead the country out of the underdeveloped world.

This issue of Islam versus the West which the NSP brought to the agenda of political discussion in recent years had its origins in the intellectual history of Ottoman Turkey in the eighteenth and nineteenth centuries. The question of how the Empire could escape from decline and disintegration haunted the Ottoman mind. The nineteenth century, especially, was a century of soul-searching as the Ottomans tried to understand the reasons for the Empire's apparent weakness *vis-à-vis* the West.

The major issue which divided Ottoman thinkers and reformers related to the question of westernisation. One school of thought argued that accepting Western technology and civilisation was the only remedy for Europe's 'sick man'. These were the Westerners and the course of

119

reform which the Empire had followed since the *Tanzimat* edict of 1839 was in line with their prescription. Critical of this school were the Islamists. They admitted the superiority of Western technology and the necessity to adopt it, but rejected the acceptance of Western civilisation itself. On the contrary, the Islamists saw in westernisation the root of the Empire's problems. For them, change in itself did not mean progress. A nation without its own laws, institutions, and customs would lose its bases of independence. Hence, they argued that the statesmen who had adopted westernisation as a model for change and the method of reform which was accordingly followed for half a century were responsible for speeding the collapse of the Ottoman state. As Şeyhü'l-İslam Mustafa Sabri put it, reformers of the *Tanzimat* and the following periods had chosen westernisation as a path of progress, but it had turned out to be a path leading the Empire into the 'deep abyss'.[1]

The collapse of the Ottoman Empire following World War One and the subsequent establishment of the Turkish Republic in 1923 signalled the end of this debate. The Kemalist period was the heyday of westernising reforms. Modernisation became the equivalent of westernisation as the new Republic settled down for a period of radical change which was designed to substitute Western culture for the Islamic.

The list of secular reforms undertaken during the initial years of the Republic is impressive in terms of their scope. The Republican government embarked on a concerted effort, often through the force of law, to eradicate the role of Islam in Turkish society. The result was the creation of a new generation of Turks whose cultural milieu was radically different from that of their fathers. They now used the Latin alphabet instead of the Arabic script. They spoke a language which was largely purified from Arabic and Persian derivatives. The men wore Western suits and the Western hat which, a few years earlier, was considered a trademark of the infidel. The women got out of their veils and the seclusion of the house as they were given equal legal and political rights with men. Gone were the polygamous families, the divided sections for men and women in tramcars, theatres, or other public places. Women now entered parliament, the public service, and the professions. They took part in sports, beauty contests, fashion shows. Working people took their day-off on Sundays, rather than the Moslem rest day, Friday. The call to prayer, the *ezan*, was recited in Turkish instead of Arabic throughout the mosques. For believing Moslems, this was nothing short of blasphemy. Also gone was the *Caliphate*, for centuries a symbol of the unity of the Moslem *ummah*. The office of the *Şeyhu'l-Islam*, giving religious sanction to state affairs, had been dissolved. The *Shari'ah*, religious law, had been replaced by Western codes. The *medreses*, important centres of religious education during the Ottoman period, had been closed down. The brotherhoods (*tarikat*), organised around various *Sufi* orders, had been outlawed. The activities at the sacred shrines and other popular places of workship had been banned. The religious organisation and the Moslem clergy had been put under the control of the state bureaucracy. Finally, the new Republic, by a constitutional amendment, had withdrawn its recognition of Islam as a state religion.

The institutional and legal reforms introduced by the Kemalist regime disestablished the influential positions of the *ulema* hierarchy in the political, judicial, and educational fields. As salaried employees of the state without an autonomous organisational base, the religious func-tionaries had no means of effective opposition to the secular foundations of the Republic. However, in later years, they did play an important role in mobilising electoral support for parties with more relaxed policies on the question of secularism. The *Sufi şeyhs*, on the other hand, enjoyed much greater independence from the state and sustained their influence among the masses. Although outlawed, the *tarikats* nevertheless continued their activities underground. Some of them were responsible for organising the uprisings against the Republic during its formative years (Özek, 1964). After the transition to democratic politics in 1946, the *şeyhs* became influential figures in party competition as they were able to draft the votes of large areas of the country for parties of their choice.

The Kemalist reforms were internalised mostly by the élite. For the rural masses, the culture of the urban-educated élite was incom-prehensible and alien. Despite the lip-service paid to the importance of the peasantry, not much was done to improve the socio-economic conditions of the countryside during the one-party years. Hence, opposition to the regime was often within a religious context, the only meaningful point of reference for a peasant population which had remained at the margin of main currents of change. During the early decades of the Republic, this opposition took the form of outright rebellions which were instigated in the name of Islam. After the Second World War, it was expressed through the party system as a number of parties emerged which sought electoral success by politicising the religious question.[2] However, despite their efforts to build a mass following by politicising the religious issue, none of these parties (founded between 1945 and 1950) was able to play a significant role in national politics. The Democratic Party (1945–60) by contrast, though remaining faithful to the principles of the Kemalist secular state, was successful in mobilising popular support and gaining power in part by appealing to the religious sentiment and through a rapprochement with religious groups such as the *Nurcus*.

The secularisation programme of the one-party period gave way to a lasting controversy. The Kemalist understanding of secularism was unique. Rather than separating church and state,[3] the new regime opted for state dominance over religious institutions. In an Islamic country, this was double heresy. The concept of secularism itself is heretical in Islam since Islamic teaching makes no differentiation between state and society, politics and religion (Gibb, 1962; Rahman, 1966). Kemalism not only made that differentiation but also reversed the order of importance between the sacred and political realms. Secularisation as state policy, therefore, had a built-in tendency to envisage oppositional politicisation of Islam.

The National Salvation Party was established in 1972 against this background. Since the mid-1960s, the importance of religion as a political issue had considerably faded away as the electorate was increasingly politicised on a Left/Right spectrum. The NSP, accordingly, emerged with a political platform which sought to place the Islamic appeal within a wider context. The NSP occupies a distinct place among other parties which have, at one time or another, entered the political arena with a similar concern for the religious question. The NSP is the only explicitly religious party in the history of the Republic with a well-defined ideology and a relatively successful electoral record.

The members of Constituent Assembly convened after the military intervention of 1960 sought to prevent the recurrence of the politicisation of religion under the Democratic Party administrations. Previous legal prohibitions on the use of religion for political purposes were reaffirmed and strengthened in Article 19 of the Constitution of 1961 which read as follows:

> No individual can exploit religion in order to change the social, economic, political, or legal structure of the state according to religious principles, neither can he use religion to further his personal or political interests.

When considering the ideology of the NSP, it is important to bear in mind that its leaders had decided to operate within the framework of the 1961 Constitution. This is especially so because the predecessor of the NSP, the National Order Party (*Milli Nizam Partisi*), founded by

Erbakan, had been dissolved by the Constitutional Court in 1972 for violating the prohibition against the use of religion for political purpose (Toprak, 1981, pp. 98–9).

The ideological stand of the NSP, to a large measure, rested on the importance it placed on history. This was in line with the Islamic emphasis on history as theologically significant: the Islamic state was said to have the historical mission of establishing a powerful community of believers which reflected divine design.[4] The NSP's view of history was central to an understanding of its political vision, a vision which saw an almost religious calling of world leadership for Turkey. In conformity with the Islamic stress on history, the NSP considered the re-establishment of a powerful Moslem nation as its major goal. However, the prerequisite of national strength for the NSP was the creation of a common historical consciousness. Reminiscent of the Islamist school at the turn of the century, the NSP pointed out the need to re-evaluate the process of westernisation. In that context, the party leadership attempted to explain the reasons for Turkey's present state of underdevelopment despite a distinguished imperial past.

According to Erbakan and other leaders of the NSP, an adequate analysis of this problem could only be undertaken after a correct appraisal of the relationship between Turkey and the West. That relationship, the NSP argued, resulted in the adoption of misplaced priorities. On the one hand, the Turks had chosen to imitate the West in an area where Western civilisation was at its weakest, namely, its cultural orientation. On the other hand, they had been unsuccessful in borrowing Western technology. The westernisation effort, therefore, had led to national decline to the extent that a common cultural heritage had been rejected while at the same time the country had failed to industrialise.

Like the Islamists of the late nineteenth and early twentieth centuries, the NSP saw no correlation between Western civilisation and technology. On the contrary, it found the present level of Western technological advancement an historical irony. Erbakan, for instance, argued that the bases of Western technology could be traced back to the scholarly achievements of the Moslem world between the seventh and fourteenth centuries. The West had borrowed this accumulation and built on it without, however, giving reference to the original sources. Hence, it was historically erroneous to claim that technical innovation had originated in the West, a claim which gained legitimacy only as a result of Western cultural imperialism. For the NSP, however, progress involved spiritual wealth. The West could not sustain its progressive development given its cultural poverty. Western knowledge and technology, therefore, could no longer advance. It was at this point that the Moslem world in general and the Turkish nation in particular could pick up their distinguished historical mission of world leadership. The unique key for the success of that mission passed through the revival of Islam's historic role in Turkish society (Erbakan, 1975a, pp. 6–42; 1975b, pp. 65–89).[5]

This plea for the re-creation of the cultural past, however, only involved matters that did not enter the realm of illegality within the framework of existing laws, laws which forbade the use of religion for political ends. This meant, for example, that the NSP could not make an appeal for a return to a theocratic state. It certainly did not express any such objective, although this could have been for tactical reasons. Islamic revival for the NSP, therefore, meant the retraditionalisation of the social and cultural milieu. In that context, the NSP strongly criticised the Western orientation of the Turkish élite in terms of social customs, mores, values, and intellectual outlook.

In addition to history, the family and social life were major components of the NSP's concept of culture. The party leadership repeatedly voiced its concern about what it considered to be an 'illness' among the élite of imitating Western cultural patterns. Such imitation the NSP argued, resulted in the disappearance of traditional family life and social relationships. Look around and witness the decadence: parents no longer had authority over their children; the young lacked respect for the old; the youth was impious; promiscuity and pornography were tolerated; women followed Western fashions which were designed to be sexually suggestive; nightclubs were mushrooming everywhere initiating the youth into drinking and sexual liberty.[6] Cultural life fared no better. Television, movie, and theatre programmes were heavily biassed in favour of Western productions which inflicted corrupt social norms. 'An actor who plays the role of an unfaithful husband', complained Erbakan, 'gets a prize for distinguished acting'. He promised that when the NSP assumed power, a yet-to-be-written play on the seige of Istanbul by Mehmed the Conqueror would replace 'Fiddler on the Roof' (Milliyet, 1 October 1973).

Indeed, the party attempted to tackle some of these issues while in power as a partner in various coalition governments. For example, the sculpture of a nude in an Istanbul square, which the party press had called 'the sculpture of shame', was lifted by the order of the Minister of the Interior, then an NSP member, on the grounds that it was a piece of pornographic material (*Milli Gazete*, 20 March 1974). A television documentary about the Amazon tribes, which included shots of naked bodies, prompted the Minister of Justice, again an NSP member, to take legal action against the General-Director of the state-owned television with the charge of encouraging obscenity (*Milli Gazete*, 24 October 1974). An application for government credit to construct a tourist resort was rejected by the Ministry of Commerce, then under NSP control, on the basis that tourists corrupt the morality of the Turkish people (*Milli Gazete* 24 March 1974). Restaurants and sandwich stands without a permit for sale of alcoholic beverages were forbidden to sell beer, which did not classify under that category previously, by a directive of the one-time Minister of the Interior of the NSP (*Milli Gazete*, 12 March 1974). The NSP's Minister of Justice started a nationwide campaign against pornography which was much publicised in the party press (*Milli Gazete*, 12 May 1974). The wives of NSP leaders started a new fashion which the party apparently saw fit for Moslem women: maxi skirts, long sleeves, and scarfed heads, with the scarf tied in a special way so as not to show the hair. NSP parliament arians with a background in law took up the defence of a woman lawyer who had been expelled from the Ankara Bar Association for dressing in the NSP fashion. One of her lawyers in the lawsuit that she filed against the Bar, a leading MP of the NSP, issued a statement in the party press in which he pointed out that 'the scarf of the Turkish woman is as sacred as the Turkish flag' (*Milli Gazete*, 25 February 1974). The NSP-controlled ministries and government offices became famous for their special rooms which were reserved as places of worship for the personnel who performed the *namaz* (daily prayers) (*Milli Gazete*, 12 September 1974).

The NSP, then, advocated the reaffirmation of a Moslem way of life. According to the party view, a right kind of educational policy was the most important vehicle for carrying out this goal. As the NSP saw it, Turkey's lag in development could be traced back to the educational philosophy adopted by Turkish governments. On the one hand, this philosophy centred on the repudiation of national history and culture. On the other hand, it was based on the imitation of Western civilisation and technology. Such warped objectives had produced an educational system which failed miserably to encourage creativity. At the same time, it had led to a lack of competence in both arts and sciences. The prerequisite of technological advancement was originality rather than imitation which in turn was the prerequisite of regaining historical greatness through rapid industrialisation (Erbakan, 1975b, pp. 61–116; *Milli Gazete*).

Indeed, the problem of industrialisation occupied the most important dimension of party ideology. It related to the NSP's assessment of Turkish history. Turkey had lost its leading position as a great power because it had failed to industrialise. The NSP promised to initiate rapid development through revitalising indigenous cultural values which would supply the necessary spiritual and moral qualities for a new work ethic (Erbakan, 1975a, pp. 68–111; 1975b, pp. 193–227; *Milli Gazete*). The NSP's commitment to industrialisation was repeatedly emphasised by the party spokesmen. During its tenure in office as a partner in three coalition governments between 1973 and 1978, the NSP controlled the Ministry of Industry and Technology. The party's vision of a powerful industrial nation found expression in a number of campaigns for the building of heavy industry and the construction of factories in each administrative district. Although such campaigns remained limited to promises for the future, the party propagandists nevertheless claimed to have initiated an unprecedented industrialisation process which was compared with mobilisation for war (*Milli Gazete*, 6 September 1975). As part of this effort, Erbakan toured the country for a number of opening ceremonies of industrial complexes. The press reports, however, discredited the party claims by pointing out that most of these complexes did not even exist on paper since they had not been included among the projects of the State Planning Organisation (*Milli Gazete*, July to September 1976). In fact, the party's emphasis on industrialisation was not backed up by sound econonic policies. The party leadership did not spell out a detailed economic programme for rapid industrialisation. In that respect, the NSP's plea for industrialisation remained largely limited to a Weberian-type expectation that the affinity between values and economic development will suffice for a break-through.

The NSP referred to its ideological stand as the 'National Outlook' (Erbakan, 1975b) with the claim that the party's point of view was the only indigenous political philosophy with historical roots. In that context, Erbakan and other NSP leaders were quite vocal in their criticisms of major parties on the Left and the Right on the grounds that both of these ideologies were Western-based and hence alien to the national experience.[7]

Indeed, the National Salvation Party occupied a unique place within the Turkish political spectrum. In a sense, the NSP reflected the voice of the Third World. Characteristically, it saw the world within the framework of the cultural and economic imperialism of the West. In foreign policy, however, this view took the form of a Moslem parochialism. Rather than unity with the Third World, the NSP favoured co-operation among the Moslem countries. Such preference was largely due to the party's analysis of foreign affairs within a religious baggage. For example, the NSP strongly opposed Turkey's entrance into the Common Market. One major reason for this opposition was the party's perception of the EEC as a Christian-dominated organisation which sought to 'melt the Moslem Turkish nation within Christian Europe' (Erbakan, 1975b, pp. 227–64). The NSP, accordingly, proposed the creation of a Moslem Economic Community. In a parallel vein, Erbakan called for the acceptance of an Islamic dinar as a common unit of currency, the founding of a United Moslem Nations as an alternative to the UN, and a Moslem version of the NATO (Erbakan, 1975b, pp. 265–70; 1979). For the NSP, the unity of the Moslem world, however, was dependent on the abandonment of a pro-Western foreign policy by the countries involved. The NSP saw the recent developments in Iran as an important step towards the realisation of close co-operation among Moslem nations and suggested that other Moslem states follow the Iranian example of cutting-off ties with the West in order to end a 'master–servant relationship' and to begin a new era of Moslem interdependence based on brotherhood (*Cumhuriyet*, 1–2 August 1979).

The National Salvation Party, then, saw the process of modernisation in unique terms. The party's stand on that issue can be seen as a revival of the pre-Republican search for an Islamic model of modernity. The NSP questioned the mainstream of Turkish political thought at its core by rejecting the definition of modernisation as synonomous with westernisation. It combined this ideological distinctiveness with sharp critiques of governmental policies concerning underprivileged groups in Turkish society. It was thus able to make a serious inroad into political competition by receiving the support of a sizeable sector of the electorate.

The NSP's relative strength within the Turkish party system, in addition to its ideological appeal, also stemmed from its organisational network. As in the case of most other Turkish parties, the NSP's branches in Turkey's sixty-seven provinces were not very active in between election periods. The party headquarters of the Istanbul branch, for example, were closed most of the time. Its chairman, Mehmet Okul, was the general-manager of a co-operative of flower growers. He accepted visits concerning party affairs at the co-operative building where he kept no documents on the party. In fact, he gave the impression that his party affiliation was a pastime hobby rather than a professional job. He seemed little informed about the party's activities and organisation, although one may suppose, however, that he did not choose to appear so as a measure of caution in conversation with non-party people.

In contrast to this typically intermittent activity which reached its peak at election periods, the NSP maintained an ongoing network of close ties with a number of youth and professional groups. Of these, the most important was the *Akıncılar* (The Raiders), a youth organisation with its headquarters in Ankara and with approximately 600 branches throughout Turkey. It was established as an NSP alternative to the highly politicised Turkish youth in various organisations on the Left and Right. The NSP also had organic ties with the National Turkish Students' Union (*Milli Türk Talebe Birliği*), the oldest organisation of university students among several others. Erbakan and other NSP parliamentarians were frequent guest-speakers at its meetings. In addition, the party opened several youth centres (*MSP Gençlik Lokalleri*) where young people who were sympathetic to the NSP were educated in the party ideology. Women's associations, on the other hand, were not established, although envisaged, probably due to the ambiguity of the party leadership on the question of women's status in a Moslem country.

There were a number of professional groups with which the NSP established close contacts although all of them were minor associations within the related professions. Several can be mentioned here: The Writers' Union of Turkey (*Türkiye Yazarlar Birliği*), not to be confused with the prestigious and powerful Syndicate of Turkish Writers (*Türk Yazarlar Sendikasi*); The Union of Technical Personnal (*Teknik Elemanlar Birliği*); The Cultural Foundation of Economists (*İktisatçılar Kültür Vakfı*); The Organisation of Idealist Teachers (*Mefkureci Öğretmenler Derneği*); and the Society for the Propagation of Knowledge (*İlim Yayma Cemiyeti*), knowledge, in this context, connoting religious studies.

The NSP also attempted to establish organisational ties with the working-class and, for this purpose, founded the NSP Workers' Commissions (*MSP İşçi Komisyonları*) with approximately 300 branches in various industrial centres. According to the party daily, *Milli Gazete*, these commissions aimed at solving job-related problems of individual workers. In addition, the party had an affiliated labour union, the *Hak-İş* Confederation, although its membership and its strength within various branches of the industry was limited. There were similar attempts to organise migrant Turkish workers in Germany through the Organisations of the National Outlook in Germany (*Milli Görüş Almanya Teşkilatları*) with headquarters in Cologne and with approximately 170 branches in other German cities. Teams of these workers visited Turkey during elections in order to help in the NSP campaign.[8]

The party appeared to have developed informal ties with the *Sufi* orders and *tarikat*-based movements. In terms of electoral mobilisation, the NSP's rumoured connections with one such movement, the *Nurcus*, during its formative years, and later with the *Naksibendi* order, probably enabled the party to strengthen its informal channels of communication. The party leadership also attempted to build a patronage network through the placement of its own clientele into the various ministerial and other governmental posts during its stay in power as a partner in three coalition governments between 1973 and 1978.

The NSP had a relatively successful electoral record. It entered elections at the national level twice, polling 11.8 per cent of the total vote in 1973 and 8.6 per cent in 1977. It emerged from the 1973 elections as the third strongest party and, despite the decreases in the percentage of its votes in the following election, it was able to keep its ranking. As such, the party was indispensable for the formation of coalition governments, a factor which led Erbakan to boast at several occasions that the NSP had the key, as on the party emblem, to open government doors. Indeed, the party participated in Bulent Ecevit's coalition government of 1973–4, and in Suleyman Demirel's first and second National Front governments of 1975–7 and 1977–8, respectively.[9] To understand this sudden prominence and success, we need to examine the social background of the leaders of the NSP and the bases of social support for the party.

The leadership ranks of the party were predominantly professional men and government employees, especially teachers. Table 6.1 shows the professions of the NSP members elected to the Assembly in 1973.

The picture presented by the professional backgrounds of the 450 NSP candidates in the 1973 election is consistent with the one presented in the Table 6.1 although the representation of industry and commerce is stronger (21.2 per cent) and that of clerics weaker (2.8 per cent) (Toprak, 1981, p. 106). In view of the disestablishment of the *ulema* half a century earlier, it is worth noting that although there were no more than six clerics among the forty-eight members of the NSP in the Assembly in 1973, more detailed background information indicates that of the forty-eight, nineteen, or 39.4 per cent were directly involved in religion, either through family background (one member, for instance, was the son of a sheikh), or through education (quite a few were graduates of *İmam-Hatip* schools or of the Faculty of Divinity) or through membership of religious associations (such as associations for the promotion of *Qur'an*

TABLE 6.1     *Professions of NSP members elected to the assembly, 1973 election*

| Profession | Number | Percentage |
|---|---|---|
| Free professions | 27 | 55.8 |
|   Lawer | 10 | (20.8) |
|   Doctor-pharmacist | 4 | (8.3) |
|   Architect-engineer | 9 | (18.7) |
|   Journalist | 1 | (2.0) |
|   Contractor | 1 | (2.0) |
|   Economist | 1 | (2.0) |
|   Accountant | 1 | (2.0) |
| Government service | 10 | 20.7 |
|   University teacher | 3 | (6.2) |
|   High school teacher | 6 | (12.5) |
|   Retired officer | 1 | (2.0) |
| Commerce and industry | 5 | 10.4 |
| Clerics | 6 | 12.5 |

SOURCE   *Milliyet*, October 19, 1973.
Note: Percentages may not add up to 100 because of rounding up.

courses or the construction of mosques) (*Milliyet*, 19 October 1973).

What these and other background data show is a group of people who are, on the whole, well-educated, professionally successful, presumably of middle or upper-middle class income, and relatively young. They do not fit the image of the stereotype religious fanatic. Neither do they fit the category of men who have been adversely affected by modernisation and turned to religion as a means of registering their discontent.

Necmettin Erbakan's own personal background reflects the general characteristics of the NSP leadership that I have outlined above. He came from a notable provincial family. His father was a civil servant, a judge, who was an ardent supporter of Republicanism. Necmettin was one of six children in the family. He had his primary-school education in Trabzon and his high-school education in Istanbul. He was an outstanding student and graduated from Istanbul *Lycée* with honours. He then went to the prestigious Technical University in Istanbul. He received his BSc in 1948 and subsequently entered into a university career. He finished his PhD within three years and, on the basis of an outstanding thesis, was awarded a grant to continue his postdoctoral studies in the Federal Republic of Germany. Upon his return, he became an associate professor in 1953 and a full professor in 1965.

It is more difficult to draw a picture of the NSP supporters because of the absence of survey data. Nevertheless, the analysis of electoral data can be indicative of the social location of the NSP supporters. Election statistics show that the National Salvation Party received its support overwhelmingly from rural areas. In the 1973 and 1977 elections, 67.2 per cent and 63.2 per cent of all the votes cast for the NSP, respectively, came from rural districts. The NSP's strength also displays an inverse relationship with higher levels of development. In both the 1973 and the 1977 elections, the NSP did better in the less-developed regions of the country, most notably in East and Central Anatolia. In addition, a distinguishing characteristic of the administrative districts which turned out a high percentage of votes for the NSP is their rapid rate of urbanisation and development.[10]

The NSP's appeal to rural and relatively underdeveloped communities which, however, are in a process of change needs some explanation. Ahmet Yücekök, in a study of religious organisations in Turkey (Yücekök, 1971), has argued that religiosity functions differently in regions with varying levels of development. In the less-developed areas, religious ties reinforce dominant power relationships. In the more-developed areas, it becomes a means of protest for individuals who have lost their economic base as a result of rapid change. In the case of NSP voters, Serif Mardin has hypothesised that individuals who have not been assimilated into the 'modernist centre' either in social or economic terms probably make up the bulk of the NSP supporters, the prototype of which is a small merchant (Mardin, 1973; Landau, 1976, pp. 1–57).

If we combine the two observations, the picture that emerges suggests that the NSP appealed either to rural people who have remained in their traditional communities or to individuals who have a marginal status in terms of their cultural orientation and economic activity. In rural, underdeveloped areas, the NSP vote probably indicated support for tradition. As I have earlier pointed out, rural communities in Turkey were much slower in accepting the secular reforms initiated by the Republican regime. With the advent of electoral competition, the peasant vote predominantly went to opposition parties which were critical of the secularisation policies of the one-party period. Although the religious issue cannot be considered the most important determinant of electoral success, it nevertheless played an important role in the mobilisation of the countryside. An explicitly Islamic party, such as the NSP, has a good chance of capturing the allegiance of some of the rural electorate. Moreover, in the traditional rural setting, the *tarikats* have powerful networks and can play an influential role in party competition by throwing their weight to a party which, for whatever reason, they choose to support. If the NSP indeed had connections with the *Naksibendi* order, this would partially explain its strength in the East Anatolia region. On the other hand, the fact that the NSP's support also came from rapidly changing communities may indicate a protest vote by individuals who have been unable to make the transition to new kinds of economic activity. For example, it is probably not by chance that the electoral districts of Istanbul where the NSP received the highest percentage of its votes are centres of small merchants, artisans, and shopkeepers.[11]

As a postscript, it should be added that the National Salvation Party's political life came to an end after the military coup of September 1980, which suspended the activities of *all* political parties. The present military authorities are resolved to re-establish the saliency of Kemalist principles in Turkish political life as they understand them and, in this context, they seem determined to follow, once again, a strict secularist line. In February 1981, a military court started a lawsuit against Erbakan and thirty-three members of the NSP's General Administrative Board with the charge that the party had worked towards the overthrow of the existing structures of the secular state in order to establish a theocracy (*Milliyet*, 25 February and 27–30 April 1981). Although the NSP neither attempted a takeover of the government by force nor voiced any overt intention to establish a theocratic state, the open-ended nature of existing laws, which forbid the use of religion for political purposes, allowed the military court to furnish enough evidence against the party. Erbakan was sentenced to four years of imprisonment and twenty-two other members of the NSP received prison sentences ranging from two to three years (*Milliyet*, 25 February 1983).

The NSP emerged on the Turkish political scene as a party which successfully defends the rights of people with religious concerns to be represented within the framework of a pluralist political system. For the first time in the history of the Republic, the NSP legitimised the demands of people who search for an Islamic alternative to Western models of development. The NSP phenomenon demonstrates that the Turkish political élite have travelled a long way in accepting that religious interests, like all others, can be legitimate and find voice in the political process. However, the NSP's end indicates the precarious nature of tolerance for Islamic parties in modern Turkey.

# NOTES

1. Sabri, 1977, p. 95. For similar views on the question of westernisation by a leading member of the Islamist school and a prominent statesman of the Second Constitutional Period, see Said Halim Paşa, n.d. For a detailed study of the Islamist movement, see Tunaya, 1962.
2. Of the twenty-four parties founded between 1945 and 1950, at least eight had explicit references to Islam in their programmes. For a list of these and their programmatic outlook, see Tunaya, 1962, pp. 190–2. The most important religious party that emerged during this period was the Nation Party founded in 1948. Although not within this category, the Democratic Party of 1945–60 also used the religious issue for electoral purposes.
3. I use the term 'church and state' here in a heuristic, technical sense. Otherwise, the church concept does not exist in Islam.
4. Donald Smith (1970) has argued that whether a religion is historical or ahistorical is theoretically significant from the standpoint of the relationship between church and state. On the historical nature of Islam, see Smith, 1957, esp. pp. 11–46.
5. Also see the text of Erbakan's speech in Erzurum in *Milli Gazete*, 9 September 1973.
6. Repeated statements of the NSP leaders on these issues can be found in the *Milli Gazete*, which is a party daily.
7. See Abdi İpekçi's interview with Erbakan in *Milliyet*, 18 October 1973.
8. The preceding information on the NSP's organisational network was gathered mostly from the *Milli Gazete*. Its reliability was checked from the archives of the Istanbul daily, *Hürriyet*. Mehmet Okul, the chairman of the party's Istanbul branch, supplied the figures for the number of branches of the *Akıncılar* and the *Milli Görüş Almanya Teşkilatları*.
9. The Republican People's Party/The National Salvation Party Coalition Government was formed in January 1974 and lasted until September 1974. The first National Front Government of Suleyman Demirel was formed in March 1975. It included the Justice Party (JP), the National Salvation Party (NSP), the National Action Party (NAP), and the Republican Reliance Party (RRP). It ended in June 1977. The Second National Front Government of Demirel was formed in August 1977, with the participation of the JP, the NSP and the NAP. It ended in January 1978.
10. For election statistics, see Başbakanlık Devlet İstatistik Enstitüsü, *14 Ekim 1973 Milletvekili Seçimi Sonuçları* (Ankara: Başbakanlık Devlet İstatistik Enstitüsü Matbaasi, 1974) and *5 Haziran 1977 Milletvekili Seçimi Sonuçları* (Ankara: Başbakanlık Devlet İstatistik Enstitüsü Matbaası, 1978). For an index of development of all Turkey's sixty-seven administrative districts which the State Planning Organisation has put out, see Türkiye Cumhuriyeti Başbakanlık Devlet Planlama Teşkilatı, *Türkiye'de İller İtibariyle Sosyo-Ekonomik Gelişmişlik Endeksi (1963–7)* (Ankara, 1970).
11. Beykoz, Eminönü, Eyüp and Fatih are the four districts in question. For election statistics, see note 10 above.

# 7 Ideology, Social Class and Islamic Radicalism in Modern Egypt

## ERIC DAVIS

One of the most significant phenomena in the contemporary Middle East is the increased strength of Islam as a political force. Under the banner of Islam, militant religious movements have toppled the Pahlavi dynasty in Iran while threatening the stability of secular regimes in Syria, the Sudan and Iraq. In Egypt, Islamic militants were responsible for the assassination of the most prominent Arab leader, Anwar al-Sadat. Even the arch-defender of Islamic orthodoxy, the Saudi monarchy, has not been immune from attack. It has found itself challenged by tribally-based religious groups which claim that Islam is not being protected from the encroachment of secular westernisation. Given their increasing political influence, the paucity of information and the conceptual confusion surrounding them underline the need for a better understanding of Islamic radical movements.

By far the most powerful radical Islamic movement in the Middle East is the Moslem Brotherhood which was founded in Egypt in 1928 and subsequently spread throughout the Arab world. Although studied from an organisational and ideological viewpoint, there is still a relatively limited understanding of the continuing attraction that the Brotherhood and its militant offshoots holds for large segments of the Egyptian populace. To broaden our understanding of the relationship between Islam and politics in Egypt, this study focuses on three central questions. First, what social strata are attracted to Islamic radicalism and why? Second, why do these strata interpret Islam in the way that they do? Third, how do radical Islamic political organisations relate to the dominant groups in Egyptian society and what chances do they have of seizing power?

134

Two types of approaches to the study of the relationship between Islamic radicalism and politics can be ascertained. One such approach or framework might be referred to as the 'ideational' model. This approach views organisations such as the Moslem Brotherhood in terms of the development of Islamic thought. In this view, the origins of Islamic militancy in Egypt are to be found in the Islamic reform movement of the late nineteenth century whose leaders were Jamal al-Din al-Afghani and Muhammad 'Abduh. The primary purpose of this movement was to return to the fundamentals of Islam. By removing centuries of unnecessary exegesis, the basic principles of Islam would once again be visible and would provide the most effective weapon with which to confront Western imperialism. Under the tutelage of Shaykh Muhammad 'Abduh, greater emphasis was placed upon the role of reason in religious interpretation. During the early part of the twentieth century, Rashid Rida and the *al-Salafiyya* movement, the disciples of al-Afghani and 'Abduh, redirected their attention away from the role of reason to a fundamentalist interpretation of Islam. It was this particular school of thought, the *al-Salafiyya* movement, which profoundly influenced the thought of the Moslem Brotherhood's founder, Hasan al-Banna.

This ideational approach to the relationship between Islam and politics was heavily influenced by the Orientalist tradition in Middle East studies and was most prominent in the writings of H. A. R. Gibb (Gibb, 1947). An implicit assumption was that tendencies towards Islamic radicalism were directly correlated with the penetration of Western values into the Moslem world. While not articulated as such, the ideational model posited a 'decay thesis' which juxtaposed a reified Islam to a dynamic system of Western values. Islam was seen as passing through various phases or stages. In its initial phase, Islam achieved its ascendency through positing a rigid belief system which inspired its adherents to victory over infidel forces. In its second phase, under the Umayyid and Abbasid caliphates, Islam attained its Golden Age. Subsequent to the closing of the door of *ijtihad* and the decline of the Abbasid caliphate, Islam entered a long period of intellectual decline and stagnation. With the Napoleonic invasion of Egypt and the penetration of Western values, the process of decay was accelerated as a rigidified Islamic world-view made a futile attempt to cope with a dynamic and secular Western system of values, but in vain. It was this process of decay which al-Afghani, and particularly 'Abduh, hoped to end by stressing the role of reason in religious interpretation. Instead of producing a reformist Islam, the logic of this movement ultimately led it to the radical fundamentalism of *Ikhwan* ideologues such as Hasan al-Banna.

At one level, this model is very seductive since it offers a very integrated argument which is placed in an historical perspective. Nevertheless, it suffers many conceptual flaws. First and foremost of these is its emphasis on seeing change in the realm of ideas. This leads to a concentration on the thought of major Islamic thinkers and hence to an élitist bias. How this thought resonates with the needs of the society at large is largely left to the imagination. As regards Moslem Brotherhood and other Islamic radical groups, this means that we learn much about the ideologues of the movement but little about its mass following.

A second conceptual flaw is the tendency to view Islamic society (assuming for a moment that such a notion is of conceptual utility) in terms of decay, breakdown and social-pathology. Rather than seeing Islamic radicalism as an attempt to regenerate a corporate unity that repairs the breakdown of traditional institutions, such as the extended family, and to help its adherents cope with rapid social change, it is viewed as a pathological and xenophobic response to alien views with which is refuses to come to terms.[1]

Finally, this approach fails to stratify Islamic societies. Thus all Moslems are lumped together as one undifferentiated social unit. This prevents an understanding of why some Moslems and not others, are attracted to Islamic political movements. It is precisely this problem which the 'sociological' model attempts to confront.

The sociological model may be designated as such because it seeks to account for the social bases and recruitment patterns of Islamic radical groups. The early studies of the Moslem Brotherhood in Egypt said little or nothing about the social composition of the movement. In the most comprehensive analysis of the Moslem Brotherhood to date, Richard Mitchell (1969) offers a limited amount of data on members arrested during the late 1940s and after the purported assassination attempt on President Nasser in 1954. In a study completed in 1969, it was possible to expand on Mitchell's data and construct a sample of over 650 Moslem Brothers arrested between 1947 and 1954. Through the analysis of these data, an effort was made to interrelate such variables as occupation, education, place of birth, age, political activity and intensity of commitment to the Moslem Brotherhood (Davis, 1970).

Most recently, Sa'd al-Din Ibrahim, conducted a similar type of study through interviews with imprisoned members of *al-Jama'at al-Muslimin* (*Jama'at al-takfir wa'l-hijra*).[2] This research illuminated many fascinating aspects about the social backgrounds of those drawn to Islamic radical movements, such as early socialisation, which are much less clear from statistical data gained from trial records (Ibrahim, 1980).

The sociological model proved to be of greater conceptual utility than the ideational approach in demonstrating that the Moslem Brotherhood and its offshoots in Egypt recruited from a particular stratum of society, and in offering hypotheses to explain this recruitment pattern. It also introduced, albeit implicitly, a notion of process or change. By arguing that Islamic militants were drawn from members of the urban lower class who were both horizontally and vertically mobile, and who were hostile to the religious establishment and Egypt's political class, these studies posed questions which could only be adequately answered by understanding the life-experiences of Islamic militants *over time*. In other words, if Islamic militants were predominantly recruited from recent migrants to urban areas, what caused these individuals to leave the countryside? What factors caused them to seek upward mobility and why were they so hostile to the *'ulama* and to those who control the state? Unlike the ideational model which posited no more than a vaguely defined struggle between the values of occident and orient, the sociological model introduced the notion of conflict among social groups within Egypt and suggested that only through a more defined historical perspective, one that was not limited to a formalistic study of ideology, could the sources and ultimate outcome of this conflict be understood.

Despite its advance over the ideational approach, the sociological model suffers its own analytic shortcomings. If the ideational approach to Islamic radicalism tells us little about the social bases of its adherents, then the sociological approach is anaemic in its ability to explain ideology. Ideology is either viewed in terms of a crude materialism or in terms of psycho-social needs. In one instance, it is a reflection of class interests – a response to thwarted ambitions for upward mobility – and in another, a reflection of the social strains caused by the difficulties facing urban migrants steeped in tradition who are trying to adapt to the pressures of city life. This means that the internal structure of Islamic radical thought, causes underlying its changes over time, its emotive power, and the political constraints and advantages it bestows on its adherents are never fully discussed.

A second criticism of the sociological model is its failure to provide an historical context within which to situate the growth and development of Islamic radicalism. Even though the hypotheses offered by this model suggest an historical perspective, it remains implicit and is never clearly articulated. The inadequacy of the sociological model becomes manifest when one asks the following question: why is it that Islamic radical thought is anti-imperialist and largely concerned with socio-economic issues during the 1940s and 1950s while during the 1960s and 1970s, such thought places primary emphasis on symbols such as corruption, family socialisation, sexual mores and cultural authenticity – symbols which are primarily cultural rather than economic in nature?

In order to confront the criticisms of the aforementioned models, and to achieve a more comprehensive understanding of Islamic radicalism in Egypt, we propose a structural model centred on the concepts of accumulation, legitimation and authenticity. At this point, it is only possible to sketch the rudiments of such a model. Its advantage over prior conceptualisations of Islamic radicalism is that first, it integrates the study of ideology and social structure; second, it studies these phenomena over time; and third, it situates the study of Islamic militancy in a global or world-market perspective. Islamic radical movements cannot be adequately studied as a phenomenon disembodied from its larger social setting. Unless one focuses on these movements in relationship to the accumulation process, and to the Egyptian class structure and the competing ideologies articulated by groups within that structure, only partial conceptualisations of Islamic radicalism will be obtained.

In seeking to integrate ideology and social class, and to place the study of Islamic radicalism within a larger historical and global perspective, our model emphasises three broad hypotheses. The first of these hypotheses centres on the problem of differential accumulation. The central dilemma facing Egyptian society during the nineteenth and especially the twentieth century has been the inability of social resources to keep pace with an ever-increasing population. In contrast to the general impoverishment of the populace, a rural notable stratum of 'umad and mashayikh was able to capitalise upon the rapid expansion of long-stable cotton cultivation and was transformed into an agrarian *bourgeoisie* by the late 1800s. The process of differential accumulation abated somewhat following the over-throw of the monarchy in 1952 and the implementation of Nasserite 'socialism'. However, the process began again in earnest following the onset of the 'open door' policy (*al-infitah*) of the 1970s. The widening gap between rich and poor needs to be seen as a key element in providing a fertile climate for the growth of militant Islamic political groups.

The problem or crisis of legitimation is directly related to that of differential accumulation. It can be argued that the impact of the global economy was the central element in the process of differential accumulation by providing the market demand for long-staple cotton. It can also be argued that world market forces, aided by the inherent difficulties of capital formation and by both colonial and neo-colonial pressures, prevented either capitalist or 'socialist' (state capitalist) policies from effectively confronting Egypt's development problems. In contributing to the de-legitimisation of both capitalist and socialist development models, world market-forces contributed to the crisis of authenticity by creating an ideological vacuum which a militant political interpretation of Islam could fill.[3] Both the liberal model of develop-ment of the pre-1952 era and the state capitalism of the Nasser period failed adequately to confront Egypt's development problems or the contradiction of the greater accumulation of wealth in relatively fewer hands and the concomitant increasing pauperisation of the bulk of society. With the deepening of underdevelopment, the political class found it more difficult to legitimate its rule as it had been unable to solve the pressing problems of the politically conscious elements outside the dominant power structure.

It is our contention that the increasing contradiction between differential accumulation and decreasing legitimacy produces a crisis of authenticity. The failure of liberalism and state capitalism (which was referred to by the Nasser regime as Arab socialism), both of which are perceived as imported development models, stimulated an introspection among the politically-conscious strata of Egyptian society that were only marginally benefiting from the accumulation process. Whether or not the attempt to characterise liberalism and secular socialism as 'imported' value systems (that is, intrinsically alien to Egyptian society) is a valid one is not the main concern here. Rather we are interested in the effort of a disaffected stratum to substitute its own ideology and development model for what Islamic militants perceive as the bankrupt ideologies of Western liberalism and secular socialism (that is, state capitalism).

Within this context, a much more comprehensive view of ideology can be articulated than is possible through either the ideational or sociologi-cal approaches. We would argue that ideology is a reflection of class interests in that Islamic radicals, as shall be seen, do come from a particular social class and do seek to acquire a greater share of society's material resources. Ideology can also be understood in terms of social strains as Islamic militants do seek refuge in Islam to sooth the alienation stemming from the status deprivation which they have experienced. The transference of their hostility on to scapegoats such as liberals, imperialists, communists and Jews, and their conviction that, by seeking refuge in 'true Islam', they will ultimately triumph over their infidel enemies is a classic syndrome associated with coping with social strains (Geertz, 1964).[4] Beyond this, however, ideology plays an important cognitive role for Islamic radicals. It does not merely offer a call to action and a palliative for their alienation. As a rich and complex cultural system which has developed over many centuries, Islam offers a vast symbolic network and thus a medium through which to interpret reality and to provide meaning for the believer. It offers a mechanism through which to re-establish a sense of community and corporate identity that will replace the fragmentation of traditional institutions, especially the extended family. In performing this cognitive function, Islam should not be viewed in the abstract. Islamic radicalism appeals to those who have suffered real or perceived deprivation. Its call to action differs sharply from the quietism of the establishment '*ulama*.

As interpreted and practised by the Moslem Brotherhood and its derivative organisations, Islamic radicalism should not be understood in terms of the concept of revival or resurgence but rather as the *politicisation* of Islam. It is not as if Egyptians have suddenly 're-discovered' Islam. Rather the power of the appeal of radical interpretations of Islam throughout the twentieth century, and especially after the Second World War, is a response to a conjuncture of processes: the increasing gap in income between rich and poor, the declining legitimacy of the political system, the rising consciousness of the urban middle class, the breakdown of traditional institutions and the need for orienting concepts that will allow disaffected sectors of Egyptian society to cope effectively with conditions of rapid social change.

## MEMBERSHIP AND RECRUITMENT

Most studies of Islamic radical movements in Egypt have told us very little about the social composition of their membership. Ideology has proved to be a poor predictor of the social bases of such movements. Given the often crude and simplistic interpretations of Islam in writings of Islamic radicals, the tendency was frequently to assume that the membership of organisations such as the Moslem Brotherhood was drawn from such traditional groups as petty religious functionaries, small merchants and artisans, or from the urban lumpenproletariat. Data obtained from trial records, newspapers, interviews and literary sources indicate that such a perception is misplaced. While it is possible to locate members of these groups in Islamic radical movements, they comprise only a small percentage of the overall membership.

Who then is the typical Moslem Brother or member of an Islamic radical organisation? A surprisingly consistent pattern that persists over almost a fifty year period is that radical groups appeal to, and recruit members from, the urban professional middle class, especially, in more recent times, engineers. Contrary to what might be expected, members seem to be those whom modernisation predicted would be secular in their world view given their high level of education, as Tables 7.1, 7.2, 7.3 and 7.4 indicate.

This occupational pattern requires important qualifications. Although the overwhelming portion of Islamic radicals are drawn from professional and white collar occupations, most are recent immigrants to urban areas.[5] Thus their occupations and educational backgrounds belie a traditional socialisation in the countryside. Another important consideration is that while radicals in urban areas tend to be professionals or part of a white collar salariat, those in the countryside tend to contain a heavy proportion of secondary school teachers.[6]

The high representation of teachers among rural members of the Moslem Brotherhood hints at the relationship between the seemingly secular occupations of urban radicals and rural social structure. Data indicate that urban members of Islamic radical groups are both horizontally and vertically mobile. In other words, these individuals are both migrants from rural areas and aspirants to higher social status as evidenced by their choice of professional education. Although the data are not conclusive, they point to a number of patterns. First, urban radicals frequently were former teachers themselves. Second, urban militants maintain links with their families in the countryside and thus with family members who continue in the teaching profession[7] Secondary school teacher-training entails considerable religious education which is an indicator of the traditional origins of religious radicals.[8] Data also indicate that urban and rural radicals come from a very conservative and tradition-oriented rural social stratum that is comprised of sub-groups of small merchant-artisans, religious functionaries and small landowners. Often the extended family contains elements of each sub-group in addition to providing members of the teaching profession.

From the emphasis on social pathology in much of the literature on 'Islamic revivalism', one would anticipate a considerable amount of disruption of family life among members of Islamic radical organisations. Indeed this is the impression that the Egyptian government

TABLE 7.1    *Occupations of members of the Guidance Council of the Moslem Brotherhood, 1934 and 1953*

| Occupation | 1934 | 1953 |
|---|---|---|
| Higher Civil Servants (inspectors/directors) | 0 | 4 |
| Lawyers | 0 | 2 |
| Men of religion | 5* | 2 |
| University professors | 0 | 2 |
| Urban notables | 2 | 0 |
| White collar employees | 3 | 0 |
| Secondary schoolteachers | 1 | 0 |
| Pharmacists | 0 | 1 |
| TOTAL | 11 | 11 |

* Three Members of this category, including Hasan al-Banna, were teachers in religious institutes.
SOURCE    Bayumi (1979) p. 87; Mitchell (1969) p. 329.

attempted to promote in the extensive press coverage which was given to the family life of Ahmad Shukri Mustafa, the leader (*al-amir*) of *Jama'at al-takfir wa'l-hijra*. While this is certainly true for some radicals, on the whole they seem to come from relatively stable family environments (Ibrahim, 1980, p. 440). The fact that those drawn to Islamic groups

TABLE 7.2    *Distribution by occupation of Moslem Brothers arrested in 1954*

| Occupation | Percentage of sample | |
|---|---|---|
| Professionals | 6.7 | (40) |
| Businessmen | 5.0 | (30) |
| Government employees | 13.1 | (76) |
| Politicians | 0.4 | (2) |
| Military men | 6.8 | (41) |
| Teachers | 12.3 | (74) |
| Men of religion | 0.5 | (3) |
| Students | 24.1 | (145) |
| Artisans/Small business/Petty functionary | 9.8 | (59) |
| Workers | 15.8 | (95) |
| Farmers | 3.0 | (18) |
| Other | 2.5 | (18) |
| TOTAL | 100.0 | (601) |

SOURCE    Newspapers: *al-Jumhuriya, al-Akhbar al-Yawm, al-Qahira;* Magazines: *al-Musawwar, Akhir Sa a,* issues for December 1954 through February 1955.

TABLE 7.3   *Distribution by occupational group of Moslem Brothers arrested in 1954*

| Occupational group | Percentage of sample | |
|---|---|---|
| Professional | 11.0 | (66) |
| White collar | 55.3 | (331) |
| Artisan/Small business/Petty functionary | 13.8 | (83) |
| Skilled worker | 9.3 | (56) |
| Unskilled worker | 10.7 | (65) |
| TOTAL | 100.0 | (601) |

SOURCE   Same as Table 7.2.

have received a traditional socialisation, have learned basic educational skills, have a knowledge of the basic tenets of Islam and an aspiration for upward mobility suggests a cohesive family structure. What does seem to be the case is that the rural *petite-bourgeoisie* from which Islamic radicals are drawn is increasingly pressurised and marginalised by Egypt's deteriorating economic conditions.

TABLE 7.4   *Occupations of Moslem Brothers brought to trial in 1965*

| Occupation | Number | Percentage |
|---|---|---|
| Professionals | 32 | (31) |
| Secondary school teachers | 16 | (16) |
| Clerks/low level bureaucrats | 14 | (14) |
| Students (science) | 9 | (9) |
| Small factory owners/shopkeepers/contractors/merchants | 5 | (5) |
| High level bureacrats/factory directors | 4 | (4) |
| Men (and women) of religion | 3 | (3) |
| Peasants | 3 | (3) |
| Students (other) | 2 | (2) |
| Skilled workers | 2 | (2) |
| Worker | 1 | (1) |
| Army officer | 1 | (1) |
| Housewife | 1 | (1) |
| Unknown | 8 | (8) |
| TOTAL | 100 | (100) |

SOURCE   *al-Ahram, al-Jumhuriya:* issues from December-February, 1965 (NB: This sample is only preliminary since over 700 Moslem Brothers were arrested during 1965.)

Even though the rural families from which Islamic radicals are drawn seem still to be cohesive, they do not seem to be able to provide material and psychological protection for their members who seek upward mobility. It is instructive to contrast this type of family with the rural notable family from which Egypt's dominant political élite recruits its members. Despite land reform, the rural notable family still possesses significant tracts of land. From its strong rural base, it has been able to situate its members in the armed forces, the state apparatus, the dominant party and parliamentary institutions, the security network and in the public sector (Binder, 1979). By contrast, the rural petty bourgeois family cannot provide the same level of protection or influence (*al-wasita*). Thus the upwardly mobile member of the family finds himself very vulnerable to the vicissitudes of Egyptian life, especially in large urban areas such as Cairo and Alexandria. Attempting to cope with urban life becomes particularly problematic if a rural migrant has received a university degree and is unable to find satisfactory employment. Even if employment is located, considerable status inconsistency can result since white collar employment often does not allow the individual to maintain a decent standard of living commensurate with his social status.

In this regard, it is not coincidental that the Moslem Brotherhood and other Islamic radical groups have chosen to refer to their primary organisational unit as 'the family' (*al-usra*). In forming cells in major urban centres and in provincial capitals, Islamic groups seek to reconstruct the corporate unity of traditional rural life. The 'Islamic family' thus provides a sense of identity and protection within what is perceived to be a hostile and capricious environment.

Despite a strong concern with socio-economic issues, much discussion among Moslem Brothers within the 'family' or cell dealt with trying to cope with the changing mores and values of Egyptian society, especially during the 1960s and 1970s. The deep concern among male radicals with finding a 'pure' woman who would be suitable as a wife, and with trying to deal with their sexuality as a result of increased sexual stimuli, point once again to the impact of traditional socialisation. Given the very conservative and closed nature of rural petty bourgeois society, the cosmopolitan and materially oriented character of urban life which allowed for more contact with members of the opposite sex, especially in the university, posed very threatening temptations not found in the village. The cell provided the opportunity to assert one's complete elevation to purity and hence a refuge from the corrupt outside world.[9]

In recruiting members, Islamic radical movements form an extensive institutional infrastructure and symbolic nexus which is not available to competing political groups. First, over one hundred Islamic fraternal and charitable organisations are officially registered in Egypt. Second, the mosque provides an additional source of recruitment, especially since this provides an opportunity to observe who are the most devout among those saying their prayers. Since the mosque is not merely a place of prayer but also a social institution, it is frequently used by Islamic militants to organise religious study circles which is frequently done after the Friday prayer.[10] It further provides an opportunity to raise money since donations can be collected for the purchase of religious texts. Third, radicals frequently invoke the obligation of the *zakat* or tax on personal wealth for the sake of charity as an additional source of funds.[11] Of course, recruitment to groups such as the Moslem Brotherhood is often based upon family networks or social ties established at the university. Nevertheless, the ability to manipulate Islam confers an organisational advantage on radical organisations over competing political groups, especially those on the left such as the Nasserites and communists.

## IDEOLOGY

Islam in radical or fundamentalist thinking reflects the social experiences and class character of its adherents but should not be reduced to these categories. Radical Islamic ideology provides a source of strengths and constraints for organisations such as the Moslem Brotherhood and the *jama'at al-takfir wa'l-hijra*. Ideology is an important determinant of these organisations' ability to mobilise support, provide an alternative to the ideological dominance of the ruling class, and ultimately their ability to seize political power.

It is important to distinguish between ideologues and activists when discussing radical interpretations of Islam. Clearly, most activists are aware of the basic tenets of Islam but are unfamiliar with the sophisticated doctrinal disputes that have characterised the discourse among prominent *'ulama* and religious thinkers over the centuries. By radical Islamic ideology, I mean the writings of prominent Moslem Brothers such as Hasan al-Banna, Sayyid Qutb and 'Umar al-Tilimsani and leaders of more radical Islamic groups such as Ahmad Shukri Mustafa and Salih al-Sirriya, the former head of the Islamic Liberation Party (*Hizb al-tahrir al-islami*).

Perhaps the most striking feature of radical Islamic ideology is its unitary or holistic character. At the social level, the tenacious emphasis on the integrated nature of Islam and the assertion that its doctrines encompass all aspects of man's existence reflect the desire to utilise Islam as a means to resist the increasing fragmentation of social life. Islam becomes a way of reasserting the corporate unity of Egyptian society which Islamic radicals perceived to exist from the vantage point of their early socialisation in the countryside.

This emphasis on a unitary, holistic Islam is very compatible with the overall world-view of the rural *petite-bourgeoisie*. It has been argued that there is no contradiction between the fact that such a large percentage of Islamic militants have been educated in the natural sciences and still subscribe to radical interpretations of Islam. Since the natural sciences stress an absolute approach to knowledge (either something is right or it is wrong), it is erroneous to assume that a 'modern' education will necessarily erode a traditional consciousness which likewise emphasises absolute categories of thought.

If there is a 'fit' between the traditional world view of the rural *petite-bourgeoisie* and the manner in which Islamic radicalism is articulated in urban centres, then such a statement still fails to explain the way in which such thought mediates reality for its followers and the advantages and shortcomings of such mediation. In emphasising the total character of Islam, radical Islamic ideology provides not only for the psychological needs of its adherents but also provides a comprehensive explanation of a complex and changing social reality. Moreover, it does this using symbols which possess strong emotive power since they are ones with which members of the lower middle class have been acquainted since early childhood and they evoke memories of a romanticised past in which life was integrated and devoid of conflict.

The strength of such symbols becomes even more apparent when juxtaposed to those of the major competing ideologies: liberalism, Arab socialism and Marxism. All three ideologies come under major attack in the writings of Islamic radicals. Liberalism is associated with capitalism, while socialist ideologies are seen as part of a conspiracy to turn Egypt into a communist society which would be beholden to the Soviet Union. Both liberal-capitalist and communist concepts are seen as belonging to imported ideologies that seek to encourage the social disintegration of Egyptian society. Capitalism fosters social decay through unprincipled competition and exploitation of the middle and working classes while communism encourages internal conflict through its doctrine of the inherent conflict between the owners of capital and the producing classes.

The symbols of liberalism do little to mediate reality for the Moslem Brother or member of more radical Islamic groups whose contacts with Western culture are minimal at best. The atomism and individualism of liberal thought offers little to the aspirant of upward mobility who finds his path to success blocked or only partially achieved. Indeed, if liberal symbols were to be taken seriously, they would suggest that failure to achieve success and the accompanying psychological trauma are the responsibility of the individual not the society at large. Politically, Egypt's experiment with liberalism since the turn of the century produced great differentials of wealth, collaboration with British imperialism, the loss of Palestine to Zionism and increasing seculari- sation and hence in the view of Islamic radicals, moral corruption of society.

Marxist symbols are equally inadequate in performing a cognitive function for the lower middle classes. Marxist symbols are most appropriate for those who have lost all ties with existing society and who have nothing to lose and everything to gain through the revolutionary transformation of society. Future-oriented rather than past-oriented symbols provide a prism through which to understand reality for the urban factory worker or agrarian wage labourer. They offer little to the political activist of rural *petite-bourgeoisie* origin who is trying to achieve social mobility but who is still tied and committed to traditional structures.

The symbols of Arab or Nasserite socialism are even less resonant with social reality than those of bourgeois liberalism and Marxism since they are much more *ad hoc*, have a shorter history and are treated with such cynicism by their own proponents. That neither freedom, socialism nor unity were ever on the verge of being implemented in Egypt or the Arab world under President Nasser was not lost on those who were attracted to the Moslem Brotherhood and its derivative organisations. The repression of the political Right and Left, the loss of two wars to Israel, the deteriorating economic situation and the corruption within the state apparatus and public sector created utter contempt among the lower middle class for Arab socialist ideology. Worse yet, Arab socialism was seen as facilitating the infiltration of more radical communist ideas and hence the ultimate takeover of Egypt by Marxist forces.[12]

Radical Islamic ideology in Egypt thus serves to interpret reality in such a way as to fulfill the material and psychological needs of its adherents. Its symbols posit the fundamental unity and integrity of society as found in the Holy Qur'an and in the application of Islamic law (*al-shari'a al-islamiya*). Radical Islamic thought informs its followers that society is experiencing difficulties because its leaders and members of the community have strayed from the path of Islam. Greed, corruption and atheism all threaten to fragment society and prevent it from effectively confronting its external enemies. Through such argumentation, the Islamic radical is given categories which both help to explain the social decay around him and his own thwarted ambitions for upward mobility. These categories provide a sense of community or group solidarity which juxtaposes the community of the faithful to the community of unbelievers. Used in this way, Islamic symbols place the militant at a higher moral level than other members of society and thus place him in the position of serving a divine mission as he seeks to restore God's will on earth. Not only does such ideology mediate reality in a very effective manner but it also holds out the prospect that time is on the side of the believer.

Although radical Islamic thought is unitary in scope, it should not be seen as a static ideology. Here the inadequacies of viewing such thought in terms of social pathology become apparent. For if Ikhwan ideology is to be seen as an irrational aberration of Islam that is meant to offer solace to its adherents, how is one to explain the organisational sophistication of radical Islamic groups which hope to seize power? Far from being totally irrational, Islamic ideology in Egypt is structured and teleological. It proffers a political programme and hence, a vision, however impractical, of a future Egyptian society under its hegemony. Radical Islamic thought stresses the unity of Islam not just to serve the psychological needs of its followers, and to help explain reality to them, but also to counterpose itself to the dominant ideologies – both in the religious and political spheres.

The notion of a rigidified Islam which refuses to confront social change, which many Orientalists see inherent in radical or fundamentalist interpretations of Islam, seems much more characteristic of the positivism of establishment Islam. Certainly relations between the Azharite *'ulama* and the Moslem Brotherhood have always been conflictual. In the case of the *takfir wa'l-hijra* group, relations became so acrimonious that they led the group to kidnap and assassinate a former minister of religious endowments and Azhar affairs. Indeed, since the rise of the Moslem Brotherhood during the 1930s the *'ulama* have come under continual attack for their ineffectiveness in confronting Western imperialism and, during the Nasser era, in rebuffing Soviet attempts to gain more influence in Egyptian society. More recently the *'ulama* have been seen as acquiescing to the renewed influence of Western capitalism over Egypt's economic and social life and its rapprochement with Israel.

The struggle between the unitary view of Islam in its radical variants and the positivist orientation of the establishment '*ulama* is perhaps best illustrated in the dispute between Shaykh Muhammad Husayn al-Dhahabi, an Azharite scholar and former minister of religious endowments and Azhar affairs, and the *Jama'at al-takfir wa'l-hijra* which kidnapped and assassinated him in 1977. While the causes for al-Dhahabi's killing are still not entirely clear, the main reason seems to be his attack on radical Islamic groups entitled, *Deviant Tendencies in Interpreting the Holy Qur'an: Their Motives and their Repudiation (al-ittijahat al-munharifa fi tafsir al-qur'an al-karim: dawafi'uha wa daf'uha)* (1976). The sources of this dispute will be discussed in greater detail below. What concerns us here is a chapter entitled, 'The deviant tendency in explanation according to those who claim that the Qur'an contains all the universal sciences in general and in detail'.

In this chapter, it is clear that al-Dhahabi seeks to dispute the notion that 'engineering, medicine and philosophy' and all sciences can be located in the Qur'an. The Qur'an is a means towards the betterment of mankind and not a comprehensive source of knowledge. The view of the Qur'an as a comprehensive source of knowledge, al-Dhahabi argues, impedes scientific and technological studies which are crucial for the betterment of humanity (al-Dhahabi, 1976, pp. 81–8).

It is clear from al-Dhahabi's arguments and those of other establishment '*ulama* that they seek to disaggregate the very categories which radical Islamic thought views in unitary terms. Thus religion, science and politics are discrete and self-contained spheres of thought and action which do not possess any necessary interrelationship. This positivist and essentially secular view of reality serves the interests of the ruling class in Egypt in two fundamental ways. First, it separates religion and politics in an attempt to prevent oppositional groups from using Islam to challenge the ruling class's ideological dominance. Second, it precludes any attempt to place constraints on the accumulation process through invoking edicts derived from Islam. If, for example, it could be argued that Qur'an did contain all necessary scientific knowledge, or even the broad outlines of such knowledge, this would place serious restrictions on economic development since such an assertion could be used to de-legitimate technological and scientific innovations borrowed from non-Islamic societies. When considered in conjunction with the political dimensions of radical Islamic ideology, it is easy to visualise how such arguments could have a significant impact on the process of accumulation in Egyptian society and the control over this process by the ruling class. In seeking to protect its class rule, the dominant forces in Egyptian society seek to promote an individualistic and apolitical concept of Islam – the direct antithesis of the world view offered in radical Islamic thought.

## ISLAMIC RADICALISM AND STATE POWER

Given the critique of existing conceptualisations of radical Islamic political organisations in Egypt and the discussion of recruitment patterns and ideology which characterise such movements, it is now possible to examine Islamic radicalism within the context of the structural approach mentioned earlier in the paper. Recruitment data point to a class base of Islamic movements in Egypt which, while unable to seize power on their own, can continue to pose a serious challenge to the political stability of the current regime. What the lower middle class possesses in members and ideological appeal is offset by its lack of influence in formal political and social institutions (e.g., among the *'ulama*, in the parliament and in the judiciary) and its lack of control over economic resources. Nevertheless, radical Islamic political organi-sations might pose the threat of seizing power were they to enter into coalition with other rightist groups. This is particularly true with regard to attempts by other Arab regimes, such as Saudi Arabia and Libya, both in the past and in the present, to use radical Islamic groups to destabilise Egypt.

While the Moslem Brotherhood first began to make foreign contacts through its participation in the Arab Revolt in Palestine between 1936 and 1939, it did not begin to have extensive contacts outside Egypt until fighting in the 1948 Arab–Israeli war (al-Sharif, n.d.) Thus, after the suppression of the Moslem Brotherhood in 1954, several of its prominent members such as Sa'id Ramadan, Salih al-Ashmawi and Mustafa al-'Alim fled to Jerusalem where they became associated with the Higher Islamic Council. With the deterioration of Egyptian–Saudi relations during the 1960s, especially after Egyptian troops came to the support of Republican forces in Yemen, the exiled Moslem Brothers transferred their operations to Saudi Arabia where they enjoyed the largesse of the Saudi royal family. It was from Saudi Arabia that the attempted *coup d'état* against the Nasser regime in 1965 was co-ordinated and financed.

While the sample of Moslem Brothers arrested in 1954 consisted almost entirely of native Egyptians, the sample of Brothers arrested in

1965 contained nationals from other Arab countries, particularly Palestinians, Libyans, and Sudanese. Contacts with Moslem Brotherhood organisations extended as far away as Kuwait and Bahrain.[13] While the Moslem Brotherhood was founded in other Arab countries (e.g. in Syria in 1934),[14] the contact of Moslem Brothers in different Arab countries was enhanced by the spread of Arab nationalism and the internationalisation of capital in the Middle East following the Second World War. The spread of Arab nationalism which led the states of the Arab League to intervene in Palestine in 1948 was one factor which expanded contact between Islamic political organisations in different Arab countries. The attempt of President Nasser to spread Egyptian influence under the banner of Arab socialism led to offers to students from all Arab countries to complete their university education in Egypt. Given the strong influence of the Moslem Brotherhood and other radical Islamic groups in Egyptian universities, many of these Arab students were recruited to them.

The internationalisation of capital likewise had a significant impact on the interaction of Egyptian Islamic radicals with those in other Arab countries. The rise in the price of petroleum products after 1970 created a demand for skilled labour in many of the Arab oil-producing states, especially in Saudi Arabia, Libya and the Persian Gulf states, all of which have small populations. This process of cross-national migration affected Egypt more than other Arab states because of its heavy surplus population and its own limited sources of petroleum.

The organisational and financial support bestowed upon the Moslem Brotherhood and its derivative organisations by states such as Saudi Arabia, and more recently by Libya, was offset, however, by developments within the Islamic movement itself. Here the importance of a structural or systemic understanding of radical Islamic movements becomes particularly apparent. Until the assassination of the founder of the Moslem Brotherhood, Hasan al-Banna, in 1949, there were no significant cleavages in the movement. Certainly, much of this unity can be attributed to the dynamic leadership of al-Banna who was a skilled orator and highly effective in political organisation. However, with the rapid growth in the ranks of the Moslem Brotherhood after 1946, it became possible to discern splits in the organisation even before al-Banna's assassination. This was particularly true once a large number of students and young professionals joined the organisation.

By the late 1940s the Moslem Brotherhood was already witnessing signs of a fissure which was only to become fully manifest during the 1970s. This split resulted in the creation of two separate organisations:

the Guidance Council (*maktab al-irshad*), on the one hand, and the Secret Organisation (*al-jihaz al-sirri*), on the other. It was the latter organisation which, under the control of Yusif Tala't, was behind the attempt to assassinate President Nasser in 1954.

This split brings us once again to the distinction between ideologues and activists. The attempt of the Palace to co-opt the Moslem Brotherhood after al-Banna's death by encouraging the appointment of Hasan al-Hudaybi, who was considered loyal to the Egyptian monarchy, as Supreme Guide, was deeply resented by the younger and more activist members. Since the Palace was already suspected of complicity in al-Banna's death, al-Hudaybi's attempt to play down the Brotherhood's involvement in domestic politics and in the anti-imperialist struggle against the British was perceived as betraying the goals of the organisation.

The situation which existed between 1949 and 1954 bears many similarities to the situation which arose in Egypt after Anwar al-Sadat came to power in 1970. Eager to establish a power-base of his own and fearful that the most effective opposition to his rule would come from the left, Sadat began to release members of the Moslem Brotherhood who had been arrested and imprisoned in 1965. Exiled Moslem Brothers in Europe and Saudi Arabia were allowed to return to the country and in 1976 the Brotherhood was formally allowed to function once again and to publish its periodicals, *al-Da'wa* and *al-I'tisam* (Grzeskowiak, 1980, p. 678; Ramadan, 1977, pp. 10–11). Sadat used the Brotherhood very effectively as a counterweight to the left which he had neutralised by the time of his visit to Israel in November, 1977.

Perhaps in no other area did Islamic radicalism regain as much strength during the 1970s as in the universities. Leftists lost almost all influence in student organisations.[15] The Islamic radical groups which gained influence in the universities and among Egyptian youth were not part of the traditional Moslem Brotherhood which they saw as too conservative and too closely allied with the Sadat regime.

Groups such as *Jama'at al-takfir wa'l-hijra*, *Hizb al-tahrir al-islami*, *Jund Allah* (God's Soldiers), *Jama'at al-jihad* (The Holy War Association), *Jama'at al-Muslimin li'l-takfir* (The Society of Moslems which Charges Society with Unbelief), and *Ansar Khumayni* (The Followers of Khomeini) were uncovered throughout the country by the state security apparatus (Grzeskowiak, 1980, p. 675; Altman, 1979, pp. 98–101; *al-Dustur*, 1 and 8, October, 1979). While some members of these groups had formerly belonged to the Moslem Brotherhood, their organisations had no formal ties to their spiritual mentors. By the 1970s, then, an important generational split had emerged in the Islamic radical movement in Egypt.

The problem with much current writing on Islamic political movements in Egypt during the 1970s is its attempt to situate the rise of groups espousing radical interpretations of Islam within the context of the defeat of Egypt by Israel in 1967. In most studies of Islamic political movements, radical or populist Islam was suppressed in 1954 only to appear again (hence the use of the notion of revival or resurgence) during the 1970s. The problem with such a conceptualisation is that it totally neglects the events of the 1960s. It is clear that almost immediately after the end of the trials of the Moslem Brotherhood in 1955 and the release of many of its younger members, attempts were begun to resurrect the organisation.[16] Groups of former Brothers were formed in Cairo, Alexandria, and the provinces which were apparently unaware of each other's existence. Meanwhile, inside the various prisons to which they had been assigned, Brothers formed study circles which allowed new social networks to be formed. By the time they began to be released during the early 1960s, new cells were formed and ties with those already released were established and re-established. Gradually, a new leadership group began to take shape which took responsibility for co-ordinating the activities of the various cells and for re-establishing links with exiled members of the organisation in Europe and in Saudi Arabia.[17]

The most prominent Moslem Brother in prison during the 1960s was Sayyid Qutb. Released by the government in 1964 for health reasons, he was soon approached by the newly constituted leadership of the Brotherhood to become the titular head of the organisation. Although Qutb had maintained ties with Brothers while still in prison through Zaynab al-Ghazzali and his sister, Hamida Qutb, he was never in actual control of the reconstituted movement. Sayyid Qutb played the role of an ideologue whose nominal leadership lent prestige and legitimacy to the Moslem Brotherhood. The important point is that the young leadership of the 1960s demonstrated little interest in and knowledge of formal Islam. When brought to trial, and questioned by the court, they showed the same ignorance of the intricacies of religious doctrine that members of the *al-jihaz al-sirri* had shown during the trials of 1954–5. Thus the 1960s represented a continuation of the process whereby formal Islamic ideology and political activism became increasingly bifurcated until, by the 1970s, they had become almost thoroughly divorced. Once legalised by the Sadat regime, the Moslem Brotherhood relegated itself primarily to the role of criticising government domestic and foreign policies while activist splinter groups, such as those mentioned above, concentrated on illegitimate and often violent political activities (Grzeskowiak, 1980, pp. 677–9; Altman, 1979, p. 104; and *al-Ahram*, 4 July 1977 *et passim*). Groups of Islamic radicals continue to be arrested. Following the Sadat assassination, large numbers of militants were arrested in Asyut after engaging in armed conflict with the Egyptian army. In November 1982, 280 members of *Jama'at al-jihad* were brought to trial for allegedly plotting to overthrow the government of President Husni Mubarak.

The increasing hiatus between ideologies and activists can be explained in part by the policies of the Moslem Brotherhood itself and along generational lines. Just as the Brotherhood was used to break strikes led by the Wafd and the leftist worker–student alliance during the late 1940s and early 1950s so it was used by the Sadat regime to attack leftist intellectuals, students and Nasserites during the 1970s. In both instances, this close association alienated the younger and more radical elements of the movement. Clearly, generational factors were also crucial in explaining the bifurcation of ideologues and activists. The older Brothers in the Guidance Council were less prone to become involved in opposing the state outside legally prescribed channels. Indeed, during the 1960s, many older Moslem Brothers rejected the appeals of younger members to rejoin the organisation.

To understand fully the fissures that came to characterise the Islamic radical movement in Egypt, it is necessary to study the changes in its ideology. The fact that the ideology changed between the 1940s and the 1970s from an emphasis on socio-economic variables to those emphasising cultural issues relates in large measure to Egypt's relationship to the world market and its domestic class structure. Whereas members of the urban middle class saw the causes of Egypt's ills as stemming from British imperialism during the 1940s and 1950s, the expulsion of the British from the Suez Canal in 1956 signified the end of formal colonial control over Egypt. Increasingly, during the 1960s and 1970s, Islamic radicals came to see Egypt's problem as stemming from domestic rather than foreign sources. Some writers were very much aware that neo-colonial influences still persisted in Egypt. Nevertheless, Islamic radicals increasingly saw Egypt's problems as caused by betrayal from within rather than control from without. No longer was it possible to argue that foreign capitalists exploited the middle and lower classes through ownership of domestic industry since, by the mid-1960s, almost all the means of production were owned by the state public sector.[19]

This shift in perception was reflected at the ideological level in the increasing prominence of the concept of withdrawal. In this sense, the period of the 1960s is a crucial, albeit unstudied, era when this concept first began to be clearly articulated. Sayyid Qutb's emphasis on the distinction between the 'community of the faithful' (*al-umma al-mu'mina*) as opposed to the 'community of unbelievers' (*al-umma al-jahiliya*) reflected the increasing alienation of Islamic radicals from their own society.[20] This hostility to the state and society at large replaced the former hostility to imperial control. By the 1970s, this alienation had reached the point in the *Jama'at al-takfir wa'l-hijra* and other radical groups where its members had completely withdrawn from society. In the case of the *takfir* group, this meant refusing to take employment in the state bureaucracy or serve in the armed forces since this, it was argued, would only strengthen the infidel forces.[21] Neighbours of *takfir* communes, which were dispersed throughout middle-class quarters of Cairo and Alexandria, reported that their members prayed separately in the mosque and even refused to speak to anyone outside the group.[22]

The Sadat regime utilised the withdrawal phenomenon to discredit the more radical of the Islamic political groups. Shaykh al-Dhahabi's book (which, given its size, was definitely meant for popular consumption) attacked groups espousing a '*Kharijite*' mentality (Dhahabi, 1976, pp. 63–9; *al-Ahram*, 8 July 1977). Of course, the tendency among youth to disengage themselves from society and, as many members of the *takfir* group had done, become peddlars and beggars, was very alarming to certain intellectuals and members of Egypt's ruling class.

These observations on the development of Islamic radicalism in Egypt during the 1970s suggest that the deepening of underdevelopment is exacerbating the contradiction between differential accumulation and legitimacy. While this contradiction bodes ill for political and economic stability in Egypt, it does not imply a zero-sum game whereby the decrease in the ruling class's legitimacy automatically represents a gain in the political power of Islamic radical movements. The ranks of these movements have clearly swelled during the 1970s but this increase in numbers has not translated itself into effective political power because of the reasons just discussed. Even the assassination of Anwar al-Sadat and the subsequent struggle between armed Islamic radicals and government troops in Asyut in Upper Egypt did not pose a serious threat to the Egyptian regime.

Beyond the urban middle class, it is difficult to see Islamic radicalism extending to the industrial working-class and peasantry which has traditionally ignored its appeals.[23] This is especially true given the shift in symbols from a socio-economic to a cultural emphasis which means that until now, Islamic political groups have offered little of substance to the lower classes. Given the presupposition of reading and writing skills which are required for even the most basic religious tracts, illiterate or semi-literate peasants and workers are unable to relate to radical Islamic writings and the study circles in which these writings are discussed. Furthermore, peasants and workers have not been socialised into a petty bourgeois consciousness which would make the symbols of Islamic radicalism relevant to their lives.

In conclusion, the chances of Islamic radical groups seizing power in Egypt seem remote in light of their own internal cleavages and their inability to form a powerful coalition with the upper middle class or to mobilise the masses behind their cause. At best, these groups seem destined to play a supporting role on the historical stage. Their power, then, ultimately seems to be determined in large measure by the extent to which they are manipulated by the dominant class which currently controls Egyptian society. This class, whose interests and destiny seem increasingly to be tied to foreign capital through the 'open door' policy, will probably only find it useful to mobilise support from Islamic radical movements if there is a strong challenge from the left. At the same time, radical Islamic groups may refuse to support the regime given their increasing alienation from it because of widespread corruption and the refusal of the state to reconstitute society according to their own interpretations of Islam. The result will most likely be a fragmented Egyptian polity pitting the 'neo-liberal' coalition of Anwar al-Sadat's successors against an increasingly vocal Islamic radical movement and a Nasserite and Marxist left.

## NOTES

1. Examples of this type of approach to the relationship between Islam and politics can be found in Safran, 1961; and Halpern, 1963: esp. the chapter on 'Neo-Islamic Totalitarianism', pp. 134–55. For a critique and attempt to transcend it, cf. Binder, 1965, p. 396, and more recently Gilsenan, 1980.
2. This organisation refers to itself as the *al-Jama'at al-Muslimin*. However, the name which the Egyptian government has attached to it—*Jama'at al-takfir wa'l-hijra* (the association which accuses society of disbelief and advocates withdrawal from it)—has come to be the one by which it is commonly known.
3. A comparative example which highlights the importance of world market-forces in fostering the growth of Islamic radical movements in Egypt can be found in the emergence of the *Gush Emunim* and other militant Jewish groups in Israel. As in Egypt, a bureaucratically top heavy 'socialist' model

of development proved unable to provide adequate capital and technological modernisation for significant economic growth. The result was the turn to a much more *laissez-faire* model of development, similar to Egypt's *infitah*, and the undermining of the legitimacy of leftist ideologies in general. The attempt by groups such as the *Gush Emunim* to recapture the 'pioneering spirit' of the early *yishuv* and to define Israeli society in more Jewish and nationalist terms suggests a crisis of authenticity which is similar to that being experienced in Egypt. These arguments are developed in greater detail in my forthcoming book-length study which compares the Moslem Brotherhood and the *Gush Emunim* and their radical offshoots.

4. For an example from the American experience, cf. Lipset, 1964, pp. 358–71.
5. All available data support this hypothesis (Davis, 1970, pp. 15, 27–31; Ibrahim, 1980, pp. 438–9; Kira, 1955, vol. I, pp. 143 ff. *Al-Ahram*, 27 February; 7 March; 18, 19, 29 April; 1, 4, 5 May; 13, 14, 15 July 1966).
6. Al-Ahram, 10, 14 February 1966; 4 May 1966; 13, 14, 15, 17, 18 July 1966.
7. Al-Ahram, 13, 14 July 1966.
8. cf. note Table 1, p. 11.
9. Interview with a former Moslem Brother from Damanhur, December, 1978; *al-Ahram*, 19 April 1906, where a young Brother met Sayyid Qutb in Ra's al-Bar to help him find a '*Zawja saliha*'.
10. *al-Ahram*, 28 April, 4, 5 May 1966; 11 July 1977; the pilgrimage also provides organisational opportunities for Islamic radical groups in bringing together large numbers of the faithful in al-Makka, *al-Ahram*, 17 May 1966.
11. *al-Ahram*, 16 February; 13, 14 July 1966.
12. *al-Ahram*, 19 April; 2, 4 May 1966; 8 July 1977.
13. *al-Ahram*, 5, 9 February; 2, 7 May 1966.
14. *al-Ahram, al-Ahzab al-siyasiya fi suriya* (Damascus: Dar al-Ruwwad, 1954) p. 11.
15. A similar phenomenon occurred in the Sudan during the 1970s as Moslem radicals were able to oust leftists from all student organisations and take control of them. Personal communication from a Sudanese professor from the University of Juba, 17 October 1981.
16. *al-Jumhuriya*, 7 March 1977.
17. *al-Ahram*, 2, 11 May; 17 July 1966.
18. *al-Ahram*, 17, 18 July 1966.
19. Compare, for example, Sayyid Qutb's earlier writings such as *Ma'rakat al-islam wa'l-ra'smaliya* (1952), with *Ma'alim fi-l-tariq* (1964).
20. *al-Ahram*, 1 May 1966.
21. *al-Ahram*, 7, 8 July 1977.
22. *al-Ahram*, 8, 9, 10, 11 July 1977; it is also interesting that all marriages within the group were arranged by its leader, Ahmad Shukri Mustafa.
23. For example, 'Organisationally the brotherhood made a concerted attempt to recruit the workers of the mill [at al-Mahalla al-Kubra] ... But the Brotherhood only succeeded in acquiring a following among the managerial employees' (Carson, 1957, p. 369).

# 8 The *Fada'iyan-e Islam*: Fanaticism, Politics and Terror

## FARHAD KAZEMI

### INTRODUCTION

Shi'ite Islam emerged as a significant force in Iranian politics with the creation of the Safavid state in 1501. With the help of the Safavids, the Shi'ite *'ulama* established an effective organisation that permeated various levels of social and political life. Since the sixteenth century, a complex set of working relationships has continued to link the religious and political systems. Although this relationship was harmonious at the beginning, important theological and political issues arose in due time which occasionally strained the basis of the religious hierarchy's interaction with the ruling dynasty. The intricacies of the clergy's relationship with the various Iranian rulers is beyond the scope of this paper. It is, however, important to point out that the Shi'ite *'ulama* suffered enormously under Nader Shah Afshar (1736–47). Nader Shah's schemes and actions challenged the pre-eminence of Shi'ism in Iran and limited some of the clerics' traditional privileges. In addition, the Shah and his lieutenants frequently plundered the clerically controlled *waqf* property. Aqa Muhammad Khan Qajar (1785–96) once again stressed the Shi'ite nature of the Iranian state and restored some of the *'ulamas'* lost power. This stable relationship between the ruling monarchs and the clergy continued throughout the Qajar period (1785–1925). Tensions, however, began to mount gradually and towards the end of the Qajar era, important coalitions led by the *'ulama* liberal reformers, and merchants challenged the absolutist monarchs on several occasions winning significant concessions.

When Reza Shah founded the Pahlavi dynasty in 1925, the religious

158

hierarchy was subjected to the superior power of the state. The *'ulama* were not able to challenge Reza Shah's rule in any effective manner. With the onset of World War Two and Muhammad Reza Shah's ascendancy to the throne in 1941, the religious establishment was able to regain certain lost prerogatives and influence the course of politics more actively. During this period several religious organisations and parties appeared and played important roles in the political arena. Although these organisations all had ties to elements within the religious hierarchy, their theological orientation, social basis, the political power varied considerably. However, similar to previous periods of religious assertiveness, two broad issues combined to help transmit the activities of these organisations to the political forefront.

The first issue concerned a set of theoretical questions, with deep roots in the Shi'ite religious tradition, about the right to rule and legitimacy of secular monarchy. Who are the legitimate wielders of political authority – the clerics or the monarchs? What is the proper role of the Shi'ite clergy in guiding the faithful? The second issue was essentially non-religious and non-theoretical. It related to the state of social and economic affairs and the sense of crisis that had beset the social order. As in the past, societal crisis, economic dislocation, and political turmoil prompted the clergy's forceful expression of theological issues and questions of political legitimacy. The crisis of the social system acted as the catalyst for the Shi'ite clergy's reiteration, reinterpretation, or reaffirmation of theological concerns. It also helped the process of mass mobilisation, particularly in the urban centres where economic problems were more severely felt.

During World War Two and in the years immediately following, the sense of societal crisis in Iran was at its peak. The experience of occupation by the Allied powers, the forced abdication of Reza Shah, and the economic dislocation caused by the war had combined to create a political vacuum as well as a deepening perception of crisis. The pervasive feeling of powerlessness of the Iranian masses was partially rectified by the attempt to wrest control of Iranian oil from the British. The issue of oil nationalisation soon emerged as the single most potent force uniting disparate elements of Iranians behind a common cause. A grand coalition composed of liberal nationalists, the religious establishment and bazaar merchants was formed with the goal of making oil nationalisation a reality. Among those who supported the oil nationalisation drive was a small fanatical religious organisation known as *Fada'iyan-e Islam* (The Devotees of Islam). The *Fada'iyan* viewed oil nationalisation as a sacred duty for the faithful Shi'ites. Their call for action was couched in a fundamentalist religious form that justified and legitimised extremist tactics and violent participation in the political arena. The pages that follow attempt to review the history, organisation, ideology, and social base of the *Fada'iyan-e Islam* from the date of its creation to the present time.

## ORIGIN AND DEVELOPMENT

The *Fada'iyan-e Islam* was formed in 1945 by Sayyed Mujtaba Navvab Safavi in Tehran.[1] Navvab Safavi was born in 1923 in Tehran in a religious family known as Mirlawhi. The family name was changed to Navvab Safavi (deputies of the Safavids) to identify with the famous Shi'ite dynasty of the Safavids, who in the sixteenth century made Shi'ism the state religion of Iran. The family was deeply religious and claimed descent from the Prophet Muhammad and on the mother's side, from the Safavids. Navvab had his early schooling in Tehran. He had completed the eighth grade when his father died. Navvab left school and for a while was employed at the Anglo-Iranian Oil Company. He then left for the well-known Shi'ite religious centre of Najaf in Iraq and became a theology student.[2]

In Najaf, Navvab became acquainted with the works of the distinguished Iranian intellectual and historian, Ahmad Kasravi. Kasravi's books and articles were antagonistic towards traditional Shi'-ism and held the religion responsible for many ills of the Iranian society. In one of his works, Kasravi reviews Shi'ism historically and concludes that through distortion and misrepresentation of facts, Shi'ism has led the Iranians astray:

> Shi'ism, in addition to being incompatible with wisdom and thus objectionable on this ground, is also a hindrance to (a meaningful) life ... This religion has led its followers astray and away from (true) religion. The Shi'ites call themselves the 'group of redeemers' and do not recognise any but their own religion. But the truth is the opposite of that and they are completely out of (the realm of true) religion.[3] (Kasravi, 1945, p. 45)

Angered and distraught by Kasravi's unorthodox views and his anti-clericalism, Navvab, now in a religious garb, returned to Tehran 'to discover whether the author was as evil as his works' (Abrahamian, 1969, p. 134). For his visit to Tehran, Navvab received the financial support and blessing of the Shi'ite *ulama* of Najaf. On the way, Navvab delivered several rousing anti-Kasravi speeches and sermons in the streets and mosques of Abadan. Once in Tehran, Navvab established contacts with the clerics of the 'Society to Combat Irreligion' – an organisation that was founded to root out the spread of Kasravi's ideas. With the support of this group, Navvab engaged Kasravi in several discussions and debates. Having become convinced of Kasravi's evil, Navvab set out to assassinate him with a weapon purchased from funds advanced by Haj Shaykh Muhammad Hasan Taleqani, a known figure among the *'ulama* of Tehran.[4] The first attempt on Kasravi's life, made in broad daylight in May 1945, was a failure. The injured Kasravi was taken to a nearby hospital pursued by his shouting and angry assailant.

The jailed Navvab was released shortly after bail was raised for him. Soon after, a broadsheet, signed by Navvab and distributed throughout Tehran, heralded the establishment of the *Fada'iyan-e Islam*. The combative tone of the broadsheet, generously sprinkled with quotations from the *Qur'an*, set the pattern for future *Fada'iyan* publications. It called upon all Moslems of the world 'to rise up, become alive, and regain your rights'.[5]

The second attempt on Kasravi's life was planned more systematically by Navvab and his followers. In March 1946 Kasravi and his secretary were assassinated in the Ministry of Justice building by two devoted followers of Navvab, the brothers Husayn and 'Ali Muhammad Imami. The assailants and conspirators left the bleeding victims with loud shouts of *Allahu Akbar*.

The assassins were swiftly rounded up and sent to jail. Navvab, however, made his way to Mashhad and from there to Najaf, safe from retribution. The trial of the Imami brothers, held in a tense and highly charged atmosphere, eventually brought them a verdict of acquittal. Pressures from the clergy and elements from the bazaar were largely responsible for the Imami brothers' freedom. It is reported that the leading cleric, Ayatollah Haj Aqa Husayn Qumi, had pointed out to a group of high ranking government officials that the murder of Kasravi was 'an obligatory act similar to prayer and required no *fatwa* (authoritative religious decree). Anyone who insults the prophet and his family must be liquidated and his blood shed'.[6] A broadsheet originating from the Tehran bazaar called the day of Kasravi's assassination 'a new Islamic day of celebration' and 'a glorious date of history'.[7]

In the *Fada'iyan* chronicles, the murder of Kasravi is described as a significant threshold event that catapulted the organisation into the forefront of politics. In an article entitled 'A Foreigner is a Foreigner' in the *Fada'iyan* newspaper, *Manshur-e Baradari* (The Brotherhood Circular), Kasravi's death is discussed in laudatory terms:

> For the first time in 1324 [1946], the sparkling fire of these manly youth burned the life and existence of Ahmad Kasravi, who was the greatest tool of the British imperialists and who was the agent assigned to create division among Moslems and to prepare the grounds for exploitive domination. . . . The bullet that struck his brain forced the British to retreat for a few years.[8]

Upon his return to Tehran, Navvab met and formed an alliance with Ayatollah Abu'l-Qasim Kashani that lasted from August 1946 until May 1951 (Faghfoory, 1978, pp. 164–203). When Kashani was arrested in July 1946 for anti-government activities, the *Fada'iyan* feverishly searched for ways to gain his release. The fall of premier Ahmad Qavam in 1947 led to Kashani's release. Kashani's freedom signalled the beginning of a new period of public protests and demonstrations by the *Fada'iyan* and Kashani's supporters. These demonstrations were staged to support a variety of specific causes ranging from the condemnation of Jewish terrorism in Palestine to the support of oil nationalisation.

In a major demonstration in favour of the Palestinian Arabs, in May 1948, the *Fada'iyan–Kashani* coalition mustered several thousand active participants. A group of youthful *Fada'iyan* members sang a poem, beginning with the words, 'We are the youth of Iran – the devotees of Islam'. The Zionists in Palestine were then publicly condemned and volunteers were requested to go to Palestine and fight for the Islamic cause. After 5000 men signed up for volunteer duty, the *Fada'iyan* issued a proclamation asking the Iranian government for permission to send the youth to Palestine. The proclamation read in part, 'the pure blood of the brave devotees of Islam is boiling to help the Moslem Palestinian brothers'.[9] The government's refusal to accede to their demand ended this phase of the *Fada'iyan*'s pro-Palestinian activity.[10]

In February 1949 an attempt was made on Shah Muhammad Reza Pahlavi's life. There were conflicting reports about the assailant's connections. The *Tudeh* (Communist Party) was officially held responsible for the act and banned by the government. But the assailant had a reporter's card from the religious newspaper, *Parcham-e Islam* (The Banner of Islam). Kashani was suspected of collusion and exiled for sixteen months to Syria and Lebanon. Although the *Fada'iyan* were not directly charged, their alliance with Kashani also made them suspect.

In the ensuing months several violent demonstrations and clashes took place in Tehran. The *Fada'iyan*, carrying the Kashani banner, were major participants. A secret letter from Kashani to Navvab, prompted the *Fada'iyan* to play a more active role in the parliamentary elections to the sixteenth Majlis (lower house of the parliament) on behalf of Kashani's candidates. The letter, according to Navvab, 'specifically ordered us to participate in the elections and a few National Front Leaders were introduced as candidates'.[11]

In these demonstrations and election contents, the *Fada'iyan* ire was frequently directed at the Minister of the Court and former prime minister, Abdu'l-Husayn Hazhir. Hazhir was assassinated in November 1949 at the Sipah Salar Mosque by Husayn Imami, one of the infamous Imami brothers. A *Fada'iyan* broadsheet, issued soon after the murder, praised the slaying and took responsibility for it. The assassination probably had Kashani's approval although he was in exile at the time. The *Fada'iyan* gave an elaborate religious rationale for the slaying of Hazhir. The *Fada'iyan* historian, Muhammad Vahedi, for example, made a distinction between two types of *jihad* (holy war) in Islamic jurisprudence, preliminary and defensive. He pointed out that preliminary *jihad* related to the historical and initial expansion of the Islamic army to lands of irreligion. Preliminary *jihad* is forbidden and should not be undertaken during the absence of the Hidden Imam. Defensive *jihad*, however, is obligatory at all times as it combats erosion of Islamic values and the religious basis of social order. True Moslems, according to Vahedi, 'must defend themselves from these attacks and root out those political leaders who are the tools and shields of the irreligious elements'.[12] From the *Fada'iyan*'s point of view, Hazhir was a prominent example of such a political leader and had to be removed.

The assassination of Hazhir exacerbated the existing political chaos. The assailant and a few leading opposition figures were arrested and martial law was declared in Tehran. The *Fada'iyan* attempt to gain Imami's release, including a plan to arrange an escape, was of no avail. During the short trial, the accused openly admitted to his act and declared 'I am ready to be executed and await martyrdom'.[13] On an early November day, just before dawn, Imami was hanged and buried in a public graveyard. The tensions, however, did not subside with this swift retribution. The holy city of Qum was in an uproar with much of the tension fuelled by the activities of Abdu'l-Husayn Vahedi, the *Fada'iyan*'s second in command.

The government finally agreed to allow Kashani to return from exile and take his seat in the sixteenth *Majlis*. Kashani was given a hero's welcome and allowed to resume political activity. Kashani's return in 1950 and the increasing public mobilisation behind the oil national-isation issue gave the *Fada'iyan* ample opportunity for political intrigue. The chief obstacle to oil nationalisation, as viewed by the *Kashani-Fada'-iyan* group, was prime minister 'Ali Razmara, who at the time was negotiating a new oil agreement with the British. The draft of the agreement was opposed by the parliament and ran counter to popular sentiments.

In March 1951, Khalil Tahmasbi, a devoted followed of Navvab, assassinated the prime minister at the Shah Mosque. Although Kashani was implicated in Razmara's assassination, no action was taken against him. A *Fada'iyan* leaflet boldly pointed out that Tahmasbi had 'sent to hell the greatest of all criminals'.[14] The leaflet also threatened the Shah and Razmara's cabinet members with death if the assassin was not released within three days.[15] The tone of the *Fada'iyan*'s statements even disturbed Kashani, who unsuccessfully asked Navvab to deny and withdraw the leaflet.[16] Tahmasbi himself declared that people like Razmara are 'sources of corruption and destruction of human life. Like cancer, they take root in one part of the body and injure the rest'.[17] In a later interview from jail, Tahmasbi maintained that he had stood up 'for God, and the implementation of the *Qur'an* and Islamic injunctions'.[18]

Twelve days after Razmara's assassination, Dr Abdu'l-Hamid Zan-ganeh, the Dean of the Law Faculty at the University of Tehran, was gunned down. Initially the *Fada'iyan* were thought to be responsible for the act. Statements by the assailant, Nusratollah Qumi smacked of similarity to the views of the *Fada'iyan*: 'All traitors must be extermi-nated'; Dr Zanganeh 'is a traitor and his presence harmful to the nation and its culture'.[19] However, it became evident that the assassin had not acted on orders from the *Fada'iyan*. Various accounts of the *Fada'iyan*, including the series by Muhammad Vahedi, all point to the absence of any direct links.[20] Nevertheless, the atmosphere of terror created by the *Fada'iyan* probably had a role in the latest assassination. After a series of noisy trials, Qumi was found guilty and hanged in April 1953.

Tahmasbi, however, was released from jail in November 1952 through a bill passed by the *Majlis* but never ratified by the Senate. The billl specified that 'because it is obvious to the public that 'Ali Razmara was a traitor, Khalil Tahmasbi will be pardoned and released from prison on the basis of this law which will go into effect as soon as it has been proved that he is Razmara's assassin'.[21] Immediately after winning his freedom, Tahmasbi made a brief pilgrimage to the nearby shrine in Ray and then set out to pay homage to Kashani. The Ayatollah warmly greeted Tahmasbi and, putting his hand on Tahmasbi's head, addressed him as 'the offspring of Islam'.[22]

Not long after Razmara's assassination, the relationship between the *Fada'iyan* and Kashani became estranged, soon to be broken off completely. The coming to power of the National Front government and the installation of Muhammad Mosaddeq as prime minister in April 1951, drastically changed Kashani's situation. The *Fada'iyan*'s 'demands for a share in executive power' was rebuffed by Kashani, who was certain Mosaddeq would deny such a request (Akhavi, 1980, p. 69; Faqhfoory, 1978, pp. 194–7). Navvab had apparently expected to be named the Minister of Religious Affairs.[23] Richard Cottam explains the break between the *Fada'iyan* and Kashani on ideological grounds. He points out that the *Fada'iyan*'s absolutism and their complete subordination of politics to religion 'made the political Kashani a natural target' (Cottam, 1964, p. 152).[24]

By June 1951 the top leadership clique of the *Fada'iyan*, including Navvab, were all arrested. Blaming Kashani and the National Front for their imprisonment, Navvab declared that the *Fada'iyan* 'have irrevocably broken away from Kashani'. He charged that Kashani's group and the National Front had 'promised to set up an Islamic country according to the precepts of the Koran. Instead they have imprisoned our brothers and suspended our newspaper'.[25] From his jail, Navvab declared:

Had it not been for my will, and my eminent brother Khalil's powerful bullet, neither the oil would have been nationalised nor the British expelled. I have performed unforgettable service for Kashani. I even swept the dust in his house. But the reward for my toil is imprisonment. Whenever I decide, the doors of jail will be opened for me. But I will stay in this place until *they* open my jail doors. I ask God not to allow us to die without bullet holes in our chests.[26]

A noisy demonstration by 500 *Fada'iyan* members protested against Navvab's arrest but failed to gain his release. Reports by the police that recently discovered *Fada'iyan* documents revealed plots to assassinate both Kashani and Mosaddeq did not improve matters.[27] Although these reports were denied in a formal letter by the *Fada'iyan* to the press, the tension between the *Fada'iyan* and the government leaders remained at a high level.[28] A sharp ideological division and differences in tactics separated the *Fada'iyan* from the secularist leaders of the National Front. The depth of this antagonism was made clear when a member of the *Fada'iyan* attempted to assassinate Dr Husayn Fatemi, the well-known publisher and National Front *Majlis* deputy (and later Dr Mosaddeq's foreign minister) in February 1952. Mosaddeq was apparently the assailant's first choice. It was rumoured that one reason for the attempted assassination of Fatemi was his omission of the final sentence 'Long Live Islam' from Tahmasbi's pronouncement against Razmara in Fatemi's newspaper, *Bakhtar-e Imruz* (Abrahamian, 1969, p. 166). The fifteen-year old assailant, Muhammad Mehdi 'Abd-e Khoda'i, was a minor attendant in a small hardware store. He had been a member of the *Fada'iyan* for only six months. Inscribed on his weapon were the slogans: 'Death to the enemies of Islam'; 'Immediate implementation of Islam's holy injunctions'; 'Immediate freedom of His Holiness Navvab Safavi and Master Tahmasbi'; 'Cut off the hands of foreigners and suppress Iran's enemies: Russia, England, and America'.[29] Navvab, however, was not released until early February 1953.[30]

The *Fada'iyan*'s final act of terrorism took place in November 1955. Muzaffar Zu'l-Qadr tried to assassinate prime minister Husayn 'Ala at the Shah Mosque just before 'Ala's departure to Iraq to represent Iran in the Baghdad Pact. Although 'Ala was injured, the attempted assassination was a failure. The assailant, a small shopowner, was wearing a white shroud underneath his garments on which a few passages were inscribed in red ink from the *Qur'an*. In the official interrogation, he repeated his belief in Islamic injunctions and maintained that since the Baghdad Pact was a military and defence pact which would result in the death of young Iranians, it should therefore be abrogated.[31]

The government quickly rounded up the top leadership of the *Fada' iyan* as well as sympathisers and former associates such as Kashani. During the course of the *Fada'iyan*'s trials new light was shed on Razmara's assassination. It was reported in one instance that Kashani had confessed to have issued a *fatwa* condoning Razmara's liquidation.[32] Kashani and others who had been arrested were soon released. The government, however, executed four of the top leaders of the *Fada'iyan*, including Navvab Safavi in January 1956. With these executions, the brief and violent history of the *Fada'iyan-e Islam* was, for the time being, closed.[33] Minor elements of the *Fada'iyan*, however, continued to operate clandestinely on a small scale. The *Fada'iyan*'s name re-emerged in the news in January 1965 when members of a secret organisation known as the Islamic Nations Party (*Hizb-e Millal-e Islami*) assassinated prime minister Hasan 'Ali Mansur at the entrance to the parliament buildings. The group's leader, Muhammad Kazem Musavi Bojnurdi, was an Iranian resident of Iraq who had previously belonged to the Iraqi party of *al-Da'wat al-Islami*. According to the Iranian government reports, the Islamic Nations Party was a conspiratorial organisation whose small group of young members was determined to re-establish the supremacy of Islam through armed struggle. The discovery of a cache of arms belonging to the party in the hills of northern Tehran gave greater weight to these charges. Forty-five of the party's members were arrested; thirteen of them were tried for the alleged role in the prime minister's assassination. The trial of the accused was conducted swiftly, and varying sentences, including four executions, were passed by the military court. During the trials it was revealed that some of the accused had been members of the *Fada'iyan* – one serving as the organisation's treasurer. There may have been other links with the *Fada'iyan* that have not come to light. However, both organisations recruited their members primarily from those in the lower socio-economic strata and had similar goals for Islamic supremacy in Iran.[34]

In the period since the Iranian revolution, the *Fada'iyan* have been officially resurrected under the leadership of Shaykh Sadeq Khalkhali, the judge of the revolutionary Islamic courts and a close associate of Ayatollah Ruhollah Khomeini. In a recent interview, Khalkhali maintained that he has been a member of the *Fada'iyan* since his days as a religious student (*talabeh*). He further stated that the *Fada'iyan*'s activities are now in the open.

We no longer need to engage in underground activities. We have a revolutionary court and can summon the guilty. The *Fada'iyan*'s operation, however, will not be limited to Iran. It will extend to all Islamic lands.[35]

The establishment of the Islamic Republic in Iran has given the *Fada'-iyan* the long-awaited opportunity to organise and operate openly. However, since at least some of the goals of the *Fada'iyan* have already been implemented by Khomeini's theocracy,[36] the *Fada'iyan*'s independent existence and influence in the government may turn out to be superfluous.

## MEMBERSHIP, ORGANISATION, AND IDEOLOGY

There are no accurate statistics about the size of the *Fada'iyan*'s membership. Adele Ferdows estimates that at its height the organisation had between 20 and 25 000 members in Tehran and between 12 and 15 000 members in other cities, notably Mashhad (Ferdows, 1967, p. 40). A recently declassified Foreign Service Despatch of the United States Government attests to the *Fada'iyan*'s relatively small size.

> The Fedayan Islam can in no way be considered a mass movement, nor is it well organised. Safavi has at various times claimed a membership of 5 000 and a following of sympathisers of 100 000. At outdoor meetings called by the Fedayan in the past, never more than a few hundred have appeared. Even these, however, must be considered more as followers of Kashani than of the Fedayan proper. After his arrest, Safavi's faction of the Fedayan was unable to gather more than 100 persons to demonstrate in front of the prison where he was being held.[37]

These figures are, at best, reasonable estimates and cannot be taken as completely reliable information. It is, however, clear that the *Fada'iyan*'s size was a far cry from a mass organisation, even in major urban centres such as Tehran and Mashhad. Their total membership is nevertheless not insignificant when compared with other terroristic organisations that have emerged elsewhere since World War Two. The number of those who sympathised with the *Fada'iyan* and their goals was much larger. The coalition with Kashani and other clerical elements made the *Fada'iyan* appear to be more powerful than their numerical strength warranted. The *Fada'iyan* membership was drawn almost exclusively from illiterate or semi-literate lower- or lower middle-class youth from the bazaar. For example, the average age of twenty-nine members of the *Fada'iyan* who were tried in 1952 was 24, and practically all of them had low status occupations (Abrahamian, 1969, p. 136).[38] Moreover, three of the *Fada'iyan* assassins, whose occupations were known, had low status jobs including a carpenter, an attendant in a small store and a small shopowner.

Navvab Safavi was the key figure in the *Fada'iyan* organisation. His position of eminence was recognised by all of his followers. The circle of top leadership included (in addition to Navvab) the Vahedi brothers. The two brothers were brought up in a clerical family and their clergyman father had been a staunch supporter of Shaykh Fazlollah Nuri's anti-parliamentarian drive of the early twentieth century.[39] The Vahedi brothers were of great importance because of their organisational ability and 'intellectual' contribution to the *Fada'iyan*. But none of them was in any way equal to Navvab. Even when an internal dispute apparently arose between the Vahedi brothers and Navvab and the temporary departure of the Vahedi brothers from the organisation was announced, the brothers explicitly stated that Navvab is their acknowledged leader and that they are of no consequence without him.[40] An intense personal relationship characterised the *Fada'iyan*'s interaction with one another. They viewed themselves as a true fraternity of devoted Islamic soldiers.

Navvab made ample use of his personal appeal to recruit members and create a devoted following. During the questioning prior to his trial, Navvab expressed admiration for the indoctrination method of legendary old man of the mountain, Hasan Sabbah and, similarly, presented himself as someone with certain extraordinary and superhuman qualities.[41] The assailant of prime minister 'Ala described an indoctrination session with Navvab before the assassination attempt:

A few hours before giving me the weapon ... Navvab presented me with a bowl of water in the middle of which there was a rolled piece of paper. Navvab said this is a talisman. After drinking this water, no one can hurt you and everyone will be under your influence and control.[42]

The organisation also had a security guard whose members all wore identical fur hats.[43] It appears that individuals in the security guard had received some training in the use of weapons. The training and practice sessions were held in the deserted areas and outskirts of greater Tehran.

Handsome financial support was provided to the *Fada'iyan* by a few known Tehran merchants. The amount was purported to be about 600 000 rials annually. In addition, the *Fada'iyan* received money from various individuals as part of Shi'ite religious 'tax' payment and, through threats, from wealthy bazaar merchants. When in need of ready cash, Navvab drafted and sent hand-delivered messages requesting financial support. In one such letter, he declared 'after having consulted the Holy *Qur'an*, I am writing to you because money is needed for Islam ... for the purchase of loudspeakers, a car, and for the publication and distribution of leaflets. Give the messenger your generous response'.[44]

There were also allegations to the effect that the *Fada'iyan* had connections with similar fraternal groups in Iraq, Turkey, and Egypt. In an announcement in 1955, the Iranian government charged the *Fada'-iyan* with having ties with the *Tudeh* military network and that Navvab and fifteen of the *Fada'iyan* terrorists had received military instructions from the *Tudeh* officers in the military. Navvab himself had claimed in an interview that 'he could wield greater influence over Iranian Communists, although himself not a Communist, than could premier Stalin'.[45] It is doubtful that any *formal* ties existed between the *Fada'iyan* and the Egyptian Moslem Brotherhood. The Iraqi connections probably consisted of a few Iranian sympathisers and members of the *Fada'iyan* who were residents of Iraq.[46] It is possible that some *Tudeh* military officers instructed a few of the *Fada'iyan* in the use of weapons, but the two organisations were diametrically opposed in their ideologies and no long-range co-operation could have worked out between them. The goal of the Tudeh military network was the creation of a communist regime, not an Islamic state. Any co-operation that may have existed between the *Fada'iyan* and the *Tudeh* military officers had to be of a purely tactical nature based on a common desire to eliminate Western influence in Iran and oppose the Pahlavi dynasty. The *Tudeh* notions of Marxism and dialectical materialism had no place in the *Fada'iyan* belief system.[47]

The *Fada'iyan* spread their message through various leaflets, broadsheets, and their weekly newspaper, *Manshur-e Baradari*. An important event in this regard was the publication of their book of ideology, *Rahnama-ye Haqayeq* (The Guide to Truth) in 1950.[48] Its ideas formed the basis of the *Fada'iyan*'s attempt to reconstruct Iran according to their version of the Shi'ite Islamic order.

The *Fada'iyan*'s ideology combined religious zeal and belief in the supremacy of Shi'ite Islam with elements of Iranian nationalism. The *Fada'iyan* sought to 'purify the Persian language' and hoped to bring the Iranian–Shi'ite lands together and establish an Islamic government (Binder, 1962, p. 82; Ferdows, 1967, p. 51).[49] They viewed secular government as a usurper of power and authority which in their view belonged to a theocratic Shi'ite leadership under a Caliphate or an Imam. As Nikki Keddie and A. H. Zarrinkub (1965) point out, the *Fada'iyan*'s

> goals included strict enforcement of the *Shari'ah* and the ending of irreligiousness. They combined fundamentalism with violent xenophobia, and considered attacks on foreigners and politicians with foreign connections a defence of *Dar al-Islam*. The Fada'iyan proclaimed the government of 'xenophiles' illegitimate, and called such men enemy spies whose blood must be shed.[50]

In their book of ideology, the *Fada'iyan* assert that 'the present government of Iran is unconstitutional and illegal' and is composed of 'traitors and usurpers . . . and the enemies of Islam'.[51] This book shows some ambivalence regarding the monarchy. Although it denounces the Shah and his government in very harsh terms, at times it gives the impression that a monarch who rules according to Islamic laws and follows religious precepts might be tolerated. In a section discussing the Shah's duties, it is said that the Shah must be guided by the rules and principles of Shi'ite Islam and must chose the first Shi'ite Imam, 'Ali, as his model. In addition, specific religious duties such as paying proper respect to the holy shrines, participation in congregational prayers, and supervision of religious endowments are assigned to him. The section is concluded with the remark that if the monarch continuously checks his 'duties and responsibilities . . . as dictated by religion . . ., then he will be the Shah'[52] (that is, the legitimate Shah).

In discussing the Iranian parliament, the *Fada'iyan* maintain that all those laws passed by the *Majlis* which are contrary to Islamic principles must be abrogated. The parliament deputies

must not pass laws and set rules for the country, because God alone has the right to make rules. Laws and rules which are based on the meagre and feeble minds of humans and which are contrary to the spirit and the wisdom of the Islamic laws and principles are unlawful and unacceptable. Iran is officially a Muslim land, and all of the rules and regulations of the society must be based strictly upon the principles of *Ja'fari* Islam.[53]

The *Fada'iyan*'s social and economic views are traditional and at times strikingly naive. They believe that the proper and best place for a woman is 'to be the manager of the house and a mother and wife'.[54] They ridicule the notion of women's rights and advocate temporary marriages to eradicate prostitution.[55]

They compare the operation of the nation's economy to the running of grocery stores and find the grocer to be the best choice for heading the ministry of economy or finance: 'If a pious grocer were to replace the corrupt minister of finance, he could manage and develop the economy of the country much better than any honest and capable minister of finance anywhere in the world who claims expertise in the science of economy and finance'.[56] Moreover, there are specific suggestions for lowering the cost of living and for instituting taxes based on Islamic principles.[57]

The *Fada'iyan* propose the establishment of a Ministry of Justice to adjudicate disputes according to Islamic laws and to apply strict religious punishments for the wrongdoers. Thus, the *Fada'iyan* expect the thief's hand to be cut off and the adulterer whipped in public.[58] The *Fada'iyan*'s militancy is also evident in their insistence that 'military instruction and war techniques ... be taught in schools during the physical education hour as a regular part of the programme'.[59] They believe that the 'military principles of *Qur'an*' must be a basic to any military training.[60] This includes the idea of the holy war against the infidels and enemies of Islam.

## CONCLUSION

The *Fada'iyan* never managed to become a mass organisation and attract a cross-section of the population. Their financial resources were too limited to allow them to expand their organisation and its various arms. Their political importance was due to their successful terroristic activities and the general social and political conditions in Iran after World War Two. The alliance with the clergy helped the *Fada'iyan* to increase their financial base, membership, and influence in the political arena. But they had to share their constituency and new members with the influential clergy. The break with Ayatollah Kashani cost the *Fada'-iyan* dearly and severely handicapped their operation. The *Fada'iyan*'s failure to extend their appeal beyond the lower- and lower middle-classes in the bazaar stands in sharp contrast to the success of the Egyptian *al-Ikhwan al-Muslimun* (The Moslem Brotherhood) in securing members from most sectors of society. Although there was much similarity between the *Ikhwan* and the *Fada'iyan* in the areas of tactics, use of terrorism, goals of an 'Islamic order', urban appeal, and anti-Western orientation, the similarity ends when one scrutinises closely the organisation or programmes of the two groups (Mitchell, 1969, esp. pp. 234–41, 254–9, 264–7, 281, 328–31). The *Ikhwan* had a vast organisation with branches, administrative offices, and sections and committees dealing with problems of labour, peasantry, students, finance, and legal and policy matters. The *Fada'iyan* could claim no such organisational apparatus. The *Ikhwan* represented their constituency directly and effectively while the *Fada'iyan* sympathisers were simultaneously represented by the politically active *'ulama'*.

The *Ikhwan* had a much more elaborate and sophisticated programme for political organisation based on Islamic law. This involved dividing the governmental sector into five distinct spheres of executive, judicial, financial, legislative, and 'control and reform' (Mitchell, 1969, p. 248). In addition, such basic principles as freedom of thought, worship, expression, education, and possession were specifically singled out as having been proclaimed by Islam (Mitchell, 1969, p. 249). The *Ikhwan* were also aware of the importance of social contract and practice of consultation with representatives of the people (Mitchell, 1969, pp. 247–8). The *Fada'iyan*'s programme for political organisation, although detailed, was simplistic and dealt essentially with the re-organisation of the existing ministries in very general terms. There was no real attempt to relate the proposed reorganisations to broader principles of politics and political community. Moreover, there was much ambiguity in their discussion of the monarchy and the *Majlis*.

The *Ikhwan*'s proposals on economic and social organisation were also more elaborate and cohesive. They agreed to the right of private ownership but modified the extent of private accumulation of wealth by forbidding monopoly and by proposing taxation on the basis of 'a statutory level of property' (Mitchell, 1969, p. 253). The *Fada'iyan*'s economic programme also emphasised taxation and private property rights, but this was coupled with simplistic analyses of the operation of the market and financial management. On the question of women's rights, the *Ikhwan* were a step ahead of the *Fada'iyan*. The *Ikhwan* at least envisaged equal political rights for women in the future and were more tolerant of women's gainful employment in law, medicine, or business.

In a fundamental way, however, the *Fada'iyan* and the *Ikhwan* had something in common. Both had emerged as severe reactions to economic, political, and cultural changes that had disturbed the social fabric of Iran and Egypt. They were responses to the economic dislocations caused by World War Two and the overwhelming presence of the 'infidel' power in their midst. Many among the disenfranchised masses shared their reactions, their sense of malaise, and their yearning to return to the 'Golden Age' of Islam when problems were not so complicated and one's position in the social order was more clearly established. Yet what distinguished the particular response of the *Fada'-iyan* and the *Ikhwan* from that of others was its pervasive religious character, its rigid intolerance, and its frequent reliance on violent terroristic acts.[61]

## NOTES

1. The exact date of the founding of the *Fada'iyan* is in dispute. Ferdows cites 1945 as the founding date, Abrahamian and the recently declassified Foreign Service Despatch of the US State Department believe it was 1946, while Keddie and Zarrinkub use 1943 as the base year for the *Fada'iyan*'s activities. Published reports of the Iranian government during the *Fada'iyan* trials cite 1945 as the founding date which appears to be correct. Furthermore, in the introduction to the 1979 reprint of the *Fada'iyan*'s book of ideology, *Rahnama-ye Haqayeq*, again 1324/1945 is given as the founding date. Finally, a series of articles published in *Khvandani-ha* by Muhammad Vahedi on the history of the *Fada'iyan* confirms 1945 as the founding date – although the first broadsheet of the *Fada'iyan* was not issued until March 1946 (Ferdows, 1967, p. 26; Abrahamian, 1969, p. 134; Keddie and Zarrinkub, 1965, p. 882). US Department of State, Foreign Service Despatch, Tehran to Washington, No. 20, 7 July 1951, p. 1. *Ettela'at*, 27 December 1955, p. 4. M. Vahedi, '*Khaterat-e Fada'iyan-e Islam az Havades-e Chand Sal-e Akhir*', *Khvandani-ha*, Mehr 4, 1334, p. 14.
2. Background information on Navvab Safavi can be found in Ferdows, p. 33; *Ettela'at*, 27 and 31 December 1955; and the Vahedi articles in *Khvandani-ha*, 1334.
3. Kasravi had also written that the Safavid dynasty's claim of descent from the Prophet was a forgery. Navvab was angered by Kasravi's charge and had further incentive to plan Kasravi's assassination. See also Abrahamian, 1980.
4. Vahedi, *Khvandani-ha*, *Mehr* 1, 1334, pp. 13, 24.
5. See the text in *Khvandani-ha*, *Mehr* 4, 1334, pp. 14, 35.
6. Vahedi, *Khvandani-ha*, *Mehr* 6, 1334, p. 35.
7. Ibid, p. 34. See also Sharif-Razi, 1979: pp. 279–86; and V. Razi, 1980 '*Fada'iyan-e Islam*', *Raha'i* (*Bahman* 9, 1359) pp. 10–12.
8. *Manshur-e Baradari*, *Urdibehesht* 5, 1332, p. 2.
9. Vahedi, *Khvandani-ha*, *Mehr* 18, 1334, p. 15.
10. There were other demonstrations later about the Palestine problem. For example, in 1949 demonstrations were held in Tehran 'against migrating Iraqi Jews *en route* to Palestine' (Bayne, 1968, p. 276).
11. '*Parvandeh-ye Mahramaneh-y Bazju'iha-ye Navvab-e Safavi Fash Mishavad*', *Khvandani-ha*, *Bahman* 5, 1334, p. 10.
12. Vahedi, *Khvandani-ha*, *Mehr* 25, 1334, pp. 15–16, and *Aban* 2, 1334, p. 31.
13. Vahedi, *Khvandani-ha*, *Mehr* 27, 1334, p. 19.
14. *New York Times*, 10 March 1951, p. 3.
15. See *Ettela'at*, 11 March 1951.
16. Vahedi, *Khvandani-ha*, *Aban* 16, 1334, p. 18.
17. '*Chira Razmara ra Koshtam*', *Taraqqi*, *Mordad* 14, 1330, p. 3.
18. *Taraqqi*, *Mordad* 28, 1330, p. 1.
19. *New York Times*, 20 March 1951, p. 3. *Asiya-ye Javan*, *Shahrivar* 13, 1330, p. 11.
20. Vahedi, *Khvandani-ha*, *Aban* 18, 1334, p. 16.
21. Text in *Taraqqi*, *Mordad* 13, 1330, p. 1; quoted in Ferdows, p. 61.

22. *Asiya-ye Javan, Aban* 28, 1331, p. 12.
23. *Ettela'at*, 13 January 1956, p. 8.
24. Cottam also points out that the cynics have maintained that this break was due to Kashani's refusal to subsidise the *Fada'iyan* for their support.
25. *New York Times*, 13 May 1951, p. 3.
26. *Asiya-ye Javan, Aban* 28, 1331, p. 12.
27. See *New York Times*, 6 June 1951, p. 6; and 21 April 1951, p. 9.
28. *Taraqqi' Khordad* 20, 1330, p. 7. See also *Taraqqi, Tir* 31, 1330, p. 5.
29. *Asiya-ye Javan, Bahman* 30, 1330, p. 12; and *Ettela'at*, 16 February 1952, p. 7. See also *Ettela'at*, 1 April 1932, p. 8 for anti-Musaddeq pronouncements of the *Fada'iyan*.
30. For a detailed account of the *Fada'iyan* activities in Qum prior to Navvab's release see *Taraqqi, Day* 22, 1331, pp. 2–4, 23.
31. See *Ettela'at*, 18 November 1955.
32. *Ettela'at*, 22 January 1956.
33. Abdu'l-Husayn Vahedi, the top intellectual and number two man of the *Fada'iyan* was killed in November 1955 after his arrest on his way to Tehran from Ahvaz while attempting to escape from the hands of the police.
34. Among those jailed in connection with the Islamic Nations Party's assassination of Mansur was Habib Allah Asgar Auladi who has become a prominent figure in Khomeini's Islamic Republic as a member of the parliament and as a one-time candidate for the presidency. He is also alleged to be a key official of the group known as *Hizb Allahis* (Partisans of God) who have frequently and violently attacked anti-Khomeini demonstrations in Tehran . . . Bijan Jazani, a key figure in the *Cherikha-ye Fada'i-ye Khalq-e Iran*, also links the assassination of Mansur to the *Fada'iyan*. His discussion of the *Hizb-e Millal-e Islami*, however, depicts an organisation somewhat different from the *Fada'iyan* (Jazani, 1978–9, pp. 63, 193–8).
35. *Omid-e Iran*, New series, *Tir* 4, 1358, p. 22. The *Fada'iyan* members received international notoriety when in May 1980, under Judge Khalkhali's direction, they succeeded in demolishing a marble mausoleum built some twenty years ago to honour the founder of the Pahlavi dynasty, Reza Shah.
36. See Chapter 10 by Arjomand.
37. US Department of State, Foreign Service Despatch, No 20, p. 4.
38. See Chapter 10 by Arjomand.
39. The occupation of fifteen of these were published in newspapers. These were: 'two shirt-tailors, a theology student, a glass-seller, a preacher, a dry-cleaner, a carpenter, an architect-builder, a weaver, a draper's apprentice, an engraver, a metal-peddlar, a grocer, a machine-owner, and a bicycle-repairer' (Abrahamian, 1969, p. 136).
40. For the text see *Ettela'at*, 13 May 1953.
41. *Ettela'at*, 1 December 1955, p. 14.
42. *Ettela'at*, 13 December 1955, p. 1.
43. *Taraqqi, Bahman* 20, 1331, p. 22.
44. *Ettela'at*, 27 December 1955, p. 16; 13 January 1956, p. 14; 14 December 1955, p. 14. See also Ferdows, p. 66.
45. *New York Times*, 13 May 1951, p. 3.
46. Keddie and Zarrinkub maintain that the *Fada'iyan* 'had ties' with the Moslem Brotherhood in Iraq and Egypt, and 'like the *Ikhwan* as well as

many co-religious groups of the past they called each other "brethren" '. See Keddie and Zarrinkub, p. 882. Richard Mitchell, however, points out that there were apparently no 'formal' ties between the *Fada'iyan* and the *Ikhwan*. He indicates that Navvab Safavi visited Egypt in January 1954 and was welcomed by the *Ikhwan*, but probably his 'stress on *Shi'ite* Islam would make him automatically a "non-ally" '. Letter from Professor Richard P. Mitchell, Department of History, University of Michigan, 5 December 1972. See also Mitchell, 1969, p. 126, note 60. For additional material on *Fada'iyan*'s alleged ties with other groups see *Khvandani-ha*, *Azar* 9, 1334, p. 9. *Taraqqi*, Day 15, 1331, p. 2. Sharif-Razi, p. 288.

47. On the *Tudeh* military network see Kazemi, 1980, pp. 224–33.
48. Vahedi, Khvandani-ha, Aban 9, 1344, pp. 15–16. Vahedi gives a vivid description of the process of publication and distribution of this book to a selected group of Iran's political and religious leaders.
49. There was apparently an 'irredentist' strain in the *Fada'iyan*'s ideology. But this, like many other of the *Fada'iyan* views, was not fully developed.
50. Keddie and Zarrinkub, p. 882. See also *Ettela'at*, 30 March 1953, p. 10.
51. *Fada'iyan-e Islam, Rahnama-ye Haqayeq* (Tehran: n.p., 1329–1950). For the sake of convenience, I have used the translation by Adele Ferdows (1967).
52. Ibid, pp. 79–80.
53. Ibid, p. 85.
54. Ibid, p. 12.
55. Ibid, p. 41.
56. Ibid, p. 49.
57. Ibid, pp. 51–2.
58. Ibid, p. 34.
59. Ibid, p. 68.
60. Ibid, p. 71.
61. For similar comments about the *Ikhwan* see Mitchell, 1969, p. 320.

# 9 Sermons, Revolutionary Pamphleteering and Mobilisation: Iran, 1978[1]

## SHAUL BAKHASH

On 6 January 1978, the Iranian Minister of Information handed to a reporter of the newspaper, *Ettela'at*, a brown manila envelope containing an article that the newspaper was ordered to publish. The imposition of officially-inspired articles on the Tehran press was at the time standard government practice. When *Ettela'at*'s editors examined the article, they were appalled. The article was a scurrilous attack on Ayatollah Khomeini. It described him as a reactionary and contentious cleric, cast aspersions on his religious scholarship and suggested that he had sought to achieve through political demagoguery a prominence he had been unable to attain on the strength of his religious learning. It accused Khomeini of having been in the pay of the large landlords, reactionary elements and even British Intelligence. It suggested Khomeini had written love-poetry under the pseudonym of 'al-Hindi'. Alluding to the fact that Khomeini's grandfather had for a time lived in Kashmir, the article sought to cast doubt on the authenticity of Khomeini's Iranian origins.[2]

Objections by *Ettela'at*'s editors failed to budge the Ministry of Information in its insistence that the article be printed. When the piece appeared in *Ettela'at* on 7 January, it caused a sensation in Qum. On 8 January, students from Qum's religious seminaries began to move in a body from the home of one Ayatollah to another, eliciting statements from the religious leaders condemning the article and expressing support for Khomeini. The seminarians, joined by townspeople, continued on their rounds the next day, when the bazaar, many shops and the seminaries were closed as a mark of protest. Other religious leaders commented on the article.

The remarks made by Qum's leading clerics, and the statements they issued, were generally mild in tone. They expressed their indignation at the article; they strongly criticised its authors. But they urged the students to protest peacefully, and they assured them they were doing what was necessary in taking up the issue with the authorities in Tehran.[3] It was the religious students who pressed their leaders for a stronger stand. For example, they urged Ayatollah Ha'eri to speak more forthrightly when, in remarks at his house and later at the A'zam mosque, he commented on the article only in guarded terms.[4] He in turn cautioned against statements or action which would cause the security authorities to attack and wreck the mosque as they had done the *Fayziyyeh* seminary two years earlier.

On the afternoon of 9 January, as the seminarians and the towns-people were moving from the house of one Ayatollah to another, they were confronted by security forces. Inevitably, clashes occurred. Before the night was over, government offices and banks had been attacked by the crowd, shots had been fired, and demonstrators had been wounded and killed. News of the clashes in Qum spread to other cities. The Isfahan bazaar closed for a week. Merchants in the bazaar in Tehran, Shiraz and other cities closed their shops in protest. Political groups, the Iranian Committee for the Defence of Human Rights and Liberty, student associations and religious figures in Tehran and other centres issued statements of solidarity with the Qum clerics.[5]

## THE PATTERN OF PROTEST

Although this was not understood at the time, the collision in Qum marked the beginning of the Iranian revolution. It inspired a chain of protest demonstrations that provided a vehicle for mass mobilisation, confrontation and 'martyrdom', and contributed powerfully to the overthrow of the Shah. It also set the pattern for the later de-monstrations and clashes with the authorities. The elements that would form and fuel the subsequent protests – the fusing of religious and political themes, the focus on the streets, the use of the mosque sermon and of political pamphlets for the articulation of demands – were already evident in Qum.

On 18 February, bazaars and universities in several towns were closed and memorial services were held to mourn the Qum dead. In Tabriz, severe rioting erupted when police shot a demonstrator. On 30 March, clashes occurred between troops and demonstrators in Yazd and other towns during memorial services and observances for the Tabriz dead. In May, rioting and demonstrations shook some thirty-four towns and cities. In July, Mashad, Rafsanjan and dozens of other centres were racked by violence. In August, Isfahan and Shiraz followed. Beginning in July and until the collapse of the monarchy in February 1979, the riots, demonstrations and clashes with government troops became endemic, spreading from town to town like a fire in the underbrush and exploding into major conflagrations in the cities and great urban centres. Almost invariably, the clashes led to considerable destruction and left many dead and wounded.

These demonstrations, the collisions with security forces and the destructive rioting tended to be regarded by officials either as the acts of rampaging mob, mindlessly destroying banks, shops and public buildings, or as deliberate acts of sabotage carefully organised by a small group of plotters. 'The rioters' said the Shah, 'receive their orders from the Communists'. In fact, the demonstrations were both spontaneous and calculated. They often grew out of the unpremeditated actions of Iranians from different walks of life giving vent to their anger against the government; and they were given shape and direction by religious leaders, small political groups and individual political activists, frequently working independently of one another, in cities, towns and hamlets across the country.

The street crowd often set the tone and pace of the early demonstrations. Yet each of the major protests rose out of specific circumstances. The crowds, in each instance, were acting on specific complaints. The ground was prepared carefully by preachers and propagandists. On each occasion, the targets attacked by the rioters were not randomly chosen but carefully selected to underline identifiable grievances.

The early demonstrations, continuing to the end of September, were almost invariably grounded in religious events. Memorial services, traditionally held on the fortieth day to honour the dead, provided the occasion for the mass demonstrations in Tabriz in February; in Yazd, Ahwaz, Jahrom and other towns in March and April and the widespread outbreaks in numerous towns in May. But other religious events provided fuel to fire a new round of protests beginning in July.

Riots broke out in Mashad on 22 July during funeral services for Shaykh Ahmad Kafi, a local religious leader who had been killed in a highway collision.[6] Since Kafi had been an outspoken critic of the government, it was widely believed that the accident had been carefully arranged by the Shah's secret police, Savak. Mourning ceremonies for

Kafi, and protests against the killing of demonstrators in Mashad, then led to further violence in Tehran, Qum and elsewhere.

Religious ceremonies to mark the birth of the sixth Imam, Ja'far Sadeq, were also the setting for riots that broke out in remote towns and hamlets around Rafsanjan in eastern Iran.[7] Crowds in the village of Jalgeh, aroused by a local cleric, Shaykh Mohammad Taqi Haq-Dust, who had been moving from village to village to preach, to denounce the Pahlavis and speak of Islamic government, clashed with security forces. A gendarmerie officer was killed. When gendarmes returned the next day to conduct house searches, make arrests and harrass the villagers, riots erupted which spread to other villages and eventually to the provincial centre, Rafsanjan. In Rafsanjan itself, the clashes erupted following the performance of a passion play and a sermon preached by another cleric, Shaykh Mohammad Hashemian.

In Isfahan in August, excitement was generated by the return from three months in exile of one of the town's leading religious figures, Ayatollah Taheri.[8] Thirty thousand people went several miles out of the city to welcome the Ayatollah and to accompany him back to Isfahan. On the following day, he visited the bazaar. Two days later, he preached his first Friday sermon. When he renewed his attacks on the government in a sermon on the following Friday, he was arrested again. Several hundred protestors staged a *bast*, or a sit-in, in the home of the city's other leading religious figure, Ayatollah Khademi. For several days, the protestors heard speeches and sermons and took part in communal prayers. On the tenth day of the *bast*, violent riots broke out in the city. For two days, Isfahan was in the hands of the crowds, before tanks rolled in, martial law was imposed and a measure of quiet returned to the city again. It was after listening to mosque sermons, in a pattern that occurred again and again, that crowds emerged in large cities like Shiraz and Yazd,[9] and small towns like Shahsavar, Jahrom and Behbahan,[10] to demonstrate, protest, clash with security forces and attack particular targets.

## THE INSTIGATORS

At least three groups of people laid the groundwork for these mass demonstrations: religious leaders with national standing, lesser clerics working at the local level, and non-clerical political activists and propagandists. National religious figures, like Ayatollahs Shari-'atmadari, Golpaygani, Ruhani and Ha'eri-Yazdi proclaimed or lent their names to the mourning ceremonies and religious observances which became vehicles for the expression of protest. They allowed the mosques under their supervision in the major cities to be used for these purposes. Yet proclamations by the leading religious figures generally remained moderate in tone. They condemned the use of troops and the resulting loss of lives. They sharply criticised the regime – though most frequently through the employment of such euphemisms as 'the ruling administration' or 'the dictatorship'. But their proclamations, with rare exceptions, avoided direct reference to the person of the Shah, and until September they issued no call for the overthrow of the regime.

This was left to the lesser ranks of the *ulama* and to largely unknown political propagandists and activists. In Qum, the more radical declarations were issued above the signature of the middle-rank seminary teachers, most of whom were followers of Khomeini. In the town of Yazd, the leading figure was Ayatollah Mohammad Sadduqi, another early Khomeini supporter.[11] A fiery speaker, he could shut down the Yazd bazaar at will. In Najafabad, near Isfahan, Ayatollah Montazeri, though often in prison, left behind a legacy of militancy. A number of middle rank clerics led agitation from towns to which they had been exiled. Mohammad Mehdi Rabbani (later to become Prosecutor-General of the Islamic Republic) issued militant statements and led protests in the small town of Shahr-e Babak. Another exiled cleric, Ali Khamene'i (who became the third president of post-revolution Iran) was active in Iranshahr; Ali Tehrani was active from exile in Saqqez.[12]

Behind these local religious figures, there emerged an army of nameless propagandists and political activists. Many of them were young students and seminarians who had made their way from the villages to the towns during the economic boom of the 1970s, and who had received their introduction to opposition political ideas in the mosques and in the Shah's rapidly expanding education system. The pamphleteering and other efforts of these activists significantly contributed to the radicalisation of the opposition movement.

When local clerics in Yazd in February and March appeared excessively restrained in issuing statements and in condemning the regime, a banner appeared above the city's Qur'an Gate with the inscription: 'Welcome to the city of unbelievers'.[13] In such ways did the activists seek to force the hand of cautious clerics and their more moderate townsmen. In Yazd, it was students who encouraged Ayatollah Sadduqi to take radical stands and issue strong statements. They helped arouse the congregation in a Yazd mosque by shouting revolutionary slogans during a sermon on 30 March, and later helped lead the congregation into the streets in a protest march that led to clashes with security forces.[14]

These activists taped and transcribed the sermons of mosque preachers. They wrote up their own accounts of collisions between troops and demonstrators. They used Xerox machines, home typewriters, office and university stencils to reproduce tracts, leaflets and proclamations; and they helped to disseminate this oppositional literature widely. Some of the activists came from the older, established political organisations, like Mehdi Bazargan's Freedom of Iran Movement, which began semi-clandestine activities, chiefly from abroad, in January. Once controls over party activity were lifted in August, adherents of other established parties, such as the National Front and the *Tudeh* (Iranian Communist Party) also grew active.

But extensive pamphleteering activity was initially carried out by large numbers of individuals and small groups operating independently, or in association with local mosques, in towns, cities and hamlets across the country. Drawing on themes and a style made popular by Khomeini, these groups and individuals produced a populist, more radical revolutionary literature. They issued declarations in the name of organisations such as the 'Revolutionary Workers of Islam', 'Army of Revolutionary Moslems', 'Dawn of Islam', 'Vengeance' and 'Seekers of God'. Most of these groups had no real political existence and represented the temporary coalescing of a few individuals for purposes of political agitation. Yet it was largely through these pamphleteering efforts that the revolutionary temperament was steeled and hardened.

## THEMES OF PAMPHLETEERING

In the wake of the widespread killing of demonstrators in Tehran on 'Black Friday', 8 September, many prominent religious and secular leaders moved closer to calling for a deposition of the Shah. In a joint declaration issued on 12 September, for example, Ayatollahs Shari'atmadari, Golpaygani and Mar'ashi-Najafi denounced 'the shameful crimes and merciless slaughter of the tyrannical regime' and stated 'the people ... desire the uprooting of the autocratic and colonial regime ... the establishment of an Islamic order and the implementation of the commandments of the glorious Qur'an'.[15] In the first week of November, following his meeting in Paris with Khomeini, the National Front leader, Karim Sanjabi, issued a statement, with Khomeini's approval, declaring the Shah's regime illegal and demanding a national referendum to determine the country's future form of government.[16]

However, until then, the National Front had continued to focus on such issues as the release of political prisoners, the return of political exiles, punishment of those responsible for the death of demonstrators and adherence to the Constitution.[17] Similarly in May, when the popular pamphlets were already denouncing the Shah in the strongest terms, Mehdi Bazargan responded to the Shah's call for a national dialogue by inviting the monarch to join representatives of the opposition in a public debate.[18] Throughout the spring, summer and early autumn of 1978, it was the popular pamphleteers and the lesser clerics who set the pace for revolutionary propaganda, working to destroy the reputation of the Pahlavi dynasty and to mobilise support for the overthrow of the monarchy.

Established religious and secular leaders, signing their names to declarations, had to exercise a degree of circumspection in order to avoid the unwelcome attention of the secret police. As responsible figures, they were committed to the idea of rational discourse and constitutional change. But the less prominent clerics felt no such constraints. Nor did the political propagandists who issued unsigned declarations, or who issued tracts in the name of fictitious political organisations. Their leaflets thus minced no words, observed no niceties. They described the Shah as a lackey and a butcher and his family as plunderers. They termed the Shah's troops 'mercenaries'. They painted the abuses of the Shah's secret police in graphic terms. A leaflet circulated after clashes in Shahsavar said:

In order to preserve and maintain his bloodthirsty and filthy authority, the pharaoh of Iran perpetrates one massacre after another ... At the express orders of the executioner Shah, his corrupt and black-hearted mercenaries have unleashed a river of blood in the avenues, streets and homes of the township of Shahsavar.[19]

The pamphleteering literature also focused on the corrupting impact of foreign influence that had grown under the Shah's rule, the plunder of the economic wealth of the country by foreigners and Iran's growing economic dependence. The Shah's cultural policies, one leaflet said, 'has cut the people off from their religion and national traditions ... The fruit of such a calamity is the destruction of social relations and morality'.[20] Another leaflet alleged that 'the wheels of the economy have come to a standstill. People need foreign goods to meet all their needs. Iranian farmers are forced to consume American wheat and Israeli eggs'.[21] In

Isfahan, where there was a large American community, including many Vietnam veterans involved in helicopter training and maintenance, and other military work, this leaflet appeared:

> The people . . . of Isfahan could see with their own eyes how a filthy foreign minority, with the co-operation of their internal servants, were looting their material and spiritual wealth and resources . . ., had flooded the city with the prostitutes, the ailing of the Vietnam war and in general the rejects of Western society.[22]

The popular pamphleteers made it a practice to disseminate stories about the alleged atrocities of the security forces. Already following the clashes in Qum in January, the pamphleteering literature reported that the government had allowed wounded demonstrators to die in hospitals by turning away blood donors, and that government doctors had put the wounded to death by injecting air bubbles in their veins. To disguise the high number of casualties, it was claimed, the Qum dead had been piled up in army trucks and taken to unknown destinations.[23] Similar allegations surfaced after clashes in other towns and cities. 'That same night', said a pamphlet after clashes in Rafsanjan:

> they took away the dead and wounded in army ambulances displaying only one identifiable cadaver and leaving two wounded persons in the hospital. After the morning call to prayer, they began to wash away the blood of our brothers that had splattered on the doors and walls.[24]

Along with pictures of the bloodied bodies and smashed skulls of those killed in the demonstrations, which were widely disseminated, such reports helped rouse public anger and drew more people into the opposition movement.

The populist pamphleteers also played an important role in directing the focus of attention on the Shah himself. 'The Shah' said one of their leaflets 'is the problem'. They called directly for the overthrow of the Shah and for the establishment of an Islamic Republic. In an early indication of the battle-lines that would be drawn between the secular liberals and the Islamic radicals in the post-revolution period, they claimed for the religious leaders and the clerical community the credit for creating and giving direction to the opposition movement. They insisted on the centrality of Islam both to the success of the revolution and to its ultimate goals. Khomeini himself set the tone. He said:

Iran's recent, sacred movement . . . is one hundred per cent Islamic. It was founded by the able hand of the clerics alone, with the support of the great, Islamic nation. It was and is directed, individually or jointly, by the leadership of the clerical community. Since this 15-year-old movement is Islamic, it continues and shall continue without the interference of others in the leadership, which belongs to the clerical community.[25]

The pamphleteers also promoted the idea of Khomeini as leader of opposition to the Shah – to the exclusion of other leaders and movements – and they widely disseminated the idea of the 'Islamic government' as the form of government which would replace the monarchy after the revolution. Some writers on the Iranian revolution have alleged that the revolutionary movement began as a secular, non-Islamic movement, that Khomeini was relatively unknown to the mass of the people in the early months, and that the idea of an 'Islamic government' was introduced only much later into revolutionary propaganda. These assertions are not borne out by the bulk of the pamphleteering literature, where both Khomeini and the idea of Islamic government already figured prominently in January and certainly by February and March.[26] 'The Islamic nation of Iran' said a leaflet issued in August 'has signed a pact of loyalty with the great leader of the world of Islam, Imam Khomeini, and towards achieving an Islamic government. It has never looked to other ideologies'.[27] The 'Moslem Women of Khorasan' spoke in a similar vein:

We have mourned the murdered martyrs of Islam, who in the Holy city of Qum, and in Tabriz, Yazd, Jahrom, Ahwaz and other townships of Iran, have fallen in blood and dust like scattered flowers in order to achieve an Islamic government under the leadership of His Holiness, the deputy of the Imam (Khomeini), may God preserve him.[28]

Radical clerics and pamphleteers also used the political tract and leaflet to attack and discredit the idea of compromise and moderation. Every gesture of conciliation by the Shah – the promise of free elections, a change of government, loosening up of controls on the press and political parties – was treated as a sham. Propaganda activity was stepped up each time the Shah moved to treat with the moderate opposition. 'Those who for years mercilessly and wickedly strove to crush and kill the lovers of freedom . . . cannot themselves be the donors of liberty', Sayyed Jallal ad-din Taheri declared in an open letter to Ayatollah Sadduqi. 'By switching around a few key officials and permitting some of his own lackeys to voice empty criticism . . . he has sought to confuse simple minds and to direct the serious attention of the mass of the people away from the fundamental sources of the evil'.[29]

Repeatedly, the pamphleteers reminded their readers that the ultimate goal was deposing the monarchy. The Shah's reprehensible actions 'leave only one item on the agenda of the honourable nation of Iran: struggle and striving to overthrow the shameful and inhuman regime of Mohammad Reza Shah',[30] one leaflet stated.

It became a prime purpose of the populist pamphlets to close the door to compromise. On 14 August, following the Isfahan riots, the three leading Ayatollahs in the country, Shari'atmadari, Golpaygani and Mar'ashi-Najafi, issued a statement deploring the bloodshed caused by the security forces. But their language was moderate and referred to 'regrettable events' and 'painful incidents'.[31] Three days later, a leaflet appeared under the signature of the 'Seekers of God', taking the clerics to task for their moderation. 'It is astonishing that your excellencies call on the people to accept the Constitution which provided for a constitutional monarchy, and for compromise with this blood-letting pharaoh and this idolatrous, tyrannical regime', the leaflet said.[32] In the debate of the pamphlets, between the moderates and the radicals, it was the rhetoric and ideas of the populist pamphleteers and the radical clerics that came to determine the shape the attitudes of the mass of the people.


## DYNAMICS OF THE CROWD

Pamphleteers and radical preachers helped shape public attitudes and encouraged protest marches. But the crowd often set its own pace and generated its own dynamics once on the street. No doubt there were those instances where activists deliberately instigated confrontations between troops and demonstrators. There were those activists who viewed street violence as a vehicle for further public mobilisation and the destruction of places of business as a means of crippling the economy. But in general, even radical preachers did not encourage street violence or condone – except retroactively – the destruction of property. It was in an attempt to end violent street demonstrations and the resulting loss of lives that in June, after three cycles of forty-day mourning ceremonies, each of which had led to widespread street clashes, shootings and deaths, that religious leaders called for a day of silent mourning and protest.

Even in the pamphleteering literature, and invariably in the mosque sermons, the emphasis was on peaceful protest and on the maintenance of discipline. When a preacher spoke in February in Qum during a memorial service for the dead of that city, he himself was highly inflammatory. But a pre-sermon announcement banned all 'unauthorised' slogans and denounced those who intended to shout slogans as agitators.[33] Often, after the major riots, pamphlets appeared blaming the violence of the crowds on *Savak* agitators, bent on discrediting the opposition. Pamphlets that circulated following the initial riots in Qum in January alleged – and their authors no doubt believed – that it was a government *agent provocateur* and not a demonstrator who had smashed the first bank window, thus giving the police the excuse to attack the crowds and spark off the rioting.[34]

Invariably, there were conflicting accounts of the circumstances surrounding the outbreak of each round of violence. In practice, once security forces and demonstrators confronted one another, a collision became highly likely. Police or army violence – the shooting of a demonstrator, a baton attack on the crowd – often provided the spark that led to a destructive rampage. At other times, street crowds seemed deliberately to invite retaliation. On 5 November in Tehran, troops did not interfere with demonstrators because a student had been shot by a soldier on the previous day and the army presumably wished to avoid further provoking public anger. Thus, while troops watched passively, small groups of demonstrators fanned out through the capital, deliberately destroying banks, liquor shops, hotels, restaurants and government offices. By noon, fires were burning throughout the city.

Although the violence of the street crowds was partly planned, partly spontaneous, the targets earmarked for destruction were carefully chosen. Headquarters of the single official party, *Rastakhiz*, offices of the Endowments Organisation and police stations were attacked as symbols of the Shah's administration. Banks were viewed not only as violators of the Islamic injunction against usury but also as instruments of a credit policy that favoured rich industrialists and discriminated against small shopkeepers. Nightclubs, cinemas, restaurants and liquor shops were treated as sources of moral corruption, and symbolic of a regime that blindly embraced the undesirable moral corruption of the West.

Revolutionary leaflets were quite explicit about the aims of the street crowds. In Isfahan, a leaflet explained:

The people directed their numerous attacks at the banks as a protest against usury and the concentration of wealth, which have widened the gap between classes; and at the hotels and cinemas, which spread corruption and destroy the Islamic character of the youth. They bombed the Shahr-e Farang Cinema and the Pol Hotel which served as the pleasure centres of foreigners; and they attacked with Molotov cocktails the Shah Abbas Hotel, where the filthy Pahlavi family resided when they came to Isfahan.[35]

While crowds destroyed much property, violence was rarely directed against individuals. Much later, in December 1978 and January 1979, when the level of casualties mounted and bitterness grew, atrocities were committed by both government troops and street crowds, particularly in Tehran and Mashad. But in the first ten months of street demonstrations such instances were rare. In Rafsanjan, a gendarmerie officer was killed in a scuffle. Police were sometimes pelted with stones. Crowds in Qum and elsewhere occasionally beat up individuals whom they identified, rightly or wrongly, as *Savak* agents. But acts of violence against persons were few and far between. During the rioting in Tabriz in February 1978, a crowd smashing up a bank branch found a group of bank clerks and customers cowering in a back room. They stopped, escorted the people out, and continued with their work of destruction.

Some of the pamphleteering literature, perhaps inspired by the example of the *Mojahedin* and *Fada'iyan* guerilla organisations, continued to call for 'armed struggle'. The Shah's actions, a March leaflet proclaimed, have shown that 'it is not possible to speak to the Pahlavi regime except with firearms'.[36] When the '*Saf*' organisation claimed responsibility for the bomb that went off in the Khwansalar Restaurant in Tehran in August, killing and maiming some seventy customers, it described the act as a revolutionary gesture that others should follow.[37] There were a number of instances of attacks on American citizens; a police station in Tehran was bombed. But such acts, and the literature that promoted them, struck no responsive chord among the mass of the population.[38]

## NEW FORMS OF PROTEST

The pattern of pamphleteering and street demonstrations set during the popular outbreaks in the early months of 1978 continued to recur down to the eve of the overthrow of the monarchy in February 1979. On 7 and 8 October, for example, there were violent demonstrations and clashes with security forces in over twenty towns and cities. But in September and early October new patterns also began to emerge. A wider spectrum of classes joined the street demonstrations. Massive peaceful demonstrations began to be organised; strike activity was utilised as a form of popular protest.

The new academic year opened in the first week of October and schools and universities formally resumed classes. University students and faculty almost immediately went on strike and posted both intra-university and political demands. The opening of the schools made available thousands of new recruits for street demonstrations. Scattered strikes by school students in provincial centres quickly spread to towns across the country. The incidence of clashes between demonstrators and troops grew. But the students did not so much march and demonstrate as harry and harrass the troops and security forces. In late November and early December, these students were able day after day to snarl traffic for hours in Tehran's modern business district by staging sit-downs in streets and forcing motorists to carry posters on their windshields proclaiming 'Death to the Shah' thus, further contributing to the general disorder and turmoil.

At the end of September, oil industry workers went on strike for better pay and conditions. They were followed by post office employees, clerks at the Bank Melli, teachers and telecommunications workers. When the government agreed to their wage demands, this merely encouraged civil servants in other sectors to go on strike; and when wage demands were met the strikers posted political demands and continued striking. By mid-October, several hundred thousand civil servants were on strike – in ministries, post and telephone offices, banks, oil and steel industries, nuclear and electric power plants, municipalities, hospitals, customs offices and the national air line. The government and the public sector of the economy gradually began to cease to function.

There were strikes in the private sector as well, primarily in industries with large concentrations of workers. But these strikes focused on wage demands in the period before the overthrow of the monarchy did not generally develop a political dimension, and were quickly settled. It was the public sector strikes that paralysed the economy.

The strike action greatly expanded the scope of pamphleteering activities. Pamphleteering was no longer preponderantly clerical. Virtually every striking group began to issue its own declarations, bulletins and newsheets. The striking teachers issued declarations demanding improvement in pay, the right to form their own associations and release from previously required participation in pro-Shah demonstrations. They also made political demands, such as the release of political prisoners, the lifting of martial law and the dissolution of parliament.[39] Workers at the Tabriz tractor factory issued declarations demanding wage increases and also denouncing the Shah as a 'blood-thirsty butcher' and demanding his overthrow.[40] Employees at the Tehran Water Board issued a regular bulletin providing news of opposition activity and setting down the latest informaton on the government's 'crimes' and 'atrocities'.[41]

The powerful influence that was exercised by this pamphleteering literature and the credibility it had gained in the public mind is illustrated by the incident of the so-called 'Central Bank list'. In November, Central Bank employees (or others claiming to be Central Bank employees) circulated a list of some 180 Iranians who had allegedly transferred $2.7 billion out of the country during a brief two-month period. The list was a fabrication. But its authenticity was widely accepted and it was reproduced and disseminated in tens of thousands of copies.

In September there also took place the first of the peaceful mass demonstrations, involving hundreds of thousands of protestors. On 4 September, to mark the *Id-e Fetr* (the Moslem Day of Sacrifice), thousands took part in communal prayers on the heights of Qaytariyyeh above Tehran and then marched in several columns for a mass meeting at one of the great city squares in south Tehran. Another massive demonstration followed on 6 September. On 10 and 11 December, coinciding with the *Shi'ite* mourning days of *tasu'a* and *'ashura*, several hundred thousand persons marched in Tehran.

These great demonstrations provided impressive evidence of the degree of co-ordination and organising ability that had been built up over the months of political agitation. They drew new groups into open protest. Large numbers from the middle classes joined the protest marches. They permitted political groups and parties across a wide spectrum to join hands. The December marches effectively sealed the Shah's fate.

These mass demonstrations also provided the Islamic elements in the revolutionary coalition with an opportunity to carry one step further their pamphleteering activities. It was at the great marches on 10 and 11 December that Khomeini's lieutenants imposed on other political groups the essential elements of their blueprint for post-Pahlavi Iran and then secured 'approval by acclamation' for these resolutions by having dozens of marshals read them out to the cheering crowds. The resolutions confirmed that 'Imam Khomeini is the leader of the community', that 'his wishes are the wishes of the entire nation', and that

the revolution sought the overthrow of the monarchy and the establishment of 'a government of Islamic justice'. The resolutions were
distributed in tens of thousands of leaflets.[42] It was on the basis of these
resolutions that Khomeini later claimed that the concept of an Islamic
Republic had already been approved by national referendum.


## CONCLUSION

Pamphleteering activity and mosque sermons, street demonstrations
and strike action in 1978 thus combined to play a significant role in
bringing about the Iranian revolution. Political pamphleteering proved
an effective means for dissemination of information and public education. It helped to undermine and finally to destroy the reputation of the
Shah and his government in the eyes of the public. Along with the
activity of pro-Khomeini preachers, it helped develop the idea of
Khomeini as spiritual and national leader. It gave wide currency to the
belief that revolution, not reform, was necessary; and it planted in the
minds of large masses of people the idea of an Islamic republic as the
desirable alternative to the Shah's rule.

The street marches and demonstrations provided concrete evidence
that the mass of the people had rejected the Shah and the monarchy and
had transferred their loyalty to other leaders and different political
systems. Where violence was practised by security forces against the
demonstrators, it created 'martyrs' for the opposition cause, fed public
anger against the regime and won new adherents to the opposition. It
eroded the discipline and ultimately the loyalty to the Shah of the army.
Where violence was generated by the crowds themselves and directed at
economic targets, it helped paralyse the economy and erode middle and
upper class confidence in the stability of the Shah. Strike action not only
shut down the government. It alienated areas of official activity, such as
electric power distribution and oil production and distribution, from
government control and placed this control in the hands of the
opposition. Even before the revolution, the administration of some
towns, such as Amol and Mashad, for short periods passed in whole or
in part into the hands of the revolutionaries. In other towns, the mosque
was often a more important centre of decision-making than the mayor's
office or the police station. Populist action was thus already creating
forms of parallel government that were to be a common feature of post-
revolution Iran.

NOTES

1. This article is based primarily on an analysis of revolutionary leaflets, proclamations and the pamphleteering literature circulated during the revolutionary year, 1978. In addition to a large collection of leaflets in the author's own possession, the following published collections have been utilised:

    *Qiyam-e Hamaseh Afarinan-e Qum va Tabriz va digar Shahr-ha-ye Iran (Nehzat-e Azadi-ye Iran*, n.p. 1356/1978*)*, three volumes in one;hereafter, *Qiyam.*

    *Pareh-i az E'lamiyyehha-ye Montashereh dar Iran dar Mahha-ye Tir va Mordad 1358* (Organisation of Iranian Moslem Students, Willmete, Illinois, 1357/1978), hereafter *Pareh.*

    *Asnad va Tasavir-i az Mobarezat-e Khalq-e Mosalman-e Iran (Entersharat-e Abu Zar*, n.p. 1358/1979); hereafter, *Asnad.*

    Leaflets are identified by their signatories, by the person or persons to whom they were addressed, and by titles if these appear on the original. Where dates were determined from internal evidence, they appear in brackets.

2. An account of the manner in which the anti-Khomeini article was imposed on *Ettela'at* is given in the 8 *Shahrivar* 1357 (30 August 1978) issue of the newspaper. The article itself appeared in the *Ettela'at* of 17 *Dey* 1356 (7 January 1978).

3. Official statements by Ayatollahs Shahab ad-Din Mar'ashi-Najafi, Kazem Shari'atmadari, Mohammad Reza Golpaygani and Mohammad Vahedi are reprinted in *Qiyam*, I, 83–89. For the mild remarks made by these and other leading religious figures to the delegations of seminary students, see ibid, pp. 40–43.

4. Ibid, pp. 43–44.

5. A detailed account of the Qum protests is given in ibid, pp. 39–73.

6. The Mashad events are described in the following leaflets: 'Message of the Women of Khorasan to the Iranian Nation', 18 *Sha'ban* 1398 (24 July 1978) *Pareh*, pp. 23–25; and '*Ali Tehrani*: To the Grand Ayatollahs, the Ulama of Islam and other Committed and Responsible Moslems', *Mashad*, 18 *Sha'ban* 1398 (24 July 1978), *Pareh*, pp. 26–7. With their emphasis on alleged atrocities committed by the security forces, condemnation of the regime and the airing of grievances, leaflets, or messages addressed by one cleric to another, regarding events in various towns and cities were themselves important examples of the pamphleteering literature of the revolution.

7. The events in Rafsanjan and surrounding villages are described in the following leaflets in *Pareh*: 'The Society of the Clerics of Rafsanjan', [July 1978], pp. 14–16; 'The United and Responsible Moslems of Rafsanjan', [July 1978], pp. 17–20; and in 'Letter from His Excellency Hojjat ol-Eslam va'l Moslemin 'Abbas Pur-Mohammadi to the Grand Ayatollahs and the Maraje'-e Taqlid', Sarvan, Baluchestan, 17 *Sha'ban* 1398 (23 July 1978), pp. 21–2.

8. The Isfahan events are described in: 'The Militant People of Isfahan', 22 *Mordad* 1357 (13 August 1978), *Pareh*, pp. 41–2; 'Guilds of Isfahan: A Brief Look at the Sit-in of the Moslems of Isfahan', [August 1978], *Pareh*, pp. 43–5; 'A detailed Report on Events', unsigned, *Pareh*, pp. 46–9; statement

by Ayatollah Hosayn Ali Khatami and 29 others, [August 1978], *Pareh*, p. 50; and 'Militant Moslem Students of Isfahan', [August 1978], *Pareh*, pp. 51–4.

9. On Shiraz, see: 'Baha ad-Din Mahallati and 15 others: Extrapolation of the Illegal Regime of Iran', 20 *Mordad* 1357 (11 August 1978), *Asnad*, 77; and 'The Moslems of Shiraz', 21 *Mordad* 1357 (12 August 1978), *Asnad*, pp. 87–9. On Yazd, see: 'Two reports on the Bloody Uprising of the People of Yazd', *Qiyam*, vol. III, pp. 9–27; 'Mohammad Sadduqi: To the Grand Ayatollahs and the Great Maraje'', 23 *Rabi'* II 1398 (2 April 1978), *Qiyam*, pp. 31–2. 'The Yazd Seminary', 12 *Farvardin* 1357 (1 April 1978), *Qiyam*, pp. 34–5; and 'Proclamation by the Teachers and Learned Men of Yazd', [April 1978], *Qiyam*, pp. 36–9.

10. On Shahsavar, see: 'Massacre and Bloodshed in Shahsavar on the Orders of the Shah', 24 *Mordad* 1357 (15 August 1978), *Pareh*, pp. 69–72; on Jahrom: 'The Militant Moslems of Jahrom', undated, pp. 37–8; on Behbahan: 'The Movement of the Moslems of Behbahan', undated, pp. 67–8.

11. For samples of Sadduqi's proclamations, see: *Pareh*, p. 98; *Ansad*, p. 70; and *Qiyam*, pp. 31–2.

12. For proclamations by Tehrani, see *Asnad*, pp. 98–9; Khamene'i, *Qiyam*, III, pp. 45–50. Rabbani leaflet is in the author's possession.

13. *Qiyam*, III, p. 11. In Persian, the inscription read: '*Beh Kafiristan khosh amadid*'.

14. Ibid, p. 23.

15. 21 *Shahrivar* 1357 (12 September 1978) (leaflet in the author's possession).

16. '*Khabarnameh-ye Jebheh-ye Melli*', No. 8, 14 *Aban* 1375 (5 November 1978).

17. For example, 'National Front of Iran: National Solidarity Week', 6 *Aban* 1357 (28 October 1978) (leaflet in author's possession).

18. 'Mehdi Bazargan to [private secretary to the Shah] Moinian', 31 *Ordibehesht* 1357 (21 May 1978) (leaflet in the author's possession).

19. 'Massacre and Bloodshed in Shahsavar at the Shah's Orders', unsigned, 24 *Mordad* 1357 (15 August 1978), *Pareh*, p. 69.

20. 'The Seekers of God: Warning to the People of Iran', 5 *Ramazan* 1398 (9 August 1978), *Asnad*, p. 133.

21. 'The Militant Movement of Moslems', 25 *Esfand* 1356 (16 March 1978), *Asnad*, p. 25.

22. 'A Brief Look at the Sit-in of the Moslems of Isfahan', [August 1978], *Pareh*, pp. 43–4.

23. *Qiyam*, I, pp. 68–9.

24. 'The Society of the Clerics of Rafsanjan: To our Moslem Brothers', [July 1978], *Pareh*, p. 15.

25. 'Khomeini', 21 *Sha'ban* 1398 (27 July 1978), *Asnad*, p. 72.

26. See, for example, 'The Mournful Message of the Moslem University Students to the Guardians of the Revolution of Mohammad, Heirs of the Blood of Hosayn', 4 *Esfand* 1356 (23 February 1976), *Qiyam*, I, pp. 121–3.

27. 'Ruhullah Khatami', 13 *Ramazan* 1398 (17 August 1978), *Asnad*, p. 127.

28. 'Message of the Women of Khorasan to the Iranian Nation', 18 *Sha'ban* 1398 (24 July 1978), *Pareh*, p. 23.

29. 'Jalal ad-Din Taheri: To His Holiness Hojjat ol-Eslam va'l Moslemin Ayatollah Sadduqi', 18 *Sha'ban* 1398 (24 July 1978), *Pareh*, p. 28.

30. 'Society of Militant Clerics', [August 1978], *Asnad*, p. 129.

31. 'Kazem Shari'atmadari, Mohammad Reza Golpaygani and Shahab ad-Din Mar'ashi-Najafi', 9 *Ramazan* 1398 (13 August 1978), *Pareh*, pp. 60–1.
32. '*Goruh-e Puya-ye Towhid*' (The Seekers of God, 12 *Ramazan* 1398 (16 August 1978), *Asnad*, pp. 131–2.
33. *Qiyam*, II, p. 12.
34. Ibid, I, p. 50.
35. *Pareh*, p. 44.
36. 'The Militant Movement of Moslems', 25 *Esfand* 1356 (16 March 1978), *Asnad*, p. 25.
37. 'The *Saf* Group: Military Communique No. 1, 22 *Mordad* 1357 (13 August 1978), *Pareh*, pp. 58–9.
38. There was also virtually no looting. Hundreds of bank branches were destroyed in 1978. But no money was taken away. During rioting in Tehran on 5 November, crowds entered stores and supermarkets and smashed liquor bottles and liquor stocks. But nothing else was removed. Such apparently calculated behaviour led officials in Tehran to conclude that the demonstrations were centrally planned and organised and masterminded by plotters and subversives. But studies of crowd behaviour elsewhere (e.g. Rude, 1959) would suggest that such controlled spontaneity or selective violence is not uncommon among revolutionary crowds.
39. 'The Teachers of Shahr-e Rayy: To the Respected Fathers and Mothers', [October 1978?] (leaflet in the author's possession).
40. 'Workers of the Tabriz Machine Tools Factory' [April 1978], *Asnad*, p. 27.
41. Tehran Water Board Newsletter, (in the author's possession).
42. 'Resolutions of the Demonstrations of *tasu'a* and '*ashura*' (leaflet in the author's possession).

# 10 Traditionalism in Twentieth-century Iran

## SAID AMIR ARJOMAND

### ISLAMIC TRADITIONALISM IN IRAN AND INDIA

By traditionalism I mean to designate the type of social thought, action or movement which arises when a tradition becomes self-conscious either in missionary rivalry with competing traditions or in the face of a serious threat of erosion or extinction emanating from its socio-political or cultural environment. Traditional social action is spontaneous and unreflective, whereas traditionalist action is self-conscious, accompanied by some apologetic or polemical rationale. Whereas traditional attitudes are dormant tendencies which the individual harbours within himself, traditionalism is conscious and reflective since it arises as a counter-movement in conscious opposition to a rival set of beliefs and mode of conduct. Whereas the traditional man is at best only dimly conscious of the sources of the tradition and of the rationale for certain concrete traditional patterns of action, the traditionalist idealises tradition and constructs a fairly rationalised set of norms which are linked to the sources of tradition and are sharply contrasted to the alien norms of the rival belief system.

As George Makdisi (1966) brilliantly argues, in Islam, traditionalism first arose in reaction to the threat of erosion posed by Mu'tazila rationalism. It triumphed in jurisprudence with al-Shafi'i (d. 820), and in theology with Ibn Hanbal (d. 855). The erosive threat of popular Sufism provoked the traditionalism of Ibn Taymiyya (d. 1328), and Shah Waliullah of Delhi (d. 1762) and Ibn 'Abdul-Wahhab of Arabia (d. 1787). In Iran, the last important instance of *Sunni* traditionalism was provoked by the millenarian Shi'ite extremism of the ascending Safavids, and championed by Fazullah ibn Ruzbihan Khunji. In *Suluk al-Muluk*, written in 1514, Khunji greatly deplores the addiction of the

*'ulama* of his time to philosophy and the rational sciences at the expense
of religious jurisprudence (*Suluk al-Muluk*: esp. pp. 61–8). In striking
contrast to the near-contemporary treatises on government, he lays
emphatic stress on the necessity of the observance and implementation
of the Sacred Law as the embodiment of the Islamic tradition. The first
major *Shi'ite* traditionalist movement arose in reaction to philosophy
and philosophical Sufism (*'irfan*) in the latter part of the seventeenth
century, culminating, significantly, in the compilation, by Muhammad
Baqir Majlisi (d. 1699), of the massive encyclopedia of Shi'ite Traditions
(sing., *hadith*), *Bihar al-Anwar* (Arjomand, 1981b).

Having indicated the existence of an endemic propensity to traditionalism with deep historical roots in Islam and in Shi'ism, let me proceed
with an examination of the conditions which, in the twentieth century,
have given this propensity an epidemic proportion, thereby generating
the traditionalist movement which culminated in the creation of the
Islamic Republic of Iran in 1979. The term 'movement' is used as a
heuristic conceptual device to describe the heightened expression of
traditionalism as an endemic propensity or impulse. No reification, nor
any exaggerated implication of continuity through time, is intended.
The Shi'ite traditionalist movement refers to a phenomenon which
greatly fluctuates in intensity over seven decades, and which is of
necessity vague and not altogether coherent or uniformly persistent
through time, nor altogether socially cohesive or unchanging in its
membership. Nevertheless, it is a recognisably coherent phenomenon
because of the constitutive ideas which form the nucleus of social action,
and because of the core social group which leads such action. It is best
conceived as a series of waves of collective action stimulated by certain
significant events. In periods of intensified, epidemic collective action,
the constitutive ideas take shape and are formulated and clarified and/or
the cadre and the organisation network come into being and are
consolidated. The ideological and organisational rudiments of the
movement resist total dissipation during the downturn of the wave of
agitation and persist through the ensuing period of endemic dormancy.

Like all social movements, Shi'ite traditionalism has had its roots in
the dissatisfaction with the present state of affairs; and it has similarly
posed an alternative model, a Golden Age. As one student of revolutions
has observed, whether the Golden Age is in the past or the future is
irrelevant as regards the revolutionary potential of a movement; what
matters is the degree to which it diverges from the present state of
affairs (Stone, 1970). At its incipient stage, in the first decade of the
twentieth century, the Shi'ite traditionalist movement posed an ideal

model which did not significantly diverge from the *status quo* and was in fact designed to prevent its change. It was therefore anti-revolutionary. In the 1970s, an elaborated version of the same basic model presented such a radical divergence from the *status quo* under the late Shah as to constitute a serious revolutionary threat to it, which, as we now know, was to actualise itself in the first traditionalist social revolution in modern times.

The distinctive feature of traditionalism in twentieth century Iran is that it has been a general movement for the defence of Islam against Western influences led by the Shi'ite *'ulama*. As such, it has an instructive parallel in the clerically-led Islamic traditionalist movements in the Indo-Pakistan subcontinent since the early years of the nineteenth century. Wilfred Cantwell Smith convincingly argues that with the collapse of the Mogul Empire in India, the meaning of the Islamic system as a whole underwent an important change. Islam 'became the ideal not existentially of an operating social system, but, in essentialist fashion, of an abstracted entity, a pattern of intellectualised norms. In this pattern only a few of the norms could be actually implemented, but the whole disembodied pattern of them could be, and was to be, reverenced. In this situation one gets the emergence of an *'ulama* class whose function in society is that of custodians of a cherished, idealised tradition, enshrined as a static essence of their books' (Smith, 1962, p. 43). Against this background, the eldest son of Shah Waliullah of Delhi, Shah 'Abdul-' Aziz (d. 1824) issued a famous *fatwa* (injunction) in 1803, suggesting that India had passed under the control of the infidels and thus become *dar al-harb* (realm of war). The *fatwa* marked the beginning of what was to become a clerically-led movement to restore the grandeur of a threatened Islam in India. The 1820s witnessed the independent launching of two militant Islamic movements in India. Hajji Shari'atullah (d. 1838), newly-returned from twenty years in the Wahhabi-dominated Hijaz, launched the *Fara'iziyya* movement in Bengal. More explicitly than Shah 'Abdul-'Aziz, Shari'atullah declared Bengal *dar-al-harb*, and was joined by the Bengali peasantry with an acute sense of grievance against Hindu landlords (*zamindars*) and British indigo planters. A few years later, Sayyed Ahmad Barelwi (d. 1831), aided by 'Abdul-'Aziz's nephew Isma'il (d. 1831), led the *Mujahidiyya* movement. Inspired by his long pilgrimage to Mecca (1821–4), Sayyed Ahmad moved to the north western tribal area and assumed the titles of Imam and *Amir al-Mu'minin* (Commander of the Faithful) in January 1827. Barelwi, believed by his followers to be at least the *mujaddid* (renewer) of the faith for his century and at most the

*Mahdi*, set up an independent but short-lived rule (khilafat) in Peshawar (1830–1) (Metcalf, 1982, pp. 10, 60–70). The unrest fomented by these movements culminated in the mutiny of 1857. After the suppression of the mutiny, the militant *'ulama* who had participated in it set up the seminary of Deoband as the apolitical alternative for the preservation of the Islamic tradition (Metcalf, 1982). In the north western frontier area, however, the tradition of militancy under clerical leadership continued. Under the menace of the presence first of the Sikhs and then of the British, the Pukhtun tribes were unified by the Akhund of Swat (d. 1877) under the banner of Islam. The Akhund's followers led the *jihad* of 1897–8 against the British infidels (see Chapter 4 by Ahmed).

In the twentieth century, the *Khilafat* movement (1918–24), once initiated, was enthusiastically supported and directed by the *'ulama* who entered the political arena to defend 'the last hope of Islam' (Qureshi, 1978, p. 152). The reason for their enthusiastic involvement was stated by one of the *'ulama* as follows: 'until the *'ulama* take the reins of politics in their own hands and cross their voices with those in authority, it will be difficult for them to establish their religious supremacy. Moreover, the fulfilment of their higher aims (that is, the protection of Islam) will remain merely an empty dream' (Qureshi, 1978, p. 156). Once the *'ulama* dominated the *Khilafat* movement, they transformed it into a mass movement, reaching audiences previously not involved in politics (Minault, 1974, pp. 168, 175–7). Given the central goal of the defence of Islamic tradition in India, the issues chosen for politicisation were singularly inept. The *hijrat* (migration) of August 1920 turned out to be a total disaster; and the Turks themselves abolished the Caliphate in March 1924, leaving the movement with nothing better than the secondary flimsy issue of the freedom of the *jazirat al-'arab* (Qureshi, 1978, pp. 157, 167).

*Jam'iyat al-'Ulama-i Hind*, organised as a political party under the leadership of the *'ulama* of Deoband, survived from the Khilafatist days to the present day to play an important role in the movement for the establishment of the *Nizam-e Mustafa* (the Prophetic Order) which overthrew the Bhutto regime in 1977 (Smith, 1943, p. 366; Ahmad, 1980). However, the decisive innovation, epitomised in the social myth of the Pakistani traditionalist movement – that is, Nizam or Order, came not from the *'ulama* of Deoband but from another scholar, Mawlana Abu'l-A'la'Mawdudi (d. 1979). As Charles Adams shows, it was Mawdudi who transformed the cherished, idealised Islamic tradition into an explicit *system*, an 'ideology'. The variegated embodiments of the Islamic tradition were thus transformed to a comprehensive system of ideas comprising a set of blue prints for 'Islamic' economics, 'Islamic' government and the like, for whose realisation Mawdudi advocated an Islamic revolution (Adams, 1966, pp. 394–5; Smith, 1957, pp. 236–7). With this innovation, the defence of Islam against the threat of erosion by modern ideas and Western ways need not be foiled by specific events or the possible inappropriateness of fortuitous issues. With the development of an ideology, the traditionalist movement thus attains full instrumental rationality. Hobsbawm would have to agree that Mawdudi and his followers had found 'a specific language in which to express their aspirations about the world' (Hobsbawm, 1959, p. 2; also p. 60). Henceforth, the aspiration of the traditionalist movement about the world was to be expressed with perfect clarity as the preservation of traditional norms and return to the traditional Islamic pattern of life.

## THE EARLY PHASE OF THE TRADITIONALIST MOVEMENT

In the nineteenth century and the first years of the twentieth century, the Shi'ite *'ulama* acted as the spokesmen for Islam as a living tradition through the routine discharge of their religious, judiciary and educational functions. Owing to this extensive involvement in the Qajar polity, unlike their Indian counterparts, they had no need to mobilise the people in defence of an abstract and idealised Islam. Such need arose once the Constitutionalists succeeded in setting up a Western-style parliamentary government. It was greatly intensified with the Pahlavi centralisation and modernisation of the state which entailed the securalisation of the judiciary and educational systems and thus put an end to the routine institutionalised involvement of the *'ulama* in the polity.

The role of the *'ulama* in the events of 1905–6 which led to the grant of a Constitution by the reigning monarch has been well publicised. At this stage, however, the aims of the incipient popular movement were ill-defined. It was only after the ratification of the Fundamental Law on 30 December 1906, that the functions and jurisdiction of the parliament, the Majlis – originally conceived as *'Adalat Khaneh* or House of Justice – were progressively defined. And on the wake of the ratification, signs of dissatisfaction of the *'ulama* with the Constitution and the turn of events made their appearance. The *'ulama*'s dissatisfaction remained unfocused and their opposition inchoate for a few months, and serious clerical agitation under the leadership of Shaykh Fazlollah Nuri (d. 1909) did not begin until some time in May 1907. Nuri ably organised the clerical opposition to the Majlis. In doing so, he created a traditionalist movement for the defence of Islam against a Western-inspired political innovation – namely, parliamentary democracy.

Nuri launched his campaign with himself acting within the Majlis, and his son posted as a liaison in Najaf. He proposed his 'principle' – subjecting all parliamentary legislation to the ratification of a committee of five *mujtaheds* of the highest rank – while organising a group of seminarians (*tollab*) to demonstrate continuously outside the Majlis in support of the principle, and to intimidate the unsympathetic deputies. In addition, Nuri formed a political society (*anjoman*) with a number of other prominent *'ulama*. Nuri's 'principle' was passed as Clause 2 of the Supplement to the Fundamental Law by the Majlis in the second week of July 1907; but not considering this parliamentary victory sufficient, he moved to the shrine of 'Abd al-'Azim. There Nuri was joined by other prominent clerics and *tollab* whose number soon reached five hundred.

One of the most important consequences of Nuri's propaganda was the mobilisation of the piously apolitical *'ulama* against parliamentarianism. Of the Shi'ite religious leaders in the holy centres in Iraq, the *'atabat*, Hajj Mirza Hosayn, son of Hajj Mirza Khalil, the bulk of whose followers were the Tehranis, and Akhund Molla Mohammad Kazem Khorasani, with a high reputation in jurisprudence rather than a numerous following, supported by the less eminent Mazandarani, responded affirmatively to the general enthusiasm and, benefiting from the independent telegraph line of the East India Company, turned Najaf into an important centre for the transmission of pro-Constitution injunctions. The other religious authorities, most notably the towering Shi'ite jurist of the present century. Sayyed Kazem Yazdi, remained neutral and refused to intervene in politics initially. After Nuri's son was sent to Najaf to enlist support, Yazdi was won over. He responded to Shaykh Fazlollah's call, and spoke out against constitutionalism. He was supported by his Arab followers, the Ottoman governor of the province, and 'the army of God'. Clashes between his supporters and those of Khorasani and Hajj Mirza Hosayn ended in the formers' complete victory. Yazdi emerged as the undisputed master of the *'atabat* (Arjomand, 1981a).

It was during the three months at the shrine of 'Abd al-Azim from mid-June to mid-September that Nuri coherently formulated the *'ulama*'s objections to parliamentarianism, thus transforming their common though unspecified orientation into a consistent traditionalist ideology. He did so in a series of open letters published and distributed from 'Abd al-'Azim which became known as the journal (*ruz-nameh*) of Shaykh Fazlollah. They were mostly written by or upon the instructions of Shaykh Fazlollah himself but also included letters and telegrams emanating from Sayyed Kazim Tabataba'i Yazdi (d. 1919), the revered *marja'* (authoritative jurist) of Najaf *and* from the constitutionalist *maraji'*, notably Akhund-e Khorasani (d. 1911).

Though the opening of schools for women and proposals to use the funds allotted to *rawza-khani* for purpose of building factories and 'European' (*farangi*) industries are not spared from attack, Nuri's chief principled objections to parliamentarianism and the action of the constitutionalists centre on the following themes: 'the inauguration of the customs and practices of the realms of infidelity', the intention to tamper with the Sacred Law which is said to belong to 1300 years ago and not to be in accordance with the requirement of the modern age, the ridiculing of the Moslems and insults directed at the *'ulama*, the equal rights of nationalities *and* religions, spread of prostitution, and the freedom of the press which is 'contrary to our Sacred Law'.

The primary aim of the campaign is 'the protection of the citadel of Islam against the deviations willed by the heretics and the apostates'. The *'ulama* wish to awaken the religious brethren and rectify their misconceptions and errors so as to protect them from the Babis and the naturalists who are engaged in beguiling 'the masses who are more benighted than cattle' (*'avamm, azall min al-an'am*). 'We shall not tolerate,' Nuri declares, 'the weakening of Islam and the distortion of the commandments of the Sacred Law.'

In marked contrast to the 'modernist' strategem of presenting Western political concepts and practices as embodiments of the true spirit of Islam, our proponent of Islamic traditionalism highlights their imported and alien quality, stressing the Europeanness of the parliament and of the Fundamental Law. 'Fireworks, receptions of the ambassadors, those foreign habits, the crying of hurrah, all those inscriptions of Long Live, Long Live! (*zendeh bad*)! Long Live Equality, Fraternity. Why not write on one of them: Long Live the Sacred Law, Long Live the Qur'an, Long Live Islam?'

No one denies the desirability of a Majlis. What had been originally demanded from the state in 1906 had been a 'Majlis of justice (*majles-e ma'delat*)' 'so as to spread justice and equity and enforce the Sacred Law; no one had heard the *shura-ye melli* or *mashruta*'. The Majlis should not be contrary to Islam, and should enjoin the good, forbid the evil and protect the citadel of Islam. But the constitutionalists

want to make Iran's Consultative Assembly the Parliament of Paris
... We see today that in the Majlis-e Shura they have brought the
legal books of the European parliament(s) and have deemed it
necessary to expand the law ... whereas we, the people of Islam, have
a heavenly and eternal Sacred Law.

In a telegram from Najaf, Sayyed Kazim Yazdi commands that the
Majlis be a Majlis for enjoining the good and forbidding the evil, that it
should not act as a 'parliament' and accept the restrictions of the '*ulama*
of 'Abd al-'Azim. Nuri also reproduces a telegram from the three
constitutionalist *maraji'* of Najaf demanding the inclusion in the
supplement to the Fundamental Law of a Clause concerning the
heretics and the execution of divine commandments. Seeking to coin a
concept for the system of government he envisages, Nuri proposes that
the qualification *mashru'a* (in accordance with the Sacred Law) be
added to the term *mashruta*. The notion of *mashruta-ye mashru'a* is thus
given currency.

Nuri's propaganda caused quite a stir. It articulated an ideology for
the opponents of parliamentary government whose interests were
threatened by the proposed judiciary and financial reforms; *and* it turned
a considerable number of those who had piously withdrawn from
politics, or were marginally interested in politics, against parliamentarianism which was not presented as a threat to the Islamic tradition. The
impact of Nuri's *ruz-nameh* was immediate. It affected the religious
craftsmen and shopkeepers, and many of the Majlis deputies with
similar social backgrounds. Above all, it gave definitive form to the
orientation of the clerical estate, a very important social group in itself,
towards parliamentarianism.[1]

Nuri's success in organising concerted political action with Mohammad 'Ali Shah was less impressive than his feat of formulating the
ideology of Islamic traditionalism. Nevertheless, emboldened by Nuri's
anti-parliamentarian agitation, the Shah destroyed the Majlis in June
1908, and, with Nuri's support and active participation, restored the
*mashru'a* autocracy. The experiment, however, failed. The autocracy
slowly collapsed, and Nuri was hanged by the constitutionalists on 31
July 1909.

The majority of the Shi'ite religious dignitaries had followed Nuri in
supporting the restoration of autocracy in 1908, but judiciously
withdrew from the royalist camp once the failure of the attempt became
evident in 1909. By 1911, the Shi'ite clergy had become disillusioned
with constitutionalism and was predominantly hostile towards it. The
Russian invasion of Northern Iran in that year brought the '*ulama* back

into national politics for a brief period on a platform of national unity 'to protect the citadel of Islam' (*hefz-e bayza-ye Eslam*). But the attempt was a failure. The anti-constitution traditionalist Yazdi, henceforth the leading religious authority until his death in 1919, advised the '*ulama* to withdraw from the political arena and preserve the Islamic tradition in their mosques and seminaries. The first phase of the nation-wide Shi'ite traditionalist movement thus came to an end. Hajj 'Abd al-Karim Ha'iri (d. 1936), Sayyed abu'l-Hasan Esfahani (d. 1945) and Hajj Aqa Husayn Borujerdi (d. 1961) who dominated the Shi'ite '*ulama* for the subsequent four decades similarly held aloof from politics and devoted themselves to the cultivation of the Shi'ite tradition in the centres of religious learning.

The memory of Nuri as the man who was the first to realise that parliamentary government was a ploy to facilitate the growth within Iran of the cancer of Western cultural domination came to be increasingly cherished with each reversal of the '*ulama*'s fortune under the Pahlavis. His formulations were certainly adequate for the purpose of opposing incipient parliamentarianism. But they did not amount to a comprehensive blueprint for the Islamic system, as the institutional bases of clerical power were not tangibly affected and therefore the need for such a model had not yet arisen.

The wave of traditionalist agitation thus ebbed in 1911. In the 1920s and especially 1930s, the endemic impulse to defend Islam against the importation of Western norms and institutions resulted in occasional outbursts led by the '*ulama*. The legally enforced adoption of European clothes and hats and the rigid restrictions on the wearing of the clerical garb met with the resistance and violent reaction of the '*ulama*. Above all, it was the unveiling of women in 1935–6 which outraged them as the most monstrous rape of Islam, and met with the strongest resistance. The most important figures in this resistance were Ayatollah Muhammad Taqi Bafqi (d. 1946) and the Grand Ayatollah Husayn Tabataba'i Qumi (d. 1947).

Bafqi had taken an active part in the anti-constitution traditionalist agitation, and had been forced to flee Iran after publicising Yazdi's injunctions against constitutional government. He was forced by the government to leave the religious city of Qum and reside in Ray, near Tehran, in the late 1920s. One of the most regular visitors to Bafqi in Ray was a young scholar named Ruhollah Khomeini (Sharif-Razi, 1974–5, pp. 619–21; Sharif-Razi, 1979, pp. 17–21). Qumi was held responsible for disturbances in Mashhad, where he resided, and exiled to Iraq in 1934 (Sharif-Razi, 1973–4, pp. 264–5).

By the time of Reza Shah's abdication in 1941, the centralisation and modernisation of the state had destroyed the nineteenth-century division of labour in the polity and expropriated the judiciary and educational prerogatives of the *'ulama* and much of their direct or delegated control over religious endowments. They had already become, to use Akhavi's phrase, a *déclassé* estate (Akhavi, 1980, p. 132). As such their social position approximated to that of the militant traditionalist *'ulama* of India in the nineteenth century. In time, their conception of Islam too was to follow the Indian pattern. However, quite some time was yet to pass, and in the intervening years the reforms of the 1960s were to increase further the disembeddedness of the *'ulama* from the Pahlavi regime.


## THE 1940S AND EARLY 1950S

Clerically-led traditionalist agitation began immediately after the departure of Reza Shah, and culminated in the uproarious welcome given to Qumi upon his visit to Iran in 1944, and in the removal by the government upon his demand of restrictions on the wearing of the veil and the clerical garb. Immediately upon his return to Qum, Bafqi began his campaign for the observance of the Sacred Law with an attempt to oust an Armenian-owned liquor store, which was finally burnt down by a mob (Fischer, 1980, p. 112). Under the direction of Ayatollah Tabataba'i Qumi, the traditionalist preachers demanded a more strict observance of the provisions of the Sacred Law on morality, and the reimposition of the veil. Imitation of the cultural patterns of the Western infidels also came under heavy attack. A letter circulated by Khomeini suggests that they may have tried to turn the agitation to an anti-Pahlavi movement by warning his colleagues that the young monarch was likely to resume his father's bid to destroy the Shi'ite religious institution (Sharif-Razi, 1979, p. 16) but with no apparent success. The role reserved for the maturing *mujtahed* in that campaign was a different one, and it was a role indicative of a new threat of erosion which activated Shi'ite traditionalist counter-offensive: religious modernism. By the 1940s, Shi'ite traditionalists had to react not only to modernisation and westernisation of institutions by the state, but also to the advocacy of Islamic religious reform by 'modernist' intellectuals. In *Kashf-e Asrar* (1943), Khomeini took up this latter challenge as a guardian of the Shi'-ite tradition. The concern about the spread of Islamic reformism, which they regarded as the importation of Wahhabi ideas, must have been felt acutely enough by the Shi'ite *'ulama* even earlier for the Grand

Ayatollah Ha'iri Qumi (d. 1939) to have written a treatise in refutation of Wahhabism (Sharif-Razi, 1973–4, p. 336). Khomeini was similarly alert to the danger posed by the advocates of Islamic reform whom he considered blind imitators of the Wahhabis – 'the savages of Najd and the camel-herders of Riyadh' (Khomeini, 1943, p. 4).[2]
At the outset of his publicistic tract, Khomeini notes with alarm that certain writers have begun to attack religion and the clergy (*ruhaniyyat*):

> with their shameful pens, they have blackened a number of sheets and distributed them among the masses, not realising that, today, to weaken the resolve of the people in religion, in religious observance and towards the clergy is amongst the greatest of crimes, as nothing is more conducive to the annihilation of the Islamic countries. (Khomeini, 1943, p. 2.)

To free themselves from the following or imitation (*taqlid*) [of the Shi'ite authoritative jurists], 'these essayists are at times imitating Ibn Taymiyya and the savages of Najd, at other times, the Babis and Abu'l-Fazl Golpayegani, the Baha'i [in rejecting possibility of performance of miracles]' (Khomeini, 1943, p. 56). Khomeini's adversaries, whom he does not deign to name, were 'Ali Akbar Hakamizadeh whose book, *Asrar-e Hezar-saleh* (Secrets of a Thousand Years) was the immediate object of Khomeini's rebuttal, and indirectly, the two notable proponents of Islamic modernism who had inspired Hakamizadeh: Ahmad Kasravi (assassinated by the *Fada'iyan-e Islam* in 1946) who saw his mission as the purification of Islam, and Shari'at-Sangelaji (d. 1943) who was referred to as the Great Reformer (*mosleh-e kabir*) by his followers. Both these Islamic modernists denounced as superstitious many of the traditional Shi'ite beliefs and practices such as the belief in miracles and in the Imam's power of intercession, and the practice of pilgrimage to the shrines of the Imams and their putative descendants, the *ta'ziyeh* and *rawzeh-khani*. At the same time, they attacked the doctrine and practice of *taqlid* (following, imitation), the very foundation of clerical authority in Shi'ism. Khomeini demonstrated his staunch traditionalism by defending every single one of the beliefs and practices which had come under the reformists' attack as superstition (Khomeini, 1943, pp. 30–51, 77–96, 173–4) and then embarks on a lengthy defence of Shi'ite clericalism.

If the following of dead authorities were to be permissible everywhere, no name would have remained of Islam by now. People would not refer to the *mullahs* in their affairs, and the clergy would have disappeared from among the people; then a few unbridled mindless individuals like you would circulate among the people, would write book[s] full of lies and exaggerations, would distribute [the books] among them, and inculcate the masses with their poisonous ideas – consisting of an invitation to the tearing of bridles and irreligion. (Khomeini, 1943, p. 196.)

You who want to reduce the power of the clergy and to eliminate its honour among the people, you are committing the greatest treason to the country. The undermining of clerical influence produces defects in the country one hundredth of which hundreds of Ministries of Justice and Police Departments cannot repair. (Khomeini, 1943, p. 203.)

Hand in hand with this polemical attack on the Islamic modernists, Khomeini, addressing the Western-oriented intelligentsia, expresses his outrage against the deleterious moral and political effects of the Western cultural penetration:

Throughout these stages [of modernising reforms], the foreigners who wanted to execute their plans and swindle you by putting the hat over your heads, [a pun in Persian] were looking at you with deriding eyes and were laughing at your infantile acts. You were strolling up and down the streets with a chamber-pot-shaped [i.e. bowler] hat, were occupied with naked girls, being proud of this state of affairs, not realising that they took your historical honours from one end of the country to the other; that your sources of wealth [natural resources] throughout the country were being appropriated, and you were being trampled upon from sea [the Caspian] to sea [the Persian Gulf] (Khomeini, 1943, p. 224).

They have put chamber-pot-shaped hats over your heads and gladdened your hearts with naked women in the middle of the streets and swimming pools (Khomeini, 1943, p. 236).

The unveiling of the women has been the ruin of female honour, the destruction of the family, and the cause of untold corruption and prostitution (Khomeini, 1943, pp. 292–5).

This shameless unveiling, or the bayonette-spurred movement, is materially and spiritually damaging to the country and is forbidden according to the Law of God and the Prophet . . . This pot-like reject hat of the foreigners is the disgrace of the Islamic nation, stains our independence, and is forbidden according to the Law of God . . . These schools mixing young girls and young passion-ridden boys kill female honour, the root of life and the power of manly valour (*javan-mardi*), are materially and spiritually damaging to the country and are forbidden by God's commandment . . . These wine-shops and liquor-producing organisations wear off the brain of the young [men] of the country and burn away the intellect, the health, the courage and the audacity of the masses; they should be closed by God's command-ment. Wine-bibbing and wine-selling is forbidden . . . Music rouses the spirit of love-making, of unlawful sexuality and of giving free reign to passion while it removes audacity, courage, and manly valour. It is [therefore] forbidden by the Sacred Law, and should not be included in the school programmes (Khomeini, 1943, pp. 213–14).

The alternative proposed by Khomeini is of course the traditional socio-political pattern, by now self-consciously depicted as Islamic and duly idealised. The rulers of pristine Islam were men who were wont:

to implement divine punishments (*hudud*) throughout their country, to cut the hand of the thief and behead the anarchists and the seditious. [These rulers] would avoid the foreigners, and not imitate them in dressing, eating and riding. They regarded even resemblance to foreigners as forbidden and were independent in their national works and religious slogans (Khomeini, 1943, pp. 6–7).

Nowadays they sing in the national anthems 'be it the command of God, be it the command of the Shah' . . . the Qur'an has restricted the laws to divine laws. The calamity of the country is that it possesses such divine laws and yet extends her hand to the countries of the foreigners, and is seeking to execute their artificial laws which have emanated from selfish and poisonous ideas . . . No one has the right to rule except God and no one has the right to legislate. Reason dictates that God should form a government for the people and enact the laws. Such Law is the Sacred Law of Islam . . . which is valid for everyone and forever (Khomeini, 1943, pp. 180–4).

'The Islamic judiciary law is a thousand times better than the tyrannous (secularised) judiciary.' Similarly, Islamic taxation is perfect. Even traditional medicine is said to be superior to European medicine (Khomeini, 1943, pp. 252–82). It is interesting to note, however, that Khomeini does not put forward a blueprint for Islamic government or political systems. He rather insists on the enforcement of Clause 2 of the Supplementary Fundamental Law which provides for supervision over all legislation by a committee of five *mujtaheds*, and demands more extensive participation of the clergy in government[3] (Khomeini, 1943, pp. 221–34). (The demand for the enforcement of Clause 2 was put forward by the Grand Ayatollah Tabataba'i Qumi but not insisted upon once the government capitulated on the issues of veiling and the clerical garb.)

Khomeini's tract is thus a highly self-conscious defence of the Shi'ite tradition. It is more comprehensive than Nuri's formulations because a wider range of traditional beliefs had to be defended against reformist criticism. It is therefore an important mark in the development of Shi'ite traditionalism. In it, traditionalism can be seen to be more rationalistic than unself-conscious adherence to tradition; a rationalising element enters the realm of discourse by virtue of the necessity of the use of reasoned notions and logical arguments with rival groups. Nevertheless, the range of topics discussed is largely determined by the reformist polemicists, and the tendency to construct a set of blueprints for the Islamic systems, to create a systematic and comprehensive Islamic ideology, does not gain the upper hand.

Once the government conceded the major demand of the traditionalists and removed the restrictions on veiling and clerical activity in 1944, concerted nationwide action ceased and the movement gradually dissolved. However, in the following decades, Ayatollah Abu'l-Qasim Kashani (d. 1962) was able to channel the propensity to traditionalist action to a campaign to defend Islam against the new state of Israel and, for a short period, the *Nahzat-e Sharq*, a pan-Islamic movement whose backbone was 'the rank and file mullahs and less significant bazaar merchants and shopkeepers' (Faghfoory, 1978, p. 151). A group of young lower middle-class Islamic radicals who put themselves under the nominal leadership of Kashani for two or three years, and who enjoyed the support of some other prominent 'ulama, the *Fada'iyan-e Islam*, preferred the more activist route of consummating their traditionalist impulse in terrorism and the assassination of the westernised enemies of Islam. The *Fada'iyan-e Islam* remained active during the decade after World War Two (see Chapter 8 by Kazemi). These traditionalist militants were led by young clerics or sons of clerics. It is worth noting that Vahedi, their second man in the line of command, was the son of a cleric who had actively participated in the first – the anti-parliamentarian – phase of the traditionalist movement under Nuri's leadership (Ferdows, 1967, p. 46).

The manifesto of the *Fada'iyan-e Islam*, written in October, 1950 by their leader, the self-styled Navvab Safavi (1923–56), is the next crucial document of twentieth-century Shi'ite traditionalism. The sense of puritanical moral indignation against the importation of polluting cultural norms, encountered in Nuri and Khomeini, is greatly intensified. The chapter sub-headings tell us that 'Flames of Passion rise from the naked bodies of immoral women and burn humanity into ashes'; or that 'cinemas, theatres, novels and songs teach crime and arouse passion'. The unveiling of women is deplored because it results in increased divorce and prostitution. 'Music is immoral and irreligious and weakens the strong nervous system of human beings and by this contributes to the breakdown of society.' (Ferdows, 1967, trans. 9, 14, 16.) The strong disposition to moral indignation and an extropunitive 'disinterested tendency to inflict punishment',[4] also becomes more explicit, a tendency which has found practical expression in the atavistic punishments decreed for moral tort by the post-revolutionary Islamic courts:

> Yes, yes, the punishment rules of Islam are also carried out [in an Islamic state]; the thief's hand is cut off, rather than him being sent to a pleasure and rest house called prisons [Safavi has previously inveighed against the lenient treatment of criminals in modern prisons]. If the crime is repeated three times, he is executed and no more thieves will remain in the community ... The adulterer is whipped in public and is executed if adultery be repeated three times; so who would insult other people's wives and daughters and cause them to end up in prostitution houses and die of syphilis? (Ferdows, 1967, trans. 6–7).

More importantly, the manifesto of *Fada'iyan* contains a detailed blueprint for a reformed Islamic government and society which is considered still as a monarchical regime. A striking passage on 'Constitutionalism and the Majlis' attests to the continuity of *Fada'-iyan*'s traditionalist activism with that of Nuri:

> Whose poisoned policy deceived the Muslims under the disguise of friendship and support of Islam and the rights of Muslims and made them the means for the achievement of their own petty goals? It is

obvious where it was from ... it stems from those who killed the honourable and dear martyred *mujtahed*, Haji Sheikh Fazlollah Nuri, by deceiving the Muslims. They were the slaves of foreigners and executed this accursed plan for the foreigners. But the poor Muslims made sacrifices based on faith and brought about this constituti-onalism. They made every sacrifice and were so deceived that they KILLED THEIR DEAREST HOLY LEADER, HIS HOLINESS HAJI SHEIKH FAZLOLLAH NURI. For years now they have realized their mistake and have finally noticed the hands behind the scenes which pushed them to commit that crime (Ferdows, 1967, trans. 84).

Safavi then proceeds to reiterate Nuri's principle of the subjugation of the Majlis to clerical control and supervision.

The representatives of the Muslim nation of Iran must void and nullify all the legislation passed since the inauguration of the Iranian constitution, those laws which are contrary to the holy principles of Islam, and throw them out of the law books. They must not pass laws and set rules for the country, because God alone has the right to make rules ... The parliamentary representatives must understand that parliament is not a place to make laws, but rather a consultation ground ... In performing their duties, they must be put under the supervision of an assembly of pious religious leaders in order to keep the activities of the Majlis deputies in line with the Islamic provisions ... YES, ELECTIONS MUST BE FREE AND REPRESENTATIVES MUST BE DEVOUT MUSLIMS. UN-ISLAMIC LAWS MUST BE ABOLISHED. THEY MUST NOT MAKE LAWS, BUT CARRY OUT LAWS PUT DOWN BY GOD. THEY MUST NOT SPEAK AGAINST THE MUSLIM IRANIAN NATION AND MUST BE CONTINUOUSLY SUPERVISED BY THE ASSEMBLY OF THE LEADING RELIGIOUS LEADERS (Ferdows, 1967, trans. 85–6).

The judiciary system is to be desecularised and put in the hands of the religious jurists (Ferdows, 1967, trans. 34–5). In addition, there are details on the organisation of various Ministries, of flags to be displayed and congregational daily prayers to be performed in adjoining mosques, on rehabilitation of prostitutes, on Islamic taxation and on interest-free banking.

Islamic traditionalist activism of the post-World War Two period came to an end when Mosaddeq fell from power in 1953. Although it made a very significant contribution to traditionalist ideology in the form of the manifesto discussed above, its activities never reached the nationwide dimension attained in 1907-8 or 1944. With the concord between the *'ulama* and the Shah from 1953 to 1960, politicised traditionalism dissipated further, manifesting itself only endemically as during the anti-Baha'i disturbances of May and June (*Ramadan*) 1955 (Akhavi, 1980, pp. 76-90).

## THE FINAL PHASE

With the spread of literacy and the gradual enlargement of the public sphere in the post-World War Two period, Shi'ite traditionalism also continued to find expression in the writings of a number of clerics and laymen. Khomeini (1943, p. 190) had noted the alienation of the youth from the Shi'ite clergy with particular concern. It was the youth, chiefly, whom the traditionalist writers and publicists set out to capture in the early 1960s with the launching, in Tehran of a society for public discussions with a periodical, *Goftar-e Mah* (the Month's Discourse). From 1960 onwards, we witness a number of *'ulama* such as Mahmud Taleqani, Mortaza Motahhari and Mohammad Beheshti combining their concern with orthodox reformism with the entry into the business of formulation and dissemination of an Islamic traditionalist ideology attractive to the intelligentsia. Beheshti sees the enterprise designed to shake the *'ulama* awake from ten centuries of slumber to resume their responsibility for leading the Shi'ite community in the real world. Motahhari writes on the *Leadership of the Young Generation (Rahbari-ye nasl-e javan)*: 'The Shi'ite clergy must create an ideology capable of attracting the youth "from its alienated state and towards a meaningful religious orientation to social reality".' To do so, the inordinate attention given to religious jurisprudence is to be moderated by a shift towards the study of *aqayid* (ideology) and *tafsir* (interpretation of the *Qur'an*). And Beheshti would not omit to add a taste of the forbidden fruit of politics for the youth's titillation: The people are 'to supervise the government, ensure that it carry out the appropriate tasks to implement, as closely as possible, the justice demanded by the [Hidden] Imam; and, if it failed, to work to establish a government that would do so' (Akhavi, 1980, pp. 118-29).

The open activities of the Islamic publicists was interrupted by the repression of 1963 to resume in 1965 with the opening of a new centre, the *Hosayniyyeh Ershad* in the north of Tehran. The activities of the new centre were keenly observed by the religious-minded in the provincial towns who sought its directors' assistance in setting up similar centres (Akhavi, 1980, p. 144). By 1968, Motahhari could write:

> In recent years our educated youth, after passing through a period of being astonished, even repulsed [by religion] are paying an attention and concern for it that defies description . . . The *Hosayniyyeh Ershad*, a new institution, in existence for less than three years, knows its task to be to answer, to the extent that it can, these needs [of youth today] and *to introduce Islamic ideology* [to them] such as it is (Akhavi, 1980, p. 144; emphasis added).

This entailed considerable politicisation of Shi'ism. In one instance, such politicisation necessitated a sharp divergence from Shi'ite traditional interpretation of sacred history. In 1968, Ni'matollah Salihi Najaf-adabi, a student of Khomeini, published *Shahid-e Javid* (The Immortal Martyr), offering an interpretation of the tragedy of Karbala as a political uprising and denying such tenets of the Shi'ite dogma as the foreknowledge of the Imam (Enayat, 1982, pp. 190–4).

The clerical traditionalists were joined by two notable modernist laymen who expressed their ideas on Islamic reform. Mehdi Bazargan was with the movement from the very beginning, and was moderate enough in his statements – perhaps even making too many concessions (Akhavi, 1980, p. 115) – to be fully accepted by the *'ulama* within the movement and in general. The same, however, could not be said of 'Ali Shari'ati (d. 1977) who joined the *Hosayniyyeh Ershad* in 1967. Shari'ati revived Shari'at-Sangelaji's emphasis on the principle of *tawhid* (unity of God) as the cornerstone of Islam, insisting that it should correspond to a monistic and classless social order. In his politicised and populist interpretation of Islam, Shari'ati naturally championed the cause of the people, doubly oppressed by the internal forces of domination, and by the external force of imperialism. He revived the graphic Qur'anic term *mustaz'afin* (the disinherited) to refer to the oppressed masses and renders Franz Fanon's *Les Damnés de la terre* in Persian translation as the Disinherited of the Earth (Shari'ati, 1971, p. 120). Shari'ati caused the leading clerical publicist Motahhari some concern by over-politicising Islam (Akhavi, 1980, p. 144) and was opposed by the more conservative Shi'ite *'ulama* much more vehemently. Like the reformist Shari'at-Sangelaji before him, he was accused of 'Wahhibism'. A number of *'ulama* proceeded to write refutations of Shari'ati's views (Ansari, 1972; M. T. Shari'ati *et al*, 1976) or upheld the traditional view on topics such as *velayat* and *imamat* as against politicised reinterpretations of Najaf-abadi and Shari'ati (Moqimi, 1977).

The inclusion of the reformists such as Bazargan and Shari'ati whose attempts to return to Islam to overcome cultural alienation partially resonated with the orthodox reformism of such figures as Taleqani and Motahhari, contrasts sharply with the excommunication of the modernists in the 1930s and 1940s period. Despite the tension it caused within the movement,[5] the affiliation of these modernists, especially that of the charismatic Shari'ati, was highly beneficial in that it greatly increased the participation of the intelligentsia in the Islamic movement.

The closure of *Hosayniyyeh Ershad* by the authorities did not put an end to the activities of the traditionalist publicists who had already been abandoning it because of the increasing predominance of Shari'ati. On the contrary, the spate of books and pamphlets presenting the 'Islamic ideology' continued throughout the 1970s. Publicists such as Hashemi-Nejad and Makarim-Sharazi would write on 'Islamic' economics or various social problems from the Islamic viewpoint. The emphasis on ideological systematisation, present in varying degrees in all these works, is perhaps best reflected in Shaykh 'Ali Tehrani's *General Design of the Islamic Order* (*Tarh'e Kolli-ye Mizam-e eslami*) which was published in 1976.

Meanwhile, Qum too, was emerging as a vital centre of traditionalist publicistic activity. The activities of Qum were conceived as the resumption of missionary *tabliq*, both abroad and within Iran, with special attention to the youth (Fischer, 1980, pp. 81–4). The *'ulama* of Qum presumably considered the revitalisation of *tabliq* as a compensatory activity for their loss of influence over the national educational system. The Grand Ayatollah Shari'at-madari, who sponsored the *Dar al-Tabliq* of Qum and its publications, saw these activities in line with the pre-modern pattern of missionary Shi'ite traditionalism (such as Majlisi's), this time called for by disenchantment with materialism and increased religious sensibility throughout the world (personal interview in 1977). (He, like all the other thirty *'ulama* I interviewed in 1977, convinced me of their absolutely unshakable faith in the inevitable spread of Islam as the youngest of the world religions.)

The increasing momentum of Shi'ite traditionalism in the public sphere is reflected in the increasing circulation of religious periodicals, and the increased popularity of religious books relative to other categories (see Table 10.1). A survey conducted in 1976 found forty-eight publishers of religious literature in Tehran alone, of whom twenty-six had begun their activities with publication of religious books during the decade 1965–75.

TABLE 10.1  *Religious books*

| Year | No. of religious titles per year | As percentage of total titles of published books | Ordinal rank (among categories of titles) (Highest = **1**) |
|---|---|---|---|
| From 1954–5 to 1963–4 (average) (1333 to 1342) | 56.7 | 10.1 | 4 |
| From 1964 to 1967–8 (average) (1342 to 1346) | 153 | — | — |
| From 1969–70 to 1971–2 (average) (1348 to 1350) | 251.7 | — | — |
| 1972–3 (1351) | 578 | 25.8 | 1 |
| 1973–4 (1352) | 576 (a: 516) | 24.8 (a: 22.3) | 1 (a: 2 [1: literature 25.7%] |
| 1974–5 (1353) | 541 (1: 438) | 33.5 (a: 23.4) | 1 (a: 1) |

SOURCE  Najafi, 1976, pp. 51–2; *Salnameh-ye Amari, 1353*, 1976, p. 171 for additional classifications (a).

As the ensuing considerations make clear, the ideas of the Islamic traditionalist ideologues fell upon fertile grounds. A number of indicators, such as the statistics on visits and donations to religious shrines, pilgrimage to Mecca, and the number of newly-built mosques attest to the increased vitality of traditional religious sentiments. In the year 1353 (1974–5), over eight million pilgrims went to the shrine of the eighth Imam in Mashhad (about a quarter of the total population; an increase of some one million over the average for the previous three years). Table 10.2 presents another indicator of increased religiosity: cash donations (*nazr*), usually for the fulfilment of a wish or in anticipation of such fulfilment, thrown into the area around the sepulchre.

Statistics on the number of pilgrims to Mecca show the same trend, (see Table 10.3) though they grossly understate the demand which, in the last three years of the period covered, was six to eight times the size of the government quota.

From 1961 to 1975, while the population of Tehran increased almost two and a half times to just under five million, the number of mosques probably increased five times. Table 10.4 is indicative of the vitality of religion in the major rapidly expanding urban centres such as Tehran. (It should, however, be considered with caution, especially regarding the

TABLE 10.2 *Cash donations to shrines (millions of Rials in current prices)*

| Year | Domestic consumption (Private sector) | Index | Mashhad | Index | 'Abd al-'Azim (near Tehran) | Index |
|---|---|---|---|---|---|---|
| 1347, 8, 9 (average) (March 1968–March 1971) | 469 800 | 100 | 19.9 | 100 | 12.0 | 100 |
| 1350 (1971–2) | 554 800 | 118 | 24.4 | 123 | — | — |
| 1351 (1972–3) | 663 700 | 141 | 34.5 | 174 | — | — |
| 1352 (1973–4) | 818 500 | 174 | 79.4 | 400 | | |
| 1353 (1974–5) | 1 127 700 | 240 | 105.5 | 531 | 48* | 400* |
| 1354 (1975–6) | — | | 123.3 | 620 | | |

\* Average over the three year period, approximately; the exact figure not quoted in the source.
Note that with prosperity, the propensity to offer cash donation at the shrines increases over twice as much as that to other types of expenditure.
SOURCE Najafi, 1976, pp. 156–7; *Salnameh-ye Amari, 1353*, 1976, p. 537.

TABLE 10.3   *The number of Pilgrims to Mecca*

| Year | Number |
|---|---|
| 1349 (1970–1) | 27 000 |
| 1350 (1971–2) | 34 500 |
| 1351 (1972–3) | 45 000 |
| 1352 (1973–4) | 57 000 |
| 1353 (1974–5) | 51 000 |
| 1354 (1975–6) | 71 851 |

SOURCE   Najafi, 1976, p. 164.

figures for all of Iran, as it is compiled on the basis of different surveys by different bodies for each of the years covered.)

It should be emphasised that all the above statistics indicate an increased propensity to *traditional* religious activities. They thus also point to a set of traditional religious beliefs and sentiments accompanying them. When conducting a set of interviews with the *'ulama* in provincial towns in 1977, I was struck by the fact that a number of times the interviews had to be interrupted because of requests for *istikhara* (*Qur'anic* bibliomancy), usually over the telephone. *Mafatih al-Jenan* (Keys to the Garden – that is, of Paradise) – a book singularly maligned by the modernist Shari'ati for representing the worst, most other-worldly aspects of fossilised traditional Shi'ism – sold 490 000 copies in 1973–4 (1352), and was second only to the perennial bestseller, the *Qur'an* (about 700 000 copies). Next came the *Rasa'il 'amaliyya*, the manuals on religious law and ritual, by the dozen leading Grand Ayatollahs, selling, *in toto*, some 400 000 copies in a country where books rarely sell more than a few thousand (Najafi, 1976, p. 152).

Hand in hand with the dramatic rise in the number of religious publications went the mushrooming of the religious centres other than mosques, typically *Hosayniyyehs*, and an astonishing growth in the number of 'Religious Associations' (singular, *hay'at mazhabi*). These were often associated with the groupings of humbler occupations or of poorer city quarters. They met mostly during the religious months of Muharram and Ramadan but occasionally also at other times. By 1974, there were 322 *Hosayniyyeh*-type centres in Tehran, 305 in Khuzestan and 731 in Azerbaijan. In addition, there were over 12 300 'Religious Associations' in Tehran alone,[6] most of which were formed after 1965. Of these Associations 1821 designated themselves formally by a title. These titles typically refer either to the guild or profession of the members, or to their geographical town or region of origin or to their

TABLE 10.4  Number of mosques

| Year | Tehran | | | All Iranian towns | | |
|---|---|---|---|---|---|---|
| | Mosques | Cinemas | Mosques per 10 000 building units | Mosques | Cinemas | Mosques per 10 000 building units |
| 1340 (1961–2) | 293 | — | — | — | — | — |
| 1341 (1962–3) | — | — | — | 3,653 | — | 27.4* |
| [1349–50 (1970–2)] | | [124] | | | | |
| 1351 (1972–3) | 700 | — | 14.7 | — | — | — |
| 1352 (1973–4) | 909 | 122 | 18.6 | 5,389 | 424 | 29.5 |
| 1353 (1974–5) | — | 113 | — | — | 430 | — |
| 1354 (1975–6) | 1,140 | — | 22.6* | — | — | — |

* Based on projections of the total number of building units for the year from the previous or subsequent years.
SOURCES  Najafi, 1976, pp. 154–5; *Salnameh-ye Amari, 1353*, 1976, pp. 163, 331; *Amar-e Montakhab*, 1973, p. 60.

aspirations. As such, they are highly revealing of the social background of their members, and of the type of religious sentiment motivating them to form these associations. The unmistakable impression given by the titles is that their members fall into two quite possibly overlapping social groups – lower-middle-class guilds and professions associated with the bazaar economy, and recent migrants from the provinces. Furthermore, there can be no mistake that their religiosity is solidly traditional. Here are some typical examples: Religious Associations of shoemakers, of workers at public baths, of the guild of fruit-juicers (on street-corners), of tailors, of the natives of Natanz resident in Tehran, of the natives of Semnan, of the Desperates (*bicharehha*) of [Imam] Husayn, of the Abjects (*Zalilha*) of [Imam] Musa ibn Ja'far (Najafi, 1976, pp. 161–2).

The vitality of traditional sentiment among the above-mentioned social group made them receptive to the propaganda of the traditionalist preachers and pamphleteers. These groups remained marginal and excluded from political processes until the early days of 1978, when with dramatic suddenness, they were massively mobilised against the Pahlavi regime by Khomeini's traditionalist party.

A religiously-inclined section of the rapidly expanding middle-class also took part in the Islamic revival. A number of 'Religious Societies' were formed in the universities and abroad, and by engineers and physicians. The conventional wisdom among Middle Eastern scholars mistakenly refers to this branch of the movement as Islamic modernism or reformism. The examination of the publications and discussions of these societies does not show any evidence of an interest in religious reform and rethinking. They were rather gatherings by newcomers to an alienating modern world to consolidate, at regular intervals, their attachment to the Islamic tradition and to reaffirm their collective socio-cultural identity.

Traditionalism, as an attempt to revitalise the tradition, is usually activated by the intrusion of alien cultural influences. Therefore, it often consists, in part, in the celebration of the pure and authentic cultural identity and thus contains a considerable element of nativism. As we have seen, being reactive to the westernism of the political élite, Shi'ite traditionalism had a pronounced nativistic aspect. In the 1960s and 1970s, the religiously-inclined intelligentsia increasingly found this nativism consonant with their rejection of Western culture. These celebrants of Islamic collective identity who gathered in the middle-class Religious Societies were engineers, physicians and schoolteachers who remained attached to primordial ties and traditional ways, and who resented certain aspects of the imported modern pattern of life. Insecure and homesick in alien lands, especially the US and West Germany, groups of unassimilated students from traditional (lower-)middle-class backgrounds, created similar networks of regular meetings and debates.

Orthodox reformists bent on the purification of the Shi'ite tradition as much as its ideologisation, did associate with the more serious of such religious associations of laymen. Ayatollah Motahhari, for instance, gave a series of talks to the Islamic Association (*Anjoman*) of Engineers which the latter published under the title of *Khadamat-e Moteqabel-e Islam va Iran* (Mutual Services of Islam and Iran) in 1970–1 (1349). In the preface to this volume, the Islamic engineers offer a fairly sophisticated analysis of increasing political awareness and national consciousness in the Third World, which is said to unfold in three stages. In the first stage, the intellectuals of under-developed countries engage in pure imitation of Western patterns of life which are assumed to lead to prosperity. In the second stage, they become aware of the nation to which they belong, but turn to its past history, folklore and myths. Nationalism, imitative of Western nationalist ideology – 'nationalism according to the classic Western definition' – is typical of this second stage of national awareness among the colonial masses. In the third stage, this is to be replaced by Islamic consciousness appropriate to a unified Islamic community of believers. In this last stage, which is said to be about to begin, the intellectual will stop daydreaming about folklore and imitating their Western masters, and they will pay heed to the real factor making for unity in the sentiments of the masses. A new and unified Islamic community, a 'new nationality of *tawhid* (unity)' (*melliyat-e jadid-e tawhid*), as foretold by the Moslem thinkers of the late nineteenth and early twentieth century, will thus be born (Motahhari, 1970–1).

Rather than orthodox reformism or modern rethinking, however, what obsessed the highly politicised segment of the new Iranian middle class who frequented the Religious Associations was the creation of an Islamic *ideology*. This meant the arrangement of readily accessible maxims constituting the source of Islamic tradition – the *Qur'an* and the *Hadith* – in accordance with a new pattern suggested by the Western total ideologies. A number of Shi'ite clerics played an important part in the provision of the requisite Islamic total ideology. Here, the influence of the Islamic ideologues abroad must be noted. Writings of Sayyid Qutb, the theoretician of the Moslem Brotherhood, and of Mawlana Mawdudi were translated into Persian and avidly read. In his Preface to

Sayyid Qutb's *Social Justice in Islam*, its clerical translator, Hadi
Khosraw-shahi, reveals the basis of the books' appeal to the young
intelligentsia:

> Sayyid Qutb is one of the few who . . . have been able to offer to the
> world Islamic issues *in the style of today*, and in the form of systematic
> books, *as a living and invaluable ideology* as against (other) social,
> political, economic schools of Communism, Imperialism, Socialism
> and Capitalism (Qutb, 1973 [1944], p. 29; emphasis added).

This group of Iranian intelligentsia, unlike their counterparts in Egypt
and Malaysia, have constituted the followers and not the leaders, the
consumers and not the producers, of the traditionalist ideology. The
clerical publicists who appeared to have lost the initiative to Shari'ati in
the late 1960s recovered it after the latter's death in 1977. They
formulated the constitutive values and ideas of the movement in the light
of their ideal and material interests as the custodians of the threatened
religious tradition. For the lay adherents to Islamic traditionalism, such
values and ideas were to remain – in Pareto's terminology – 'derivatives'
decorating the 'residue' of the sentiment of collective identity. The
members of the Islamic Societies did listen to and read Bazargan and
Shari'ati alongside a host of traditionalist pamphleteers. Values and
ideas being derivatives superimposed on the psychological residue of
reaffirmed collective identity, modernist elements were readily added to
the traditionalist tenets of the clerical writers to produce a more
pleasing, albeit an increasingly less consistent, ideological collage.

However, if we looked for a firm imprint of the intellectual content of
Shi'ite modernism, by the late 1970s, it could only be detected among a
group of radical students who formed the *Mujahedin Khalq*. The
*Mujahedin* for some time constituted the radical branch of the Islamic
movement, and did some of the decisive fighting which resulted in the
final success of the popular uprising in February 1979.

Wallace (1956, p. 278) notes that the nativistic component is usually
lower at the initial stages of 'revitalisation' movements but increases
later. This tendency seems especially pronounced during a revolutionary
phase when the process of simplification through intensity and rejection
of all complexity sets in. After the revolution of February 1979,
increasing nativism soon set in and modernistic paraphernalia were
shorn off. It soon became clear that individuals such as the former Prime
Minister Bazargan and the former President Bani-Sadr – a modernist
exponent of Islamic monistic (*tawhidi*) economics – and especially the

*Mujahedin* as an organised group became dissonant political forces and had to be suppressed or eliminated.


## REVOLUTIONARY POLITICISATION OF SHI'ITE TRADITIONALISM

Two chief factors can be singled out to account for the politicisation of the Shi'ite traditionalist movement in the 1970s: the repressive policies of the Pahlavi state, and the determination of Ayatollah Ruhollah Khomeini.

Once he felt securely in control, Muhammad Reza Shah put an end to the *rapprochement* with the Shi'ite clergy who had helped restore him to the throne in 1953, and initiated a ruthless attack on the religious institution. This attack produced a series of crucially significant events which punctuate the progressive revolutionary politicisation of the Shi'ite traditionalism.

It is true that, after the death of the apolitical Borujerdi (1961), Khomeini, the 'decisive experience' of whose generation was Reza Shah's repression and the betrayal of the westernised intellectuals and who saw the reassertion of royal power and initiation of a new reform programme as replete with *motifs* encountered during the dreadful reign of the first Pahlavi, had begun to make a bid to take the place of Kashani in the political arena. Furthermore, the Shah's suddenly increasing popularity after the successful Peasants' Congress of January 1963 must have alarmed Khomeini and roused his apprehension. Nevertheless, he was not proposing any revolutionary programme at that time. In March 1963, he was accusing the Shah of violating his oath to defend Islam and the Constitution, opposing the enfranchisement of women, and attacking the Shah for maintaining relations with Israel. Like Kashani a decade earlier, he was upholding the legitimacy of the Constitution.[7] The critical event which changed the situation drastically was the violent sack of the main theological college of Qum, Fayziyyeh, in March 1963, an event which, according to the testimony of one of his most important aids and students, made a deep impression on Khomeini (Algar, 1980). As is made clear by the Preamble of the Constitution of the Islamic Republic of Iran, in reaction to these events, Khomeini set out to create, in contradistinction to the nationalist and the socialist political parties, a traditionalist political movement which was to be led by the clergy as the guardians of the Shi'ite tradition. The following statement is made in the Preamble of the Constitution of the Islamic Republic:

Although the Islamic way of thinking and militant clerical leadership played a major and fundamental role in [the constitutional and the nationalist/anti-imperialist] movements, these movements rapidly disintegrated because they became increasingly distant from the true Islamic position.

At this point, the alert conscience of the nation, led by ... the Grand Ayatollah Imam Khomeini, realised the necessity of adhering to the true ideological and Islamic path of struggle.

A bold innovation by Khomeini consolidated the traditionalist movement and gave it a definite direction. Around the year 1970, Khomeini took the unprecedented step of assuming the title of Imam,[8] and put forward a political theory which advocated direct hierocratic rule on behalf of the Hidden Imam. (Here, one should mention the influence of the activities of the Shi'ite leaders in the Arab land. The Lebanese leader, Musa Sadr, was also assuming the title of Imam which, however, is a good deal less elevated in Arabic and in Persian.) At the same time, Khomeini elaborated a blueprint for the ideal of Shi'ite government, an Islamic theocracy, to be realised by the movement he had launched. Thus, as the Preamble declares:

The plan for an Islamic Government based upon the concept of the Mandate of the Clergy, which was introduced by Imam Khomeini ... gave a fresh, strong incentive to the Muslim people and opened the way for a genuine ideological Islamic struggle. This plan consolidated the efforts of those dedicated Muslims who were fighting both at home and abroad.

Khomeini's theory of the *Velayat-e Faqih* (Mandate of the Clergy, or the Sovereignty of the Jurist), published in 1971, is a major innovation in the history of Shi'ism. He converts a highly technical and specific legal discussion of the rights of the gerent into a theocratic political theory. Although Khomeini cites Mullah Ahmad Naraqi (d. 1828–9) as a forerunner, the latter's '*Awayid al-Ayyam*, the only legal work to which Khomeini refers in support of his theory of the Mandate of the Clergy, pointed only to an implicit invidious contrast between religious and political authority. The primary objective of Naraqi's discussion of the 'mandate of the jurist' was to strengthen the *juristic* authority of the Shi'-ite doctors on behalf of the Hidden Imam. The bulk of the discussion was devoted to the 'delimitation' of the scope of the authority of the jurists as the vicegerents of the Imam, and their authority was delimited to the exclusion of temporal rule.

Khomeini extends the early *Usuli* arguments such as Naraqi's, which were designed to establish the legal authority of the Shi'ite doctors, to eliminate the duality of hierocratic and temporal authority altogether. For him, Islamic government will differ from representative and/or constitutional monarchies in its elimination of the separation of powers. Khomeini categorically states that 'the Mandate [of the clergy] means governing and administering the country and implementing the provisions of the Sacred Law'. Thus, having firmly rejected the separation of religion and politics, he argues that in the absence of the divinely inspired supreme leader of the community of believers, the infallible Imam – that is, from AD 874 to the end of time – sovereignty devolves upon the qualified jurists or the Shi'ite religious leaders. It is therefore the religious leaders as the authoritative interpreters of the Sacred Law of Islam who are entitled to sovereignty. Furthermore by assuming the title of Imam, he paves the way for the eventual restriction of the Mandate of the Clergy to that of *one* jurist as its presumed *supreme leader* (Arjomand, 1980).

Not only did the Islamic traditionalist movement of the 1970s consider itself to have superseded the imperfect and misconceived nationalist movements of the earlier periods, but it was also fully on guard against any possible tapping of the energy of the movement by nationalist and other intellectuals. Writing in the summer of 1978, Motahhari, a chief architect of the movement sardonically states:

I regret to say that these respected intellectuals have woken up a bit too late because the old custodians of this immense source of movement and energy have demonstrated that they themselves know very well how to utilise this immense source, and will give no one the opportunity for a take-over (*khal'-e yadd*).

He went on to add that the Shi'ite clergy must write books themselves so that others 'could not fish in murky waters' (Motahhari, 1978, pp. 84, 92).

The assumption of the title Aryamehr (Sun of the Aryans) by the Shah and the celebration of the 2500th anniversary of the founding of the Persian Empire provoked Khomeini into a vehement denunciation of the institution of monarchy. In a speech in anticipation of the celebration made on 22 June 1971, Khomeini, having adduced the tradition 'king of Kings is the vilest of words' cites the recurrent *Qur'anic* verse '*Lahu'l-mulk*' as meaning that sovereignty belongs to God alone. He proceeds to tell his audience that rising against the Pahlavi monarchy is incumbent upon them by Sacred Law. Meanwhile Khomeini had taken up the anti-foreign and anti-Zionist traditionalist themes. He vigorously protested against the granting of extra-territorial judiciary rights to American Advisers in 1964, and had issued constant invectives against the agents of the foreign powers and of Zionism.

The critically significant events of the 1970s consisted of a series of repressive measures against the religious instituion. Already in 1964, Khomeini had reacted violently against a proposal by the regime to set up an Islamic university which was taken to signal the state's intention to encroach upon the religious sphere proper (Khomeini, 1977, pp. 66–7). Such direct encroachments materialised in the 1970s. Totally disregarding its political costs, the Shah embarked on an attempt to invade the religious sphere proper by creating a 'Religion Corps' (modelled after the 'Literacy Corps'), and a group of 'Propagators of Religion'. Despite their inefficiency and lack of vigour, the religious leaders perceived these measures as a bid to liquidate the religious institution and annihilate Shi'ism altogether. In 1975 under the pretext of the creation of green space around the shrine of the eighth Imam, the government demolished most of the theological seminaries of the holy city of Mashhad, a measure which caused a good deal of apprehension in Qum (Fischer, 1980, p. 123). In the same year, the Fayziyyeh seminary was attacked by the troops during a prolonged commemoration, by pro-Khomeini students, of the sack of 1963. Furthermore, the Shah replaced the Islamic calendar with a fictitious imperial one. With their backs to the wall, the clergy within Iran increasingly heeded Khomeini's incessant appeals, and the latter's position among the Grand Ayatollahs was strengthened. Clerical reaction to the Shah's aggressive encroachments was to prove decisive. In an interview conducted in 1975, a prominent cleric spoke of 'the awakening of Iran's religious community after the frontal attack of His Majesty'. (He went on to boast about the clergy's new political maturity: in the 1960s the eligibility of women for elections was a major preoccupation of the religious leaders, now they would not lose any popularity by incautiously opposing women's electoral rights [Arjomand, 1981c].)

Throughout the 1970s, Khomeini's sense of alarm at the destruction of the Shi'ite culture and mores was augmenting. In March 1975, he would refer to the Shah's 'White Revolution' as 'the revolution intended to spread the colonial culture to the remotest towns and villages and pollute the youth of the country' (Khomeini, 1977, p. 94). Reacting to the public performance of explicit sexual acts by an *avant-garde* theatre group in the Shiraz festival, he would be moved to say, in a speech made in September 1977 in Najaf, that the function of this government:

is tyranny and oppression and the spread of prostitution. You do not know what prostitution has begun in Iran. You are not informed: the prostitution which has begun in Iran, and was implemented in Shiraz – and they say it is to be implemented in Tehran, too – cannot be retold. Is this the ultimate – or can they go even further – to perform sexual acts among a crowd and under the eyes of the people? (the speech of 14 Shawwal 1397Q).

One final significant event, or rather the anticipation thereof, should be mentioned as of utmost importance in turning politicised traditionalism into an intransigently revolutionary movement: the imminent beginning of the fifteenth century of Islam. The Shi'ite scholars' long-established tradition of the designation of a great *Mojaddid* (Renovator) for each century, against the background of the sudden explosion of popular rage and the crumbling of the Pahlavi monarchical edifice, can safely be assumed to have changed the clerical estate's conception of time (and certainly Khomeini's) from a chronological to a kairotic one; the moment when time was to be pervaded by eternity seemed at hand, empirically and numerologically.

Like Nuri in the first decade of the century, Khomeini was primarily addressing the clerical estate:

I know what dangerous dreams the tyrannical establishment has for Islam and the Moslems. You, the *'ulama* and the clergy (*ruhaniyyun*) are the culprits in their eyes ... You must be conscripted into compulsory military service, spend your time in jails, under torture and oppression and humiliation, and in exile, so that the way would be open for the agents of the foreigners and of Israel.

However, he also instructed a large number of preachers and clerical publicists to spread his message in Iran, and among the Iranian pilgrims abroad (for example, in Mecca) (Sharif-Razi, 1974, pp. 422–3 and 1979, pp. 88–9, 98–9, 149, 162–5, 175–6, 224, 254–71, 308). Furthermore, Khomeini put much emphasis on preaching, an activity confined, as he himself had stressed in 1943 (p. 211) to the lower ranks of the Shi'ite clergy. Not only did he urge preachers to spread the traditionalist propaganda, but also, unlike the other Grand Ayatollah, he personally delivered a large number of sermons.

The separation of political and religious authority, *de jure* and *de facto*, had become the distinctive feature of Shi'ite Islam by the early decades of the nineteenth century. The Shi'ite clergy's separation from the state, and especially their championship of the Shi'ite nation against a state subservient to the foreign imperial powers in the period 1890–1906, disposed them towards some measure of populism. However, the measure of paternalistic populism, which made them differentiate the community of believers from the ruling élite, sold to the foreign infidels, went hand-in-hand with a pronounced élitist attitude as regards the stratification of the community of believers into the élite (*khavass*) and the common masses (*'avamm*). Nuri's phrase, 'the masses more benighted than cattle' is indeed a recurrent one in the writings of the Shi'ite *'ulama* of the period. Elitism pervades the manifesto of the *Fada'iyan*: 'We are capable of sending these traitors [the ruling élite] to hell and of avenging Islam. But we delayed action to prevent probable dangers, and prevented forcefully the revolt of foolish ignoramuses' (Ferdows, 1967, p. trans. 114). Furthermore, by 1950, a marked status consciousness, typical of declining social strata, finds expression in certain recommendations of Navvab Safavi which were subsequently to be faithfully implemented in the Islamic regime's recruitment policies. Proposing schools of political science for the training of the Islamic ruling élite, Navvab Safavi writes:

> The students in this field must be selected from among pious families that are well-known for honesty, and unknown applicants from low-classes or dishonest families should not be allowed to register for it ... Yes, only the children from honest and pious Muslim families who will not betray their country can be trusted with the political missions and management of the country's political affairs ... Yes. Every applicant's family background must be studied before his acceptance, and only the children of honest and pious families will be admitted (Ferdows, 1967, trans. 66–7).

The situation changed drastically in the period 1963–78 when the Shi'ite clergy came under relentless attack and had to appeal to the masses more assiduously in order to mobilise them against the Pahlavi state. It is crucially important to note that this period was witnessing the rapid and enormous growth, through migration from the rural areas, in the size of the urban masses who came to constitute a new clientele and a new audience for the Shi'ite clergy. Meanwhile, the land reform of the 1960s was completing the process of disengagement of the Shi'ite clergy from the Pahlavi state which had already gone very far as a result of Reza Shah's reforms of the 1930s. It has already been pointed out that this disengagement, and the consequent separation of religious and political powers, put the Shi'ite clergy in a very similar position to the

Indian *'ulama* in the nineteenth century, and similarly disposed them to leading nationwide Islamic traditionalist movements. It should now be added that the same disengagement from the Pahlavi regime not only dispossessed the Shi'ite clergy but also oriented it towards the growing urban masses; its populism became markedly more pronounced owing to its acute sense of dispossession.

In his study of social movements, Heberle makes an important distinction between the constitutive ideas of a movement, which form the foundation of group cohesion, and those ideas which are of merely accidental or pragmatic significance (Heberle, 1951, pp. 13, 24). To the persistent constitutive ideas of the traditionalist movement expressed in the writings of Nuri, Khomeini and Navvab Safavi were now added an emphasis on social justice, and a host of secondary and demagogical ideas and rhetoric. The preachers and clerical publicists readily borrowed from Shari'ati, and from the translation of such works as the Moslem Brotherhood leader Sayyid Qutb's *Social Justice in Islam*. Above all, Shari'ati's apt term, the Disinherited, with its enormous appeal to the uprooted masses, came to occupy a prominent place in the revolutionary rhetoric of the traditionalist party, and to enahnce the paternalistic populism of its leaders.

Early in January 1978, in reaction to a slanderous government-instigated personal attack in a leading newspaper's editorial, following the somewhat mysterious death of his son, Khomeini decided the time was at hand and inaugurated a thirteen-month period of nationwide revolutionary agitation whose outcome is well-known. After the revolution of February 1979, Khomeini and the other leaders of the movement set out to implement the blueprints contained in the writings of Khomeini and Navvab Safavi with unswerving determination and consummate Machiavellian skill. A 'Council of Constitutional Experts', along the lines foreseen in *Kashf-e Asrar* (Khomeini, 1943, p. 233) was set up, and incorporated Khomeini's theory of the Mandate of Clergy into the Constitution of the Islamic Republic, taking the step which Khomeini had not dared to make explicit in 1971: the restriction of the collective office of the Shi'ite jurists, the General Viceregency (*Niyabat-e 'Amma*), to *the* jurist as the supreme leader of the community of believers. The state was put under the firmest possible domination of the clergy, as Nuri would have wished, and the preparations were made for the dismantling of the un-Islamic laws, as Navvab Safavi had recommended. Music was banned, sexual desegregation and virtual re-veiling were reimposed, adulterers and sodomites were executed or stoned in anticipation of triple repetition of the crimes, and a

host of *Qur'anic* and pseudo-*Qur'anic* atavistic punishment reintro-
duced. Above all, the westernised intelligentsia was gradually but
decisively liquidated.

With the clerical *coup d'état* of November 1979, the desecularisation
of the judiciary, the closure of universities and the suspension of secular
higher education, the 'Islamicising' purges of summer 1980 and the
installing of the lay traditionalist activists in the highest executive offices
of the state, the Shi'ite traditionalist movement spent itself in creating
Khomeini's chaotic theo-ochlocracy, with the turbanned juristochloc-
rats fulfilling both functions of rousing the club-wielding mobs –
suitably designated as the Party of God (*Hezbollah*) – and representing
God by leading the Friday congregational prayers and by presiding over
the administration of the Sacred Law through the all-powerful religious
tribunals. (This passage was written in 1981.)


## REVOLUTIONARY TRADITIONALISM IN
## COMPARATIVE PERSPECTIVE

This paper is an attempt to trace the development of Shi'ite traditionalism in twentieth-century Iran. Traditionalism is viewed as a broad
cultural movement, a 'revitalisation' movement in Wallace's (1956)
terminology. In the preceding pages, I have sketched (i) the factors
which transformed its bearers, the *'ulama*, from one of the two organs of
pre-modern government into publicists, ideologues, and finally revolutionaries; (ii) the socio-demographic and organisational factors
which facilitated its widening appeal and consequent growth; and (iii)
the political factors and critical events which caused its irrevocable
politicisation by the 1970s. Other collateral economic and social factors
were excluded from consideration because of their insufficient analytical
pertinence. As the above procedure highlights the overriding salience of
the cultural factor, it seems appropriate to conclude with a typological
characterisation of contemporary Shi'ite traditionalism as a cultural
movement, a movement for revitalisation.

A meaningful typological characterisation of Shi'ite traditionalism
can proceed along two mutually complementary lines, the one approach
locating it within the cultural and historical context of Islam, the other,
in the contemporary global perspective. A highly selective contrast with
comparable movements at the broadest possible level of generality
suggests the following ideal types as significant points of reference: from
the first perspective, revivalist traditionalism or puritanical revivalism,

especially though not exclusively notable in the *Hanbali* tradition, and Islamic radicalism of the variety espoused by the Moslem Brotherhood; from the second, commodity millenialism of contemporary Melanesia, and revolutionary reaction in the form of Western fascism.

One need not be an Hegelian to appreciate Mannheim's remark that 'no antithesis escapes conditioning by the thesis it sets out to oppose' (Mannheim, 1953, p. 89). Of course the common reference to the sources of the Islamic tradition gives all revitalisation movements within Islam a strong family resemblance. Indeed, the Islamic activists, whether they are partisans of Ayatollah Khomeini or Sayyid Qutb or Maulana Mawdudi, regard themselves as participants in *the* Islamic movement of our time. Nevertheless, one would expect significant differences among the Islamic movements corresponding to differences in their respective antithetical conditioning. Such antithetical conditioning can vary fundamentally depending on whether the revitalisation of tradition takes place under the threat of erosion from popular Sufism or from Western culture. Islamic traditionalism oriented towards popular Sufism and unorthodox religious practices of the masses may conveniently be designated 'revivalism'. The distinctive feature of revivalism as an ideal type is its puritanical reaction to popular laxity and supernaturalism which takes the form of insistence on orthopraxis and the purification of 'associationist' practices (*shirk*), and on the reiteration of the pristine Abrahamic message of monotheism. As instances of revivalism, we may mention the Almohad movement in twelfth century north-western Africa and the revivalism of the Wahhabi *Muwahhidun* in eighteenth and twentieth century Arabia. In contrast to revivalism, the *ideological* quality of Shi'ite traditionalism – its presentation of an authentic, consistent and 'total way of life' in opposition to 'Western materialism' – emerges as distinctive.

On the other hand, the ideological quality of Shi'ite traditionalism, stemming from the threat of erosion posed by Western influences, is shared by the Moslem Brotherhood and its currently active offshoots whose movement may be characterised as 'Islamic fundamentalism' or, in deference to Eric Davis (see Chapter 7) 'Islamic radicalism'. The key contrast between the two types of Islamic movements is that the former is dominated and led by the clergy, the latter, by laymen. Islamic fundamentalism represents the revitalising synthesis not of the '*ulama* but of Moslem laymen. Consequently, it does not share the pronounced clericalism of Shi'ite traditionalism and in fact is usually critically oriented towards the '*ulama*. The latter synthesis involves a somewhat greater dissociation from the immediately transmitted pattern of the

Islamic tradition, and gives greater attention to its sources, especially the *Qur'an*.

Shi'ite traditionalism is a contemporary movement generated from within a world-religion. As such, it is instructive to contrast it with ideal types of contemporary movements which are *either* nurtured by a primitive religion (a pre-world-religion belief system) *or* which attempt to transcend a world-religion. From this perspective, let us consider the marginal individuals who have emerged as the charismatic leaders of the Melanesian cargo cults, of 'commodity millennialism'. They have done so in the context of Melanesian materialistic cosgmogonies tinged with the ideas of Christian missionaries, (Wilson, 1973, pp. 209–347). Their Golden Age was in the future; and it contained venerated elements of Western culture as shown by the cults of cargo. Commodity millenialism can thus be seen as an extreme case of maximal receptivity and absorption of Western cultural elements. By contrast, the dispossessed estate which created and directed Shi'ite traditionalism, did so with emphatic reference to the heritage of the past. They were the custodians of a world religion with a dogmatically-formulated belief system and a consolidated ethos. This means that we are dealing with the opposite extreme case of minimal absorption and maximal rejection. The revitalising synthesis, therefore, did not entail the meaningful absorption of any Western beliefs and ideas through the reinterpretation of the sources of the Shi'ite tradition, but rather the mere adoption of the *ideological* frame of thought, a frame of thought which tends to present itself whenever a tradition becomes self-conscious.[9] A systematising tendency thus set in and Shi'ite Islam was presented as 'a total way of life', with a set of blueprints and of vaguer outlines of Islamic economic, administrative social, educational and governmental 'systems'.

'Revolutionary reaction,' writes Ernst Nolte, 'this is the underlying characteristic of fascism.' (Nolte, 1965, p. 81.) Western European fascism was, according to Nolte's interpretation, a reaction from within a tradition against its latest stage of development – that is, a reaction from within the Western tradition in the form of 'the denial of transcendence'. It is hard to see how the level of symbolic differentiation, and consequently the theoretical accommodation of transcendence, could be increased beyond that attained by the world-religions of salvation. As a teacher of philosophy and '*irfan*, Khomeini recognises and endorses the kind of theoretical transcendence Maurras and Hitler sought to repudiate and overcome (Nolte, 1965, pp. 182–9). Despite the similarity of the techniques of mobilisation and other features, therefore, the overworked term 'fascism' seems typologically inappropriate (in part owing to the fact that we have no satisfactory typology of fascism, one which would contrast the intensely Christian fascism of Romania and Hungary with the anti-religious Western fascism on which Nolte's characterisation is based). What Nolte terms 'resistance to practical transcendence', on the other hand, does not distinguish the Islamic movement in Iran from the other conservative movements, and therefore does not need to be built into our ideal-typical characterisation of it.

To conclude, therefore, I propose 'revolutionary traditionalism' as a contrasting typological characterisation of the Islamic movement in Iran. The term conceives of Shi'ite traditionalism as a reaction to an external cultural tradition, which reaction entails the repudiation of any change consequent upon its imposition by a Western-oriented ruling élite. This repudiation is tantamount to a revolutionary change in political institutions and the social structure. Such revolutionary changes have been and will continue to be insisted upon as a result of the transformation of ingrained traditional sentiments and dormant attitudes into an explicit and adequately systematised traditionalist ideology.

## NOTES

1. A few of the prominent *mujtaheds* who were firmly convinced of the virtues of parliamentary democracy supported the constitutionalist cause unflinchingly. Others lent their support when convenient. But in all these cases, the sympathetic '*ulama*'s support was henceforth implicitly conditional, and they too insisted on the supervisory veto power of religious authority, the restriction of freedom of the press and the disavowal of any reforms entailing the secularisation of the judiciary and educational systems.
2. There is some logic to the Shi'ite '*ulama*'s identification of the ideas of the proponents of Islamic reforms as 'Wahhabi'. The views of the Indian thinker of the second half of the nineteenth century, Sir Sayyed Ahmad Khan, can certainly be considered the quintessence of rationalist apologetic modernism. He adopted Western canons of moral Judgement, made the operation of the laws of nature the central feature of his 'Islamic' cosmology, and stressed the identity of reason and revelation (Ahmad, 1967, Chapter 2). Yet he could in all seriousness describe himself as a 'Wahhabi multiplied' – i.e., many times more radical and fundamentalist than the Wahhabi revivalists of Arabia (Rahman, 1958, p. 83).
   Sir Sayyed Ahmad Khan's paradoxical assertion stems from the fact that, in contradistinction to traditionalism, both revivalism and modernism are fundamentalist in the sense that they advocate *radical* reinterpretation of the *sources* of the Islamic tradition and dissociate themselves from its im-

mediately transmitted pattern. But the similarity does not go very deep; radical reinterpretations of revivalists and modernists are undertaken along widely divergent paths.

3. In the light of subsequent developments, it is also highly interesting to note that Khomeini does not question the legitimacy of monarchy and specifically rejects the interpretation of the political authority of the jurists he himself was to use as the basis for his model of 'Islamic government': 'No jurist has said, nor is it written in any book, that we are kings and that sovereignty is our right.' (What is true is that if a political system is organised on the basis of divine commandments and divine justice, it would be the best of political organisations.) (Khomeini, 1943, p. 186, also p. 225.)

4. 'The disinterested tendency to inflict punishment is a distinctive feature of the lower middle class.' (Ranulf, 1964 [1938], p. 198.) Ranulf maintains that this tendency, characteristic of Nazism of his time, was shared by Calvinism and a wide variety of cultures dominated by middle and lower middle classes since classical Athens and Ancient Judaism.

5. A striking manifestation of such tension was the murder of Ayatollah Shams-abadi of Isfahan in April 1976 by an Islamic radical apparently inspired by the author of Shahid-e Javid (Sharif-Razi, 1979, p. 202).

6. If one looked hard for comparable non-religious associations, one could come up with sixty 'Literary Societies' for the entire country, 20 per cent of which were in Tehran, in 1353 (1974–5) (*Salnameh-ye Amari*, 1353, 1976, p. 167).

7. At least as late as March 1975 (28 *Safar* 1395Q), Khomeini would still appeal to the Constitution when denouncing the obligatory membership of all Iranians in the Shah's *Rastakhiz* (Resurrection) Party. But at that time, the appeal was being made opportunistically and out of pragmatic political considerations.

   Khomeini's opposition to women's rights is the subject of a letter he wrote to the Shah in November 1962. (Reproduced in *Iran va Jahan*, No. 39, 7 June 1981.)

8. Khomeini has never proclaimed himself Imam, but has allowed his followers to confer this title upon him since 1970. (The earliest reference to Khomeini as the Imam known to this author occurs in a poem dated *Tir* 1349/June–July 1970.) In an interview with Ayatollah Khomeini on 2 January 1979, I asked him about the significance of the title 'Imam' conferred on him by his followers. Having pointed out that in the earlier periods, Imam was a common designation, as it still is in Arabic (as opposed to Persian), he added smilingly: 'I do not know; ask those who call me Imam. The [elevated] rank of the Holy Imams is clear; and I am a student (*talaba*) of their teachings.'

9. The one important exception is the acceptance of limited parliamentary legislation. Other apparent exceptions are certain Marxist-inspired ideas on nationalisation of foreign trade and land distribution. These, however, can hardly be regarded as constitutive ideas, and are in fact in the process of losing their appeal to the new clerical rulers of Iran. Populism, especially in its paternalistic version espoused by Shi'ite traditionalism, is not distinctively Western; and basic notions of social justice can certainly be found in Islam itself.

# References

## NEWSPAPERS, PERIODICALS AND MAGAZINES

al-Ahram
al-Akhbar
al-Ajyal
Akhbar al-Yawm
Asiya-ye Javan
Atlas
al-Barq
al-Da'wa
al-Dustur
Ettela'at
Falastin
al-Hawadith
Hürriyet
al-I'tisam
al-Ittihad al'Uthmani
al-Jumhuriya
Jeune Afrique
al-Karmil

Khvandani-ha
Lisan al-Hal
al-Mabahith
Manshur-e Baradaran
Milli Gazete
Milliyet
Le Monde
al-Mufid
al-Musawwar
al-Muqtabas
al-Nadhir
New York Times al-Nalher
Omid-e Iran
al-Qahira
al-Sha'b
al-Watan
al-Taqqaddum
Taraqqi

## OFFICIAL DOCUMENTS

Bruce, C. E. (1929) *The Tribes of Waziristan: Notes on Mahsuds, Wazirs, Daurs, etc.*, His Majesty's Stationery Office for the India Office, Confidential.

*Commandement de la IV^eme Armée* (1916) *La Vérité la question syrienne*, Istanbul, Tanin.

Curtis, G. S. C. (1946) *Monograph on Mahsud Tribes*, Government of NWFP, Confidential.

Foreign Office Political and Consular Correspondence (1908a) FO 195/2287/84: Blech to Lowther, 26 October.

Foreign Office Political and Consular Correspondence (1908b) FO 195/2277/200: Cumberbatch to Lowther, 12 November.

Foreign Office Political and Consular Correspondence (1908c) FO 195/2277/212: Devey to Lowther, 24 November.

Foreign Office Political and Consular Correspondence (1910a) FO 195/2342/87: Young to Lowther, 10 June.

Foreign Office Political and Consular Correspondence (1910b) FO 371/1002/3391/28562: Devey to Lowther, 12 July.

Foreign Office Political and Consular Correspondence (1911a) FO 195/2370/25: Cumberbatch to Lowther, 3 February.

Foreign Office Political and Consular Correspondence (1911b) FO 195/2371/151: Devey to Lowther, 2 October.

Foreign Office Political and Consular Correspondence (1912a) FO 195/2389/24/885: Fontana to Lowther, 19 February.

Foreign Office Political and Consular Correspondence (1912b) FO 195/2389/1341: Devey to Lowther, 11 March.

Foreign Office Political and Consular Correspondence (1912c) FO 195/2389/24/1338: Cumberbatch to Lowther, 13 March.

General Staff (1921) *Operations in Waziristan 1919–1920*, Calcutta, India: General Staff, Army Headquarters, India.

General Staff (1932) *Summary of Events in North–West Frontier Tribal Territory. 1st January, 1931 to 31st December, 1931*, Simla, India, Government of India Press.

General Staff (1936) *Military Report on Waziristan 1935*, Fifth Edition, Calcutta, India, Government of India Press.

Howell, E. B. (1925) *Waziristan Border Administration Report for 1924–25*, Government of India, Confidential.

Johnson, Major H. H. (1934a) *Major Notes on Wana*, Government of India, Confidential.

Johnson, Major H. H. (1934b) *Mahsud Notes*, Government of India, Confidential.

Johnston, F. W. (1903) *Notes on Wana*, Government of India, Confidential.

*al-Mu'tamar al-'arabi al-awwal* (1913) Cairo: al-Lujna al-'Ulya li-Hizb al-Lamarkaziya.

*Ministère des Affaires Etrangères, Turquie* (1912a) NS 116: Couget to Poincaré, 29 January.

*Ministère des Affaires Etrangères, Turquie* (1912b) NS 116: Grapin to Poincaré, 31 January.

*Ministère des Affaires Etrangères, Turquie* (1912c) NS 116: Couget to Poincaré, 15 February.

*Ministère des Affaires Etrangères, Turquie* (1912d) NS 116: Couget to Poincaré, 23 February.

*Ministère des Affaires Etrangères, Turquie* (1913a) NS 120: Defrance to Jonnart, 13 March.

*Ministère des Affaires Etrangères, Turquie* (1913b) NS 130: Couget to Pichon, 15 April.

*Ministère des Affaires Etrangères, Turquie* (1913c) NS 120: Bompard to Pichon, 19 April.

*Ministère des Affaires Etrangères, Turquie* (1913d) NS 121: Guy to Pichon, 30 April.

*Ministère des Affaires Etrangères, Turquie* (1913e) NS 120: Couget to Pichon, 20 May.

Sazeman-e Barnameh va Budgeh (1973/1352) *Amar-e Montakhab (1351)*, Tehran.
Sazeman-e Barnameh va Budgeh (1976/1354) *Salnameh-ye Amari-ye 1353 Keshvar*, Tehran.
Turkey (1948/1328) *Salnamé 1328*, Istanbul, Tanin.
US Department of State (1951) *Foreign Service Despatch Tehran to Washington*, *20*, 7 July.


## BOOKS AND ARTICLES

(1978/1356) *Qiyam-e Hamaseh Afarinan-e Qum va Tabriz va digar Shahrha-ye Iran*, Nehzat-e Azadi-ye Iran, three volumes in one. [Date uncertain.]
(1978/1357) *Pareh-i az E'lamiyyehha-ye Montashereh dar Iran dar Mahha-ye Tir va Mordad 1358*, Organisation of Iranian Moslem Students, Willmete, Illinois. [Date uncertain.]
(1979/1358) *Asnad va Tasavir-i az Mobarezat-e Khalq-e Mosalman-e Iran*, Entersharat-e Abu-Zar. [Date uncertain.]
Abdi, N. (1973) '*Perspectives d'évolution de la propriété privative des terres agricoles*', *Revue algérien des sciences juridiques, économiques et politiques (RASJEP)* 10, pp. 223–37.
Abdi, N. (1975) '*Réforme agraire en Algérie*', *Maghreb-Machrek* 69, pp. 33–41.
Abdi, N. (1976) '*Réforme agraire et voie algérienne de développement*', *Revue Tiers Monde* 17, pp. 663–74.
Abrahamian, E. (1980) 'Kasravi: The Integrative Nationalist of Iran', Elie Kedourie and Sylvia Haim (eds), *Towards A Modern Iran: Studies in Thought Politics and Society*, London: Frank Cass.
Abun-Nasr, J. (1963) 'The *Salafiyya* Movement in Morocco: The Religious Bases of the Moroccan Nationalist Movement', *St Antony's Papers*, No. 16. *Middle Eastern Affairs*, No. 3.
Adams, C. J. (1966) 'The Ideology of Mawlana Mawdudi', in D. E. Smith (ed.) *South Asian Politics and Religion*, Princeton: Princeton University Press.
Ahmad, Aziz (1967) *Islamic Modernism in India and Pakistan 1857–1964*. London: Oxford University Press.
Ahmed, F. (1969) *The Young Turks: The Committee of Union and Progress in Turkish Politics 1908–1914*, Oxford: Oxford University Press.
Ahmad, F. (1980) 'Vanguard of a nascent *bourgeoisie*: the social and economic policy of the Young Turks 1908–1918', *Social and Economic History of Turkey 1071–1920*, Ankara: Meteksan.
Ahmed, A. S. (1973) *Mataloona: Pukhto Proverbs*, Peshawar: Pakistan Academy for Rural Development, 1975; Reprinted, Karachi: Oxford University Press.
Ahmed, A. S. (1976) *Millennium and Charisma among Pathans: A Critical Essay in Social Anthropology*, London: Routledge & Kegan Paul.
Ahmed, A. S. (1977) *Social and Economic Change in the Tribal Areas*, Karachi: Oxford University Press.
Ahmed, A. S. (1978a) 'The Colonial Encounter on the NWFP: Myth and Mystification', in *Journal of the Anthropological Society*, Oxford, 9, p. 3; (1978b) Revised version 'An Aspect of the Colonial Encounter in the NWFP', in *Asian Affairs*, 9, p. 3, London.

Ahmed, A. S. (1980a) 'Tribes and States in Central and South Asia', in *Asian Affairs*, 11, p. 2 (OS Vol. 67).

Ahmed, A. S. (1980b) *Pukhtun Economy and Society: Traditional Structure and Economic Development in a Tribal Society*, London: Routledge & Kegan Paul.

Ahmed, A. S. (1980c) 'How to Aid Afghan Refugees', *Royal Anthropological Institute News* 39.

Ahmed, A. S. (1981a) 'The Arab Connection: Emergent Models of Social Structure and Organization among Pakistani Tribesmen', *Asian Affairs*, June 1981.

Ahmed, A. S. (1981b) 'Nomadism as Ideological Expression: The Case of the Gomal Nomads', *Nomadic Peoples* (IUAES), Summer 1981.

Ahmed, A. S. (1983) *Religion and Politics in Muslim Society: Order and Conflict in Pakistan*, Cambridge: Cambridge University Press.

Ahmed, A. S. and D. M. Hart (eds) (1981) *From the Atlas to the Indus: The Tribes of Islam*, London: Routledge & Kegan Paul.

al-Ahram (1954) *al-Ahzab al-siyasiya fi suriya*, Damascus: Dar al-Ruwwad.

Ait-Amara, H. (1973) '*Quelques aspects de la restructuration agraire*', *RASJEP* 10, pp. 161–76.

Ait-Amara, H. (1974) '*L'impact de la production des salaires et des revenus sur l'emploi agricole*', *RASJEP* 11, pp. 35–62.

Akhavi, S. (1980) *Religion and Politics in Contemporary Iran. Clergy–State Relations in the Pahlavi Period*, Albany: State University of New York Press.

Algar, H. (1969) *Religion and State in Iran 1785–1906*, Berkeley: University of California Press.

Algar, H. (1980) 'Khomeini and Shari'ati'. Lecture delivered to the Conference on Islamic Revival, University of Chicago, (29 May).

Altman, I. (1979) 'Islamic movements in Egypt', *Jerusalem Quarterly*, 10, (Winter), pp. 87–105.

Ammour, K., Leucate, C. and Moulin, J. (1974) *La voie algérienne. Les contradictions d'un développement national*, Paris: Maspero.

Ansari, M. A. (1972/1351) *Defa' as Eslam va Ruhaniyyat. Pasokh beh Doctor Shari'ati*, 2 vols, Qum.

Antonius, G. (1939) *The Arab Awakening*, Philadelphia: Lippincott.

Antoine, P. and Labbé, D. (1976) '*Inflation et développement en Algérie*', *RASJEP* 13, pp. 505–56.

Arjomand, S. A. (1980) 'The State and Khomeini's Islamic Order', Iranian Studies, 13, pp. 1–4, 147–64.

Arjomand, S. A. (1981a) 'The '*Ulama's* Traditionalist Opposition to Parliamentarianism: 1907–1909', *Middle Eastern Studies*, 17, 2, pp. 174–190.

Arjomand, S. A. (1981b) 'Religious Extremism (*Ghuluww*), Sufism and Sunnism in Safavid Iran: 1501–1722', *Journal of Asian History* 15, 1, pp. 1–35.

Arjomand, S. A. (1981c) '*Shi'ite Islam and the Revolution in Iran*', *Government and Opposition. A Journal of Comparative Politics*, 16, 3, pp. 293–316.

Asad, T. (ed) (1973) *Anthropology and the Colonial Encounter*, London: Ithaca Press.

Bailey, F. G. (1972) 'Conceptual Systems of the Study of Politics', in *Rural Politics and Social Change in the Middle East*, R. Antoun and I. Harik (eds) Indiana University Press.

al-Banna, H. (1965) *Majmu'at rasa'il al-shahid Hasan al-Banna* (The Collected

Letters of the Martyr Hasan al-Banna) Beirut: Dar al-Andalus.

al-Banna, H. (1966) *Mudhakkirat al-da'wah*, (Memoirs) Beirut: Dar al-Andalus.

al-Banna, H. (1978) *Five Tracts of Hasan Al-Banna'* (1906–1949), (Tr. C. Wendell), University of California Publications, Near Eastern Studies, vol. 20, University of California Press.

Barth, F. (1972) *Political Leadership among Swat Pathans*, London: Athlone Press.

Barth, F. (1981) *Selected Essays of Fredrik Barth: Features of Person and Society in Swat; Collected Essays on Pathans*, vol. II, London: Routledge & Kegan Paul.

Batatu, H. (1978) *The Old Social Class and the Revolutionary Movements of Iraq. A Study of Iraq's Old Landed and Commercial Classes and of its Communists, Ba'thists, and Free Officers*, Princeton: Princeton University Press.

Bayne, E. A. (1968) *Persian Kingship in Transition*, New York: American Universities Field Staff.

Bayumi, Z. S. (1979) *al-Ikhwan al-muslimum wa'l-jam'iyat al-islamiya fi'l-hayat al-siyasiya al-misriya, 1928–1948*, (*The Role of the Muslim Brotherhood and Islamic Organisations in Egyptian Political Life, 1928–1948*) Cairo: Wahba Press.

Benissad, M. E. (1978) 'L'inflation algérienne: symptomes et causes', *RASJEP* 15, pp. 11–34.

Benachenhou (1975) 'Reflexions sur la politique des revenues en Algérie', *RASJEP* 12, pp. 7–45.

Benguergoura, C. (1976) 'Villages socialistes et perception des paysans', *Lybica* 24, pp. 242–9.

Benissad, M. E. (1979) *Evolution et développement de l'Algerie*, Paris.

Bessaoud, O. (1980) 'La révolution agraire en Algérie', *Revue Tiers Monde* 21, pp. 605–26.

Binder, L. (1962) *Iran: Political Development in a Changing Society*, Berkeley: University of California Press.

Binder, L. (1965) 'Egypt: The Integrative Revolution', in Pye, L. and Verba, S. (eds) *Political Culture and Political Development*, Princeton, New Jersey: Princeton University Press.

Binder, L. (1979) *In a Moment of Enthusiasm: Political Power and the Second Stratum of Egypt*, Chicago: University of Chicago Press.

Birru, T. (1960) *Al-'Arab wa'l-Turkfi'l-'ahd al-dusturi al-'uthmani 1908–1914*, Cairo: Arab League.

al-Bishari, T. (1972) *al-Haraka al-siyasiya fi misr 1945–1953*, (*The Egyptian Political Movement, 1945–1952*) Cairo: Dar al-kutub Press.

Blumer, H. (1951 [1939]) 'Collective Behavior', in A. M. Lee (ed.) *Principles of Sociology*, New York: Barnes and Noble.

Boserup, E. (1975) 'The Impact of Population Growth on Agricultural Output', *Quarterly Journal of Economics*, pp. 257–70.

Bouzidi, A. (1977) 'Productivité du travail dans l'agriculture algérienne et problèmes de la commercialisation des produits agricoles', *RASJEP* 14, pp. 502–39.

Buheiri, M. (1980) 'Al-sadirat al-zira'iya li-mutasarafiyyat al-Quds al-Sharif 1885–1914', *Samid al-Iqtisadi* 3, 22 (November) pp. 3–22.

Buheiri, M. (ed) (1981) *Intellectual Life in the Arab East 1890–1939*, Beirut: American University of Beirut.

Burgat, F. (1979) '*Villages socialistes algériens a l'épreuve des réalités*', *Maghreb-Machrek* 86, pp. 56–62.

Carson, W. M. (1957) 'The Social History of an Egyptian Factory', *Middle East Journal*, 11.

Cecconi, O. (1974) '*Rapports de l'économique et du politique dans la croissance de l'agriculture: le cas de l'Algérie*', *Homme et société* 33/34, pp. 89–110.

Chevallier, D. (1960) '*Lyon et la Syrie en 1919: les bases d'une intervention*', *Revue Historique* 224, pp. 275–320.

Chevallier, D. (1968) 'Western development and Eastern crisis in the mid-nineteenth century: Syria confronted with the European economy', in Polk, W. and Chambers, R. (eds), *Beginnings of Modernization in the Middle East: The Nineteenth Century*, pp. 205–22, Chicago: University of Chicago.

Chevallier, D. (1971) *La société du Mont Liban a l'époque de la révolution industielle en Europe*, Paris: *Librairie Orientaliste* Paul Geuthner.

Churchill, W. S. (1972) *Frontiers and Wars*, Harmondsworth: Penguin Books.

Clement, J. (1980) '*Lectures de Khomeinism*', *Esprit*, January.

Corrèze, F. (1976) *Femmes des mechtas*, Paris: *Editeurs français réunis*.

Cote, M. (1975) '*Révolution agraire et sociétés agraires: le cas de l'Est algérien*', *Annuaire de l'Afrique du Nord (AAN)* 14, pp. 173–84.

Cottam, R. (1964) *Nationalism in Iran*, Pittsburgh: University of Pittsburgh Press.

Couderc, R. and Desiré, G. (1975) '*Croissance urbaine et milieu rural: la désorganisation de l'agriculture autogérée entre Oran et Arzew, Algérie*', *Espace géographique* 4, pp. 17–30.

Coutsinas, G. (1975) '*A propos des deux circuits de l'économie urbaine*', *Revue Tiers Monde* 16, pp. 773–81.

Daghir, A. (1916) *Thawrat al-'Arab*, Cairo, *al-Muqattam*.

Dahmani, M. (1979) *Algérie. Légitimité historique et continuité politique*, Paris: Le Sycomore.

Darity, W. A. (1980) 'The Boserup Theory of Agricultural Growth', *Journal of Development Economics* 7, pp. 137–57.

Darwazah, M. (1950) *Hawl al-harakat al-'arabiya al-haditha*, 1, Sidon: al-Matba'a al-'Asriya.

Dawn, C. E. (1973) *From Ottomanism to Arabism: Essays on the Origins of Arab Nationalism*, Urbana: University of Illinois.

Deutsch, K. W. (1953) *Nationalism and Social Communications*, Cambridge, Mass: MIT Press.

Deutsch, K. W. (1980) *Politics and Government*, Boston: Houghton Mifflin, Itd.

al-Dhahabi, M. H. (1976) *al-Ittijahat al-munharifa fi tafsir al-qur'an al-karim: dawafi'uha wa daf'uha*, (*Deviant Tendencies in Interpreting the Holy Qur'an: Their Motives and their Repudiation*) Cairo: *Dar al-I'tisam*.

Djemal, A. (1922) *Memories of a Turkish Statesman 1913–1919*, New York: Doran.

Donohue, J. J. and Esposito, J. L. (eds) (1982) *Islam in Transition. Muslim Perspectives*, New York and Oxford: Oxford University Press.

Doucy, A. and Monheim, F. (1971) *Les révolutions algériennes*, Paris: Fayard.

Durand, J. (1977) '*Exacerbation des contradictions sociales et reserrement des alliances politiques en Algérie*', *AAN* 16, pp. 123–40.

Durkheim, E. (1964 [1915]) *The Elementary Forms of Religious Life*, London: George Allen & Unwin.

Ecrement, M. (1979) '*Le programme de l'industrialisation locale de l'Algérie*', *Tiers-Monde* 20, pp. 821–32.

Elaidi, A. (1980) '*Le processus de constitution d'une organisation paysanne*', *Revue Tiers Monde* 21, pp. 627–47.

Elsenhans, H. (1977) *Algerien. Koloniale und postkoloniale Reformpolitik*, Hamburg: Inst. f. Afrikakunde.

Enayat, H. (1982) *Modern Islamic Political Thought*, London: Macmillan.

Erbakan, N. (1975a) *Üç konferans*, Istanbul: Fetih Yayinevi.

Erbakan, N. (1975b) *Milli Görüş*, Istanbul: Dergah Yayinlari.

Erbakan, N. (1979a) 'Interview with Erbakan', *Comhuriyet*, 1–2 (August).

Erbakan, N. (1979b) '*İslam Uyaniyor ve Diriliyor*', *Bayram Gazetesi* (26 August).

Espisito, J. (ed) (1969) *Islam and Development*, Syracuse, New York: Syracuse University Press.

Étienne, B. (1975) '*La paysannerie dans le discours et la pratique*', *ANN* 14, pp. 3–44.

Étienne, B. (1977) *Algérie. Cultures et révolution*, Paris: Seuil.

Etzioni, A. (1961) *A Comparative Analysis of Complex Organizations*, Glencoe, Illinois: Free Press.

Fada'iyan-e Islam (1950/1329) *Rahnama-yi Haqayeq*, Tehran, n.p.

Fazlullah ibn Ruzbihan al-Isfahani (Khunji) (1966/1386 [1514/920]) *Suluk al-Muluk*, M. Nizamuddin and M. Ghouse (eds), Hyderabad: J. M. Printing Press.

Fiedler, M. (1976) 'The Agricultural Reform in Algeria', *Archiv Orientalni* 44, pp. 126–48.

Fischer, M. J. J. (1980) *Iran: From Religious Dispute to Revolution*, Cambridge, Mass: Harvard University Press.

Fortes, M. and Evans-Pritchard, E. E. (eds) (1970) *African Political Systems*, Oxford University Press.

Gauthier, A. (1976) *L'Algérie. Décolonisation, socialism, industrialisation*, Montreuil: Bréal.

Gauthier, Y. (1978) *Naissance et croissance de la République algérienne*, Paris: Editions marketing.

Geertz, C. (1963) *Old Societies and New States. The Quest for Modernity in Asia and Africa*, New York: Free Press of Glencoe.

Geertz, C. (1964) 'Ideology as a Cultural System', in Apter, D. (ed.), *Ideology and Discontent*, New York: The Free Press.

Geertz, C. (1968) *Islam Observed*, Yale University Press.

Geertz, C., Geertz, H. and Rosen, L. (1979) *Meaning and Order in Moroccan Society: Three Essays in Cultural Analysis*, Cambridge University Press.

Gellner, E. (1964) *Thought and Change*, Chicago: Chicago University Press.

Gellner, E. (1969a) *Saints of the Atlas*, London: Weidenfeld & Nicolson.

Gellner, E. (1969b) 'A Pendulum Swing Theory of Islam', in Robertson, R. (ed), *Sociology of Religion*, Harmondsworth: Penguin Books.

Gellner, E. (1975) 'The Unknown Apollo of Biskra: The Social Base of Algerian Puritanism', *Government and Opposition. A Journal of Comparative Politics*. Reprinted in Gellner, 1981.

Gellner, E. (1981) *Muslim Society*, Cambridge: Cambridge University Press.

Ghani, A. (1978) 'Islam and State-Building in a Tribal Society: Afghanistan 1880–1901', *Modern Asian Studies*, 12, pp. 269–84, Cambridge University Press.

Gibb, H. A. R. (1962 [1949]) *Mohammedanism: An Historical Survey*, Oxford University Press.

Gibb, H. A. R. (1947) *Modern Trends in Islam*, Chicago: University of Chicago Press.

Gilsenan, M. (1980) '*L'Islam dans L'Egypte contemporaire: Religion d'état, religion populaire*', *Annales E.S.C.*, mai-aout; 3–4, pp. 598–614.

Gluckman, M. (1971) *Politics, Law and Ritual in Tribal Society*, Oxford: Basil Blackwell.

Gordon, Milton (1964) *Assimilation in American Life*, New York: Oxford University Press.

Grandgouillaume, G. (1980) '*Relance de l'arabisation en Algérie?*' *Maghreb-Machrek* 88, pp. 51–62.

Grigg, D. (1979) 'Ester Boserup's Theory of Agrarian Change: A Critical Review', *Progress in Human Geography* 12, pp. 64–84.

Grimaud, N. (1976) '*Une Algérie en mutation, a l'heure de la charte nationale*', *Maghreb-Machrek* 73, pp. 70–7.

Grzeskowiak, M. (1980) '*Extremistische Islamische Gruppierungen in Agypten nach 1970*', *Asien, Afrika, Latin-Amerika*, 4, pp. 671–82.

Guetzkow, H. (1963) *Simulation in International Relations*, Englewood Cliffs, New Jersey: Prentice-Hall.

Guichaoua, A. (1977)'*Politique agricole et transformations sociales*', *Revue Tiers Monde* 18, pp. 583–601.

Guillermou, Y. (1977) '*Les exploitations familiales. Eléments d'analyse régionale*', *Revue Tiers Monde* 18, pp. 603–13.

Haddab, M. (1976) '*Changement socio-culturel et systeme scholaire en Algérie*', *RASJEP* 13, pp. 957–70.

Haddad, R. (1970) *Syrian Christians in Muslim Society: An Interpretation*, Princeton: Princeton University.

Halpern, M. (1963) *The Politics of Social Change in the Middle East and North Africa*, Princeton, New Jersey: Princeton University Press.

Hayes, C. (1948) *The Historical Evolution of Modern Nationalism*, New York: Macmillan.

Heberle, R. (1951) *Social Movements: An Introduction to Political Sociology*, New York: Appleton–Century–Crofts.

Hobsbawm, E. J. (1959) *Primitive Rebels. Studies in Archaic Forms of Social Movement in 19th and 20th Centuries*, New York: Norton.

Hofstadter, R. (1964 [1955]) 'The Pseudo-Conservative Revolt', in *The Radical Right*, D. Bell (ed.) New York: Doubleday.

Hopwood, D. (1969) *The Russian Presence in Syria and Palestine 1843–1914: Church and Politics in the Near East*, Oxford: Oxford University.

Hourani, A. (1947) *Minorities in the Arab World*, London: Oxford University.

Hourani, A. (1968) 'Ottoman reform and the politics of the notables', in Polk, W. and Chambers, R. (eds), *Beginnings of Modernization in the Middle East*, Chicago: Chicago University Press, pp. 41–8.

Hourani, A. (1980) *Europe and the Middle East*, London: Macmillan.

Hunt, R. and Harrison, J. (1980) *The District Officer in India 1930–1947*, London: Scholar Press.

Ibrahim, S. (1980) 'Anatomy of Egypt's Militant Islamic Groups: Methodological Note and Preliminary Findings', *International Journal of Middle East Studies*, 12, 4, pp. 423–53.

Issawi, C. (1966) *The Economic History of the Middle East 1800–1914*, Chicago: University of Chicago.

Issawi, C. (1977) 'British trade and the rise of Beirut 1830–1860', *International Journal of Middle East Studies*, 8, 1, pp. 91–101.

al-Ittihad al-'Uthmani (1911) '*Al-Islam, din al-tadamun wa'l-takamul wa asas al-hadara wa'l-tamaddun: sirr al-Islam fi'l-lughat al-'arabiya*', 798, 1, 6 January.

Jazani, B. (1978/1357) *Tarh-e Jame'ehshenasi va Mabani-ye Estratezhi-ye Junbesh-e Engelabi-ye Iran*, Tehran.

Jönsson, L. (1978) *La révolution agraire en Algérie* 21 Uppsala: Scandinavian Institute of African Studies.

Karsenty, J. (1975) '*Les investissements dans l'agriculture algérienne*', AAN 14, pp. 115–42.

Karsenty, J. (1977) '*La politique agricole*', *Maghreb-Machrek* 77, pp. 31–9.

Kasravi, Ahmad (1945/1324) *Bekhvanand va Davari Konand*, Tehran: Payman Press.

Kazemi, F. (1980) 'The military and politics in Iran: the uneasy symbiosis', in Kedourie and Haim (eds), *Towards a Modern Iran*, London: Frank Cass.

Keddie, N. R. (1969) 'Pan-Islam as Proto-Nationalism', *Journal of Modern History*, 41, pp. 17–28.

Keddie, N. and Zarrinkub, A. H. (1965) '*Fada'iyan-e Islam*', in *Encyclopedia of Islam*, New edn.

Kennedy, R. (1969) *Thirteen Days*, New York: Norton.

Khalidi, R. (1977) 'Arab nationalism in Syria: the formative years, 1908–1914', in Haddad, W. and Ochsenwald, W. (eds), *Nationalism in a Non-National State: The Dissolution of the Ottoman Empire*, Columbus: Ohio State University.

Khadduri, M. (1965) 'Aziz 'Ali al-Masri and the Arab nationalist movement', Hourani, A. (ed.), *St Antony's Papers*, 17, *Middle Eastern Affairs*, 4, pp. 140–63, Oxford: Oxford University Press.

Khalidi, R. (1980) *British Policy towards Syria and Palestine 1906–1914*, London: Ithaca.

Khalidi, R. (1981a) 'The Role of the Press in the Early Arab Reaction to Zionism', *Peuples Méditerranéennes/Mediterranean Peoples*.

Khalidi, R. (1981b) ''*Abd al-Ghani al-'Uraisi* and *al-Mufid:* The Press and Arab Nationalism before 1914', in Buheiri, M. (ed.) pp. 38–61 (modified version in *Arab Studies Quarterly* 3, 1 (Winter) pp. 22–42.

Khomeini, R. (1943/1363Q) *Kashf-e Asrar*, n.p.

Khomeini, R. (1971/1391Q) *Hukumat-e Eslami*, Najaf.

Khomeini, R. (1977/1355) *Ava-ye Enqelab* (Selections from speeches). n.p.

Kira, Kamal (1955) *Mahkamat al-sha'b*, (The People's Court) 9 vols, Cairo: The Nile Company for Publication and Distribution.

Kornhauser, W. (1959) *The Politics of Mass Society*, New York: Free Press of Glencoe.

Koulytchizky, S. (1974) *L'Autogestion, l'homme et l'état*, Paris: Mouton.

Kutschera, C. (1979) *Le Movement nationale kurde*, Paris: Flammarion.

Lacoste-Dujardin, C. (1976) *Un village algérien. Structures et evolution recente*, Algiers: SNED.

Landau, J. M. (1976) 'The National Salvation Party in Turkey', *Asian and African Studies*, 11, 1, pp. 1–57.

Leca, J. and Vatin, J. (1975) *L'Algérie politique. Institutions et régime*, Paris: Foundation nationale des Sciences politiques.

Leca, J. and Vatin, J. (1977) '*Le système politique algérien*', *ANN* 16, pp. 15–18.

Lepoul, G. (1977) '*1000 villages socialistes en Algérie*', *Maghreb-Machrek* 77, pp. 40–7.

Lipset, S. M. (1964) 'The Sources of the "Radical Right"', in Bell, D. (ed.) *The Radical Right*, New York: Doubleday.

Lipset, S. M. and Raab, E. (1970) *The Politics of Unreason: Right-Wing Extremism in America, 1790–1970*, New York: Harper & Row.

Lo, C. (1982) 'Countermovements and Conservative Movements in the Contemporary US', *Annual Review of Sociology*, vol. 8.

Lucas, P. (1978) *Problème de la transition au socialisme. Le 'transformisme algérien'*, Paris: Anthropos.

Mahsud, M. (1970) *Impact of Education on Social Change in South Waziristan Agency*, Punjab University, MA thesis.

Makdisi, G. (1966) 'Remark on Traditionalism in Islamic Religious History', in C. Leiden (ed.) *The Conflict of Traditionalism and Modernism in the Muslim Middle East*, Austin: Texas University Press.

van Malder, R. (1975) '*La révolution agraire en Algérie*', *Civilisations* 25, pp. 251–71.

Mallarde, E. (1975) *L'Algérie depuis*, Paris: Table ronde.

Mandel, N. J. (1976) *The Arabs and Zionism before World War I*, Berkeley: University of California.

Mannheim, K. (1953) 'Conservative Thought', in *Essays on Sociology and Social Psychology*, Kecskemeti, P. (ed.). London: Routledge & Kegan Paul.

Martens, J. (1973) *Le modèle algérien de développement*, Algiers: SNED.

Marx, G. T. and Wood, J. L. (1975) 'Strands of Theory and Research in Collective Behavior', *Annual Review of Sociology* 1.

Masters, J. (1965) *Bugles and a Tiger*, London: Four square.

McCarthy, J. D. and Zald, M. N. (1973) *The Trends of Social Movements in America: Professionalization and Resource Mobilization*, Morristown, New Jersey: General Learning Press.

Meeker, M. E. (1980) 'The Twilight of South Asia Heroic Age: A Rereading of Barth's Study of Swat', *Man* 15, 4, (December).

Megdiche, C. and Doret, C. (1977) '*Un village socialiste en Mitidja: Tessala El Merdja*', *Lybica* 25, pp. 255–96.

Merad, A. (1967) *Le Réformisme musulman en Algérie de 1925 a 1940. Essai d'histoire religieuse et social*, the Hague and Paris: Mouton & Co.

Metcalf, B. D. (1982) *Islamic Revival in British India, 1860–1900*, Princeton: Princeton University Press.

Michel, H. (1973) '*La formation des élites politiques maghrébines. Analyse des données: L'Algérie*, in Charles Debbasch *et al.*, *La formation des élites politiques maghrébines*, Paris: Libraire generale de droit et jurisprudence, pp. 87–122.

Michel, H. (1975) '*Les élites politiques du Maghrèb: L'Algérie*', in M. Flory *et al.*, *Introduction à l'Afrique du Nord comtemporaine*, Paris: CNRS, pp. 98–106.

Middleton, J. and Tait, D. (eds) (1970) *Tribes Without Rules*, London: Routledge & Kegan Paul.

Minault, G. (1974) 'Islam and Mass Politics: The Indian '*Ulama* and the *Khilafat Movement*', in D. E. Smith (ed) *Religion and Political Modernization*, New Haven and London: Yale University Press.

Mitchell, R. P. (1969) *The Society of the Muslim Brothers*, London: Oxford University Press.

Miyaji, K. (1976) '*Kacem Ali*'. *Monographie d'un domaine autogéré de la plaine de Mitidja (Algérie)*, Tokyo: Institute for Study of Languages and Cultures of Asia and Africa.

Moqimi, M. (1977/1355) *Velayat az Didgah-e Marja'iyyat-e Shi'a*, Tehran: Amir.

Mortimer, E. (1982) *Faith and Power, The Politics of Islam*, New York: Vintage Books.

Motahhari, M. (1970–71/1349) *Khadamat-e Motaqabel-e Eslam va Iran*, Tehran: Anjoman-e Eslami-ye Mohandesin.

Motahhari, M. (1978/1357) *Nahzatha-ye Eslami dar Sad Saleh-ye Akhir*, Qum.

al-*Mufid* (1911a) '*Mawlid Nabina 'alayhi al-salat wal-salam*', '*Abd al-Ghani al-'Uraisi*, 638, pp. 1–2 (2 March).

al-*Mufid* (1911b) '*Shukri al-'Asali: khitab muhim fi majlis al-umma 'an al-sihyuniyin*', 706, pp. 1–2 (31 May).

al-*Mufid* (1911c) '*Khalid al-Barazi: khitab muhim li-mab'uth Hama*', 707, pp. 1–2 (1 June).

al-*Mufid* (1911d) '*Allahu akbar*', '*Abd al-Ghani al-'Uraisi*, 723, pp. 1–2 (20 June).

al-*Mufid* (1912a) '*Qudum al-nawwab*', 903, p. 2 (8 February).

al-*Mufid* (1912b) '*Khitab Lutfi Fikri Bey*', 905, p. 2 (11 February).

al-*Mufid* (1912c) '*Lutfi Fikri Bey fi Dimashq*', 906, p. 2 (12 February).

al-*Mufid* (1912d) '*Muhadarat Lutfi Fikri Bey*', 907, p. 1–3 (13 February).

al-*Muqtabas* (1910a) 'al-Nasraniya fi 'l-'Arab wa sahib jaridat al-'Arab', Faris al-Khuri, 386, pp. 1–2, 2 June.

al-*Muqtabas* (1910b) 'al-'Arab al-masihiyun', 386, pp. 3–4, 2 June.

al-*Muqtabas* (1910c) 'al-Da'w' al-dawa': li kul umma mufsidun', 387, pp. 1–2, 4 June.

al-*Muqtabas* (1911a) 'Sawt na'ib Dimashq fi majlis al-nawwab', 644, pp. 1–2, 6 April.

al-*Muqtabas* (1911b) 'Shukri al-'Asali', 651, pp. 2–3, 15 April.

al-*Muqtabas* (1911c) 'al-Hizb al-'arab al-mu'allat min al-nawwab', 656, p. 2, 20 April.

al-*Muqtabas* (1912a) 'al-Majlis w'al-intikhabat at-jadida', Haqqi al-'Azm, 888, p. 1, 28 January.

al-*Muqtabas* (1912b) 'al-Majlis w'al-intikhabat al-atiya', Haqqi al-'Azm, 891, pp. 1–2, 31 January.

al-*Muqtabas* (1912c) 'al-Majlis w'al-intikhabat al-atiya', Haqqi al-'Azm, 894, pp. 1–3, 15 February.

Musa, S. (1970) *al-Haraka al-'arabiya: Sirat al-marhala al-uwla li'l-nahda al-'arabiya al-haditha 1908–1924*, Beirut: Dar al-Nahar.

Mutin, G. (1975) '*L'agriculture de la Mitidja ou les difficultes d'une reconversion*', *AAN* 14, pp. 143–71.

Mutin, G. (1977) *La Mitidja. Décolonisation et espace géographique*, Paris.

Najafi, S. M. B. (1976/1355) 'Appendix (Peyvast) on religious media, centers and organizations', in Asadi, A. and Mehrdad, M. (eds), *Naqsh-e Rasanehha dar*

*Poshtibani-ye Tause'a-ye Farhangi*, Tehran: Iran Communications and Development Institute.

Nellis, J. R. (1980) 'Maladministration: Cause or Result of Underdevelopment in Algeria?', *Canadian Journal of African Studies* 13: pp. 407–22.

Nolte, E. (1965) *Three Faces of Fascism*, New York: New American Library.

Ollivier, M. (1973) 'Révolution agraire et mobilisation des masses', *RASJEP* 10, pp. 33–140.

Ollivier, M. (1975) '*Place de la révolution agraire dans la strategie algérienne de développement*', Annuaire de l'Afrique du Nord 14, pp. 91–114.

Özek, Ç. (1964) *Türkiyede Gerici Akimlar ve Nurculuğun İçyüzü*, Istanbul: Varlik Yayinevi.

Palloix, C. (1980) '*Un essai sur la formation de la classe ouvrière algérienne*', *Revue Tiers Monde* 21, pp. 557–76.

Parsons, T. (1964 [1942]) 'Some Sociological Aspects of the Fascist Movements', in *Essays in Sociological Theory*, New York: The Free Press.

Qureshi, M. N. (1978) 'The Indian *Khilafat* Movement (1918–1924)', *Journal of Asian History*, vol. 2, p. 2.

Qutb, Sayyid (1952) *Ma'rakat al-islam wa'l-ra'smaliya (The Struggle of Islam and Capitalism)* Cairo: Wahba Library.

Qutb, Sayyid (1964) *Ma'alim fi'l-tariq (Signposts Along the Path)* Cairo: Dar al-kitab al-'Arabi.

Qutb, Sayyid (1973 [1944]) '*Adalat-e Ejtema'i dar Islam*, Persian translation of *al'Adalat al-Ijtima'iyya fi'l-Islam* (1944) by M. H. Gerami and S. H. Khosraw-Shahi, Qum: *Resalat*.

Raffinot, M. and Jacquemot, P. (1977) *Le capitalisme d'état algérien*, Paris: Maspero.

Rahman, F. (1958) 'Muslim Modernism in the Indo-Pakistan Sub-Continent', *Bulletin of the School of Oriental and African Studies*, 21.

Ramadan, A. A. (1977) '*Le Nouvel élan des Frères musulmans*', *Le Monde diplomatique*, 281 (August) pp. 10–11.

Rahman, F. (1966) *Islam*, New York: Doubleday.

Rahman, F. (1980) *Major Themes of the Qur'an*, Chicago: *Bibliotheca Islamica*.

Ramsaur, E. (1957) *The Young Turks: Prelude to the Revolution of 1908*, Princeton: Princeton University.

Ranulf, S. (1964 [1938]) *Moral Indignation and Middle Class Psychology*, New York: Schocken.

Razi, V. (1980/1359) '*Fada'iyan-e Islam*', *Raha'i*, Bahman 9, pp. 10–12.

Rida, M. R. (1910) '*Kayf tunal al-umma huqquqaha*', *al-Ittihad al-'Uthmani*, 495, p. 1 (5 May).

Rodinson, M. (1980) *Muhammad*, translated by Carter, A., New York: Pantheon Books.

Romero, E. F. (1976) *Autogestión y revolución agraria en Argelia*, Bilbao: Zero.

Rudé, G. (1959) *The Crowd in the French Revolution*, Oxford University Press.

Sabri, Şeyhülislam M. (1977) *Dini Mücedditler*. Istanbul: Sebil Yayinevi.

Safran, N. (1961) *Egypt in Search of Political Community*, Cambridge, Mass: Harvard University Press.

Sa'id, A. (1934) *al-Thawra al-'arabiya al-kubra*, 1, Cairo: 'Isa al-Babi al-Halabi.

Said Halim Paşa (n.d.) 'Mukallitliklerimiz', and 'Meşrutiyet', in M. Ertuğrul Düzdağ (ed.) *Buhranlaicmiz*, Istanbul, Tercüman 1001 Temel Eser.

Salibi, K. (1976) 'Beirut under the Young Turks: As depicted in the Political

Memoirs of Salim 'Ali Salam (1868–1938)', in Berque, J. and Chevallier, D. (eds) *Les Arabes par Leurs Archives (XVIᵉ-XXᵉ siècles)*, Paris: Centre Nationale de la Recherche Scientifique.

Sari, D. (1972) '*La désorganisation de l'agriculture traditionelle dans l'Ouarsenis*', *Etudes rurales* 47, pp. 39–72.

Sari, D. (1975) '*L'évolution de l'emploi en Algérie*', *Maghreb-Machrek* 69, pp. 42–50.

Sari, D. (1977) '*L'évolution de la production agricole en Algérie*', *Afrique et Asie modernes* 114, pp. 11–24.

Schliephake, K. (1972) '*Die algerische Agrarrevolution*', *Afrika-Spectrum* 1, pp. 44–59.

Schnetzler, J. (1980) '*Les effets pervers du sous-emploi a travers l'exemple algérien*', *Revue canadienne des études africaines* 14, pp. 451–71.

Shafer, B. C. (1972) *Faces of Nationalism*, New York: Harcourt Brace.

Shari'ati, A. (1971/1350) *Hajj*, Tehran: reproduced by the Islamic Society of students in America.

Shari'ati, M. T. *et al.* (1976/1354) *Miz-e Gerd. Pasokh beh So'alat va Enteqadat*, Tehran: *Hosayniyyeh Ershad.*

al-Sharif, K. I. *(n. d.) al-Ikhwan al-muslimun fi harb falastin*, (*The Muslim Brothers in the Palestine War*) Cairo: Wahba Library.

Sharif-Razi, M. (1973–4/1352) *Ganjineh-ye Daneshmandan, vol. 1*, Tehran: *Eslamiyyeh.*

Sharif-Razi, M. (1974/1353a) *Ganjineh-ye Daneshmandan*, vol. 2, Tehran: *Eslamiyyeh.*

Sharif-Razi, M. (1974–5/1353b) *Ganjineh-ye Daneshmandan*, vol. 4, Tehran: *Eslamiyyeh.*

Sharif-Razi, M. (1979) *Ganjineh-yi Daneshmandan*, vol. 8, Tehran: *Eslamiyyeh.*

Shils, E. (1972) *The Intellectuals and the Powers and Other Essays*, Chicago: University of Chicago Press.

Shils, E. (1974) *Center and Periphery. Essays in Macrosociology*, Chicago: University of Chicago Press.

Shorrock, W. (1976) *French Imperialism in the Middle East: The Failure of Policy in Syria and Lebanon 1900–1914*, Madison: University of Wisconsin.

Smith, A. D. (1971) *Theories of Nationalism*, London: Duckworth.

Smith, A. D. (ed.) (1976) *Nationalist Movement*, London: Macmillan.

Smith, A. D. (1979) *Nationalism in the Twentieth Century*, New York: New York University Press.

Smith, D. E. (1970) *Religion and Political Development*, Boston: Little, Brown.

Smith, T. (1975) 'The Political and Economic Ambitions of Algerian Land Reform', *Middle East Journal* 29, pp. 259–78.

Smith, W. C. (1946 [1943]) *Modern Islam in India: A Social Analysis*, London [Lahore].

Smith, W. C. (1957) *Islam in Modern History*, New York: Mentor Books.

Smith, W. C. (1962) 'The '*ulama* in Indian Politics', in C. H. Philips (ed.) *Politics and Society in India*, London: George Allen & Unwin.

Souriau, C. (1975) '*L'arabisation en Algérie*', in M. Flory *et al.*, *Introduction à l'Afrique du Nord Contemporaine* (Paris: CNRS), pp. 359–74.

Stone, L. (1970) 'The English Revolution', in R. Forster and J. P. Greene (eds) *Preconditions of Revolution in Early Modern Europe*, Baltimore: John Hopkins Press.

Sutton, K. (1974) 'Agricultural Reform in Algeria', *Afrika-Spectrum* 1, pp. 50–68.

Tahmasbi, Kh. (1951/1330) 'Chira Razmara ra Kushtam', *Taraqqi, Murdad* 14.

Tamimi, R. and Bahjat, M. (1917) *Wilayat Beirut*, 2, Beirut: *al-Iqbal*.

Tammar, H. (1974) *Structures et modèle de développement de l'économie de l'Algérie*, Algiers: SNED.

Tarazi, P. (1933) *Tarikh al-sahafa al-'arabiya*, 4, Beirut: American University.

Tibawi, A. L. (1969) *A Modern History of Syria including Lebanon and Palestine*, London: Macmillan.

Tilly, C. (1978) *From Mobilization to Revolution Reading*, Mass: Addison-Wesley.

Toprak, B. (1981) *Islam and Political Development in Turkey*, Leiden: E. J. Brill.

Trautmann, W. (1979) '*Entwicklung und Probleme der Agrarreform in Algerien*', *Erdkunde* 33, pp. 215–226.

Treydte, K. (1979) *Agrarreform und Entwicklung*, Bonn: *Neue Gesellschaft*.

Tunaya, T. Z. (1962) *Islamcilik Cereyani*, Istanbul: *Baha Matbaasi*.

Turner, R. and Killian, L. M. (1972) *Collective Behavior*, 2nd edn, New Jersey: Prentice-Hall.

Vahedi, M. (1955/1334a) articles in *Khvandani-ha, Mehr*, 6, 18, 25, 27, *Aban* 2 and 18.

Vahedi, M. (1955/1334b) '*Khatirat-i Fada'iyan-e Islam az Havades-e Chand Sal-e Akhir*', *Khvandani-ha, Mehr* 4.

Vassilis, D. (1976) '*L'introduction de la technologie moderne dans le secteur agricole*', *RASJEP* 13, pp. 985–94.

Vatin, J.-C. (1980) Introduction to *Islam, Réligion et Politique, Revue de l'occident Musulman et la Méditerranée*, 1.

von Sivers, P. (1980) '*Les plaisirs du collectionneur: capitalisme fiscal et chefs indigènes en Algérie (1840–60)*', *Annales ESC* 35, pp. 679–99.

von Sivers, P. (1981) 'Work, Leisure and Religion: The Social Roots of the Revival of Fundamentalism in North Africa', in Gellner, E. and Vatin, J.-C. (eds), *L'Islam et politique au Maghreb*, Paris: CNRS, pp. 355–70.

Wallace, A. F. C. (1956) 'Revitalization Movements: Some Theoretical Considerations for their Comparative Study', *American Anthropologist*, 58.

Wilson, B. R. (1973) *Magic and the Millennium*, London: Heinemann.

Woodruff, P. (1965) *The Men who Ruled India*, vol. 1; *The Founders*, vol. 2; *The Guardians*, London: Jonathan Cape.

Yücekök, A. N. (1971) *Türkiye' de Örgütlenmis Dinin Sosyo-Ekonomik Tabani 1946–1968*, Ankara: *Sevinc Matbassı*.

Zghal, A. (1975) 'Pourquoi la réforme agraire ne mobilise-t-il pas les paysans maghrébins?' *AAN* 14, pp. 295–311.

## UNPUBLISHED ARTICLES AND THESES

Abrahamian, E. (1969) 'Social bases of Iranian politics: The Tudeh Party, 1941–1953', (unpublished Ph.D. thesis) Columbia University.

Ahmad, M. (1980) 'Class, Power and Religion: Some Aspects of Islamic Fundamentalism in Pakistan', presented to the Conference on Islamic Revival, 28–31 May, University of Chicago.

Ahmed, A. S. *The Forest Dwellers of Pakistan: Problems in Ethnicity and the Sociology of Development* (forthcoming book).

Ahmed, A. S. 'The Reconsideration of Swat Pathans: A Reply to Fredrik Barth', (forthcoming paper).

Anderson, J. W. (1980) 'How Afghans Define Themselves in Relation to Islam', paper presented to American Anthropological Association, Washington, DC, December.

Beattie, H. (1980) 'Effects of the Saor Revolution in the Nahrin Area of Northern Afghanistan', paper presented to the American Anthropological Association, Washington, DC, December.

Canfield, R. L. (1980) 'Religious Networks and Traditional Culture in Afghanistan', paper presented to the American Anthropological Association, Washington, DC, December.

Davis, E. (1970) *The Social Bases of the Muslim Brotherhood in Egypt*, (unpublished MA paper, Department of Political Science), Chicago, The University of Chicago.

Faghfoory, M. H. (1978) *The Role of the 'Ulama in Twentieth Century Iran With Particular Reference to Ayatollah Haj Sayyid Abul-Qasim Kashani*, Unpublished Ph.D. Dissertation, Madison, University of Wisconsin.

Ferdows, A. K. (1967) *Religion in Iranian Nationalism: The Study of the Fada' iyan-e Islam*, Unpublished Ph.D. Dissertation, Indiana University. Its Part II consists of a translation of *Rahnama-ye Haqayeq*.

Ghani, A., 'Disputes in a Court of *Sharia*', (forthcoming paper).

Ghani, A., '*Sharia* in the Process of State-Building: Afghanistan 1880–1901' (forthcoming paper).

Ismail, Mahmoud and Ismail, Mohamed (1962) *Nationalism in Egypt Before Nasser's Revolution*, Ph.D. Dissertation, University of Pittsburgh.

Mardin, S. (1973) 'Religion and the Turkish Social Transformation', paper presented at the conference on The Republic of Turkey, 1923–73: Studies in 20th Century Nation-Building (December), University of Chicargo.

Sa'doun, F. (1977) *al-Haraka al-islahiya fi Beirut fi awakhir al-'ahd al-'uthmani*, Beirut: Lebanese University Education Faculty (MA Thesis).

Talhami, G. (1981) 'The Muslim–African Experience', paper presented to 'The Islamic Alternative', Conference, the Arab Institute (June).

Tavakolian, B. (1980) 'Sheikhanzai Nomads and the Afghan State', paper presented to the American Anthropological Association, Washington, DC, December.

Tunçay, M. (1981) 'Marxism in Turkey', paper presented to the Conference on Social Movements and Political Culture in the Contemporary Middle and Near East, Mt Kisco, New York.

Voll, J. (1981) 'Wahhabism and Mahdism', paper presented to 'The Islamic Alternative', Conference 5–6, the Arab Institute, June.

Collection of leaflets and pamphlets distributed in Iran in 1978, in possession of Dr Shaul Bakhash.

# Index